My Story

My Story

Vietnam 1968
196th Light Infantry Brigade

Gary L Lyles

E-BookTime, LLC
Montgomery, Alabama

My Story
Vietnam 1968
196th Light Infantry Brigade

Copyright © 2014 by Gary L Lyles

All rights reserved. No part of this book may be reproduced or transmitted in any form or by any means, electronic or mechanical, including photocopying, recording, or by any information storage and retrieval system, without permission in writing from the copyright owner.

ISBN: 978-1-60862-539-0

First Edition
Published March 2014
E-BookTime, LLC
6598 Pumpkin Road
Montgomery, AL 36108
www.e-booktime.com

Contents

Preface 7

Chapter 1	*Processing In-Country*	9
Chapter 2	*First Firefight*	15
Chapter 3	*Field Stand-Down*	26
Chapter 4	*Long Range Observation Post*	33
Chapter 5	*LZ Colt*	36
Chapter 6	*The NVA*	45
Chapter 7	*Stand-Down in Chu Lai*	69
Chapter 8	*NCO School*	76
Chapter 9	*The DMZ*	87
Chapter 10	*Defending Nhi Ha*	106
Chapter 11	*The Trail Junction*	131
Chapter 12	*Home in the Mountains*	144
Chapter 13	*Squad Patrols*	159
Chapter 14	*Mines and Booby Traps*	165
Chapter 15	*The Rigors of the Trail*	170
Chapter 16	*LZ West*	182
Chapter 17	*LZ Baldy*	198
Chapter 18	*Another Long Range Observation Post*	205
Chapter 19	*Helping Vietnamese Civilians*	213
Chapter 20	*Ambush in AK Valley*	219
Chapter 21	*The Monsoon*	228
Chapter 22	*The River*	240
Chapter 23	*Ambush*	247
Chapter 24	*Short-Timer*	254

Glossary 262

Preface

I had originally attempted to capture my Vietnam experience on paper a few years after the war when I realized that my story was slowly being erased by time. My efforts were mostly unproductive and resulted in nothing more than a barely legible pile of handwritten pages. Having been pulled out of the trash several times, the pile of paper survived the years.

I eventually wrote *My Story* some twenty years later. I had no command chronologies or official sources to help me piece the story together. I had only the pile of paper, a shoe box full of memories, some pictures, old letters, and a full-page map of Vietnam from the December 19, 1967 issue of the *Memphis Press-Scimitar* on which my mama's handwritten notes detailed my travels. I was a grunt and wasn't privy to the big picture, the battle plans, or the war's strategies. I knew nothing for sure except for my own personal experiences. Although the pile of paper was nothing more than a bunch of random handwritten thoughts, the pile did capture the major events of my experience and a lot of small details that I never wanted to forget. After developing a timeline, I did my best to position and stitch the events together to create my manuscript. Over the years I have added a few words here and there and a number of footnotes to the book.

As military records, documents, and chronologies became available in later years, I considered rewriting *My Story* to include what I had learned about the war. As I collected material, I began to realize just how difficult it was going to be to accurately incorporate the information into my book. I also realized that the effort was going to add little to the personal story I wanted to tell. I finally decided to leave *My Story* as originally written.

In my manuscript I used the names of the men involved, except for a few places where I could no longer put a name with a face. For this published version of *My Story*, I substituted fictitious names for many individuals because I thought it was best given the circumstances.

Although the actual sequence of events may have varied somewhat from what is written here, every event described in this book actually took place, and *My Story* is how I remember them.

Chapter One

Processing In-Country

It was mid-morning on December 19, 1967 when the plane touched ground at an airfield in Cam Ranh Bay, South Vietnam. I had just turned twenty years old a week earlier and had come to Vietnam to stop the spread of communism, or at least that was what I was told. I had dropped out of school at Memphis State because I simply couldn't afford school on the $1.05 an hour I was making sacking groceries at Big "D." I knew it wouldn't be long before I was drafted, and if so, I would surely end up in the boonies of Vietnam with a rifle in my hands. I was told that if I volunteered for the draft, I would have some say about what I would be doing and still only have to serve two years of military duty. My plans were to volunteer for the draft, pound a typewriter for two years, and then go back to college on the GI Bill. Somehow my plans had gone astray. I was in Vietnam with an 11B10 MOS (infantry) and would soon have a rifle in my hands.

"Gentleman, I want to welcome you to Cam Ranh Bay, South Vietnam," announced the pilot as the door of the commercial airliner was opened. As I made my way toward the door, I had no idea what to expect. The thought of going to war had always produced visions in my mind of rushing the beaches on Iwo Jima or Okinawa, and yet here I was waiting in line to get off a commercial airliner with a pretty stewardess telling me to have a nice day.

As I stepped out of the plane into the hot, moist air, all I could see was sand. Cam Ranh looked to me like a large sandbox with buildings randomly placed here and there. The sand stretched inland from the South China Sea all the way to the rolling green hills to the west.

I thought I was going to war, so I was puzzled by the fact that no one I saw was armed. The military police had 45s, but hell, they carried them in the States. I knew I was in a rear area, but even so, I expected it to be more "war like" – artillery, bunkers, trenches, barbed wire, and all.

We were bused to an in-country reception center where we were to wait for our orders to come down. After a formation and some words of wisdom from one of the NCOs, I was assigned to one of the large, wood-framed-canvas-covered buildings. Inside I threw my duffle bag on one of the empty cots and then followed a group of soldiers headed for the mess hall.

As I stood in the chow line, I watched several Vietnamese civilians busily washing the metal trays and silverware in a drum of hot, soapy water, which was being heated by the gas flames below. They wore coolie hats and black pajamas just like the pictures I had seen. They paid no attention to us. I had come thirteen thousand miles to help them, and I wanted to be friends. My first opportunity came when I handed over my empty tray to the papa-san working at the end of the line. I made a helping gesture so he wouldn't have to reach for my tray and added a polite comment and a smile, hoping for a response from the elderly Vietnamese man. He said nothing and never acknowledged my presence, and went about his business of cleaning my tray.

Processing In-Country

At each of the three formations of the day, the names of those receiving orders assigning them to the various units in Vietnam were called. I listened intently for my name but had mixed emotions about whether or not I wanted to hear it. I prayed each night that I would be assigned to a unit someplace in the south close to a large city or major base camp, a unit that wouldn't be seeing any real action.

Although I wanted to know where in Vietnam I was going, I had quickly become comfortable with the routine at Cam Ranh and was perfectly willing to spend as much of the war as I could right there. The morning work details were typical State-side Army bullshit, mostly filling sandbags, policing the area, and pulling KP. I dismissed the familiar harassment that came with each job as just part of the game. We never really worked very hard, so I didn't mind it, and besides, it helped pass the time.

Other than the three formations a day and the work details in the morning, I had a considerably good time. I played cards in the afternoon and drank beer and listened to a live band at the EM (Enlisted Men's) club in the evening. I even hit the jackpot on one of the slot machines in the EM Club. I had watched this one machine pay off twice in a row and figured it was out of order and just might do it again. It was and it did, and I bought a round of beer for the guys. My strongest memory of Cam Ranh comes rushing back to me every time I hear the hit song by the Animals, "We Gotta Get Out of This Place." We all sang along with the band at the EM club every time they played it. It didn't matter whether you were drunk, sober, in uniform or out, you hit an emotional high as you put everything you had into it, *"We gotta get out of this place if it's the last thing we ever do....!"* The song would later take on much more meaning for me.

I remember feeling somewhat guilty for having such a good time. My mama and dad thought I was at war risking my life, and yet here I was enjoying being grown-up and away from home. I even began to look for things that would ease my conscience and prove that I was at war. Most of the buildings and tents were surrounded by a waist-high wall of sandbags, which meant that the potential for an enemy attack did exist, or at least somebody thought so. And there was another thing; we all wore olive green underwear instead of white underwear like the soldiers wore back in the States. When I walked from my barracks along the decked walkway to the showers in my cammo undies, it would be harder for the enemy to see me. All the sandbags and my "green underwear" helped prove that I was at war, and in my mind, provided some justification for my parents' worries. I spent Christmas 1967 in Cam Ranh and even got to see Bob Hope's Christmas show.

About the time I decided that war wasn't exactly hell, I received orders assigning me to the Americal Division up north in I CORP. A few hours later, I was getting off a camouflaged C-130 turbo-prop at an airfield in a place called Chu Lai. I could tell right away that I wasn't going to like this place as well as Cam Ranh; the guys here were carrying weapons just like in a real war.

We were loaded on trucks and taken to the Americal Division's Orientation Center. All new replacements were to attend the Division's school on jungle warfare. The first couple of days were spent attending classes on weapons, explosives, survival, and so on. The course was topped off by an actual ambush, or so I thought at the time. Later I found out that before the enemy could have crossed our ambush site, he would have had to fight his way through the 196th Infantry, the 198th Infantry, the Navy patrolling the coast, the Air Force, and the Chu Lai perimeter guards. Then, if Charlie (Viet Cong – VC – Victor Charlie, or just Charlie for short) came from the right direction, we green-horns would get a crack at him.

Processing In-Country

  I finally finished the course, and word had it that all infantry were going to be sent to the 11th Brigade. I was pleased because the 11th was new in-country and wasn't supposed to see any real action for quite some time. There was a slim chance I could be sent to the 198th, whose area of operation was around Chu Lai, which wouldn't be too bad, but from what I heard, anything would be better than to be assigned to the 196th Light Infantry. They were known as the fire brigade of the Americal Division. The 196th was always sent to the Division's hot spots.

  A day or so later, my orders came down, and sure enough, I had been assigned to the 11th Brigade. I slept well that night, that is, until a NCO calling names woke me. PFC Gary Lyles was one of them. I was told to get my things together and get on the "deuce and a half" waiting in front. Sitting in the back of the truck a few minutes later with about ten other guys, I asked where we were going. I was told that I had been reassigned to "A" Company, 3rd Battalion, 21st Infantry, 196th Light Infantry Brigade. Alpha Annihilator, as the company was called, had been chewed up by the NVA in the Que Son Valley and needed replacements. We were taken to the 196th rear headquarters there in Chu Lai and given a cot in a large, sandbag-surrounded tent for the remainder of the night.

  The next morning after chow, we replacements were standing in front of the company's supply room where we were to be issued our field gear. Two hours later, I was still standing in front of "supply," but now with so much equipment on my back that I could hardly move, let alone jump around like John Wayne does in his war movies. The supply sergeant told us that later each of us would be issued three hand grenades, twenty-five magazines of ammo, one smoke grenade, one claymore mine, and twelve meals of C-rations. Surely this was a joke; they couldn't expect a man to carry all this stuff and still be able to fight.

My Story, Vietnam 1968, 196th Light Infantry Brigade

"Supply" was given such short notice that, to say the least, they issued some used – very used – equipment. One M-16 actually had a piece of wood in place of a missing hinge pin to hold it together. My weapon was in somewhat better condition, but not much. I figured there was about a 50-50 chance that it would even fire. There weren't enough rucksacks to go around, so I ended up with two regular size army backpacks tied together with string. Even two packs wouldn't hold everything, so I put the excess into long, wool socks and tied them to my packs and pistol belt. I looked more like a junk collector than a soldier.

After the morning's ordeal, we were fed a hot lunch and then taken to the chopper pad where we were to wait for a ride to a fire support base in the mountains called Landing Zone (LZ) Center. One thing I didn't understand at the time was why we were being treated so well. We were given a lot of personal attention and even called by our first names, which wasn't like the army I knew at all. Later I realized that it was all because they knew where they were sending us, and they knew that some of us wouldn't be coming back.

Chapter Two

First Firefight

It wasn't long and I was on my way; first time in a chopper (UH-1 Helicopter, Huey) for me. It was a real experience. Through the misty rain, I could see the jungle and rice paddies below, and the outline of the mountains off in the distance. The beauty was breathtaking. The wide-open side doors of the chopper let in all of Vietnam's beauty. I was sitting on the floor next to the open door, and as I looked down, I thought of how easy it would be to fall out. The Huey was terribly loud, and the strong vibrations coming though the floor seemed to be working me toward the edge. I knew that transporting troops in this manner was routine, so I tried not to show my fear as I appeared to be casually holding on to a brace, but in actuality, I had a death grip on it. My thoughts were interrupted when the door gunner cocked his M-60. That's when it hit me; I was going to war. This time it was for real; not just training or war games, but the real thing.

    The chopper crossed the flatland and paddies to the northwest and headed into the mountains; up over a ridge and down into a lush valley, and then toward a small brown bald spot high atop a green mountain ridge.

My Story, Vietnam 1968, 196th Light Infantry Brigade

A few minutes later I was standing in a foot of mud on top of Landing Zone Center, or the "Mud Monster" as it was known during the monsoon season. The fire support base sat between the Song Chang and Heip Duc valleys, which were main NVA infiltration routes to the Da Nang and Chu Lai areas.

The mist had given way to a pouring rain, and I and everything I carried was soaked. I sloshed through the mud to get out of the way of another incoming chopper. LZ Center looked like a scene right out of a war movie. The 155 and 105 millimeter howitzers, pits of four-duce mortars, and several 81 millimeter mortar positions were on the west and easier-to-defend side of the mountain. A circular wall of sandbags surrounded each gun emplacement. The mess tent, supply bunker, medic bunker, and chopper pad were on the east side. There were fighting bunkers spread about 25 to 30 meters apart around the perimeter and rolls of concertina (military barbed wire) encircled the entire top of the mountain. LZ Center was sandbags, mud, wire, and guns. I felt my heart pounding as I looked around and I thought to myself, "How could I be here? How could this have happened to me?"

I was taken to the supply bunker and given ammo and C-rations, and then taken to the east side of Center to test and supposedly zero my weapon. No grid target, no 25 meter range, just firing 20 rounds down the side of the mountain was all it took to zero your weapon. I was relieved to find that my M-16 fired much better than it looked.

We hung loose that afternoon waiting for what was to happen next. I was still in a state of disbelief as I sat in the mud, leaning back against the mud-covered sandbags of a bunker wall. I was miserably cold and wet and felt like crying. I stared down the side of the mountain watching the rain drops drip from the rusty perimeter wire. Beyond the wire, scattered rocks and boulders protruded above waist-

First Firefight

high grass that had been washed shiny green by the continuous rain. I could see numerous scars on the rocks, and a queasy feeling settled into the pit of my stomach when I realized bullets had made them. About halfway down the waist-high grass gave way to a thick, green jungle that eventually melted into the mist-filled valley hundreds of feet below.

I watched as a soldier made his way along the narrow, muddy footpath leading toward the mess tent. Although he was draped in a poncho and his helmet was pulled down low over his eyes, there was something familiar about him. I wiped the rain from my face and stared in the soldier's direction. It was Gene Tilson. He had been in my AIT (Advanced Infantry Training) Company at Fort Polk Louisiana, or Tiger Land as it was called. At Tiger Land we learned to growl out loud on command, "Grrrrrrrrrrrrrr!" And the answer to everything was, "To Kill!" Gene was an easygoing, likeable fellow. He was from Tennessee and spoke with an extremely slow, southern drawl. I splashed through the mud as I hurried to catch up with him. "Hey Tilson!" I yelled.

I felt good. I had found somebody I knew, something familiar in this strange world I had been thrust into. He turned and looked at me. I had a smile on my face, and he didn't. He was looking in my direction, but I felt as if he was looking straight through me. I offered my hand, but it went unnoticed as Tilson said, "It's... bad... real bad... I... was... with... Alpha... and... it... was... bad." He showed no emotion, and with a certain mental vagueness, told me that he had been caught in an ambush. Tilson had made it to the field a week or so ahead of me. He didn't say why he had left the field, but now he was on his way back out to the company. In the middle of one of his long, drawn-out sentences, Tilson simply turned and walked away, leaving me horrified. "Surely this must be a nightmare," I thought to myself.

My Story, Vietnam 1968, 196th Light Infantry Brigade

We were told that the ten or so of us replacements were going to receive some OJT before being sent out to our companies. That evening six or seven men from the battalion's Long-Range Reconnaissance Patrol (LRRP) Team were to take us down the side of the mountain into the valley and establish a defensive perimeter for the night. They were to show us how to dig-in and set up for the night, and provide us with tips on how to survive in the jungle. The thought of leaving the perimeter and walking down the mountain into the misty fog frightened me.

It wasn't long before we were saddled up and following the LRRPs (called "Lurps") out of the perimeter wire and along a trail that snaked its way down the side of the mountain toward the valley below. The muddy trail was slick and steep. I took advantage of the scattered rocks to secure my footing and help balance my load as I worked my way down the trail. One of the boys ahead of me slipped and was pulled down hard to the earth by his overfilled rucksack. He struggled back to his feet and continued down the trail as the rain worked to wash the mud from his fatigues, rucksack, and weapon.

Once on the valley floor, we followed a trail through a rain-glistened jungle a short distance to a clearing of short green grass about 30 meters across. The area was perfectly flat and had once been a terraced rice paddy, but was now dry and would provide us with a place to spend the night. There was thick, waist-high brush surrounding the area, and hazy jungle beyond that. The Lurps paired us up and then positioned us to establish a perimeter around the clearing. I was soon busy digging the first of many foxholes I would dig during the coming year.

The Lurps took turns instructing us on the "do's and the don'ts" of jungle warfare. They had no problem getting our attention, and I guess that was the idea behind the OJT. I

First Firefight

knew I had better listen. I needed to know this stuff if I ever wanted to see home again.

Needless to say, I didn't sleep a wink that night. It was a long night, and I was scared, cold, and wet. The rain never let up. I was soaked right down to the bone, and I wondered if my crinkled fingers would ever recover. As I sat at the edge of my foxhole in the mud with my teeth chattering, watching the blackness in front of me, and listening for the enemy, I heard a whimper come from the position on my right. I heard it again, and then the whimper turned into a sniffling cry. One of the new boys had started to cry. It was so dark I couldn't see exactly what happened next, but I heard it. One of the Lurp NCOs grabbed the boy by the neck and in a low growl said, "Shut the fuck up or I'll kill you dead! Fuckin' green is going to get us all killed!" I wanted to go home. I didn't want to be here. The Lurps referred to us as greens; not greenhorns, but just greens. We apparently weren't worth the extra effort required to add "h-o-r-n-s" to the word.

It was a long night, but morning finally came. A little sun, and then more rain, and then came the long climb back up Center. I didn't think I was going to make it. The gear on my back weighed almost as much as I did. I carried water, food, poncho, poncho liner, toiletries, writing paper, pen, weapon, ammo, hand grenades, smoke grenades, claymore mine, and an entrenching tool. I carried it all up the trail toward the top of the mountain. I made it, but as I reached the top and made my way through the concertina wire, my legs felt like rubber. I was totally exhausted, miserable, and soaked to the bone with sweat and rain. After everyone had reached the top, we were told to hang loose until a chopper was available to take us out to the company.

Later that day I boarded a supply ship headed for Alpha Company. We flew across several mountains and down a valley to a small, grass-covered hill. As I stepped off the

My Story, Vietnam 1968, 196th Light Infantry Brigade

chopper and looked around, I immediately felt out of place. My helmet cover was crispy green, my fatigues a sharp, olive green, and my boots were black. The uniforms of the soldiers staring at me were more brownish than green, and the black dye on their boots had long since worn away, leaving them a suede brown.

The first man to greet me was the company commander, Captain Yurchak. He welcomed me to the company in an extremely polite manner and then introduced me to Sergeant Hanna, the platoon sergeant and acting platoon leader of the First Platoon. The platoon leader had been killed in an ambush. Sergeant Hanna was a Korean War veteran who looked the part with his handlebar mustache and large physique. I looked up at him, and he looked down at me and said, "You're kind of small, but I guess you'll do." I followed Sergeant Hanna through the tall grass to a clearing where four guys were sitting around two freshly dug foxholes. Sergeant Hanna pointed to the position, so that's where I went. As he turned to walk away, he ordered, "Take care of the green."

I was told that I was to pull guard with the command section of the platoon that night, and the next day I would be assigned to a squad. There was a medic, RTO (radio-telephone-operator), and two other guys. All of them were friendly; they must have known how I felt. "Sit down and fix yourself something to eat; it's that time of day you know." They shared in showing me how to make a little stove from a C-ration can to heat my C's and how to get set up for the night.

After supper we all sat around the foxholes shooting the bull and enjoying a break from the rain. Thanks to the guys, I began to feel relaxed for the first time since climbing aboard the chopper in Chu Lai. The medic had been in-country for six months and had earned a Bronze Star for something; he never did say. The other guys had only been

First Firefight

in-country a couple of months but had seen quite a bit of action. All four were originally with the Second Platoon, but after the action in Que Son Valley, the experienced men were divided among the platoons. I commented on how polite the CO had been to me. I was told that Captain Yurchak had spent several tours in Vietnam and was an excellent company commander. He was taking the recent loss of so many men extremely hard. The company had been chewed up in Que Son Valley when they walked into a well-placed NVA ambush. Nobody wanted to talk much about the ambush, but I did hear enough to pray that I would never have to experience anything like it.

Guard duty was divided into shifts, and because I was new, the guys were considerate and gave me the first shift. It was another long, wet, and sleepless night.

The next morning Sergeant Hanna assigned me to the Second Squad. I was the fifth man of a five-man squad, which now consisted of four greens and a SP-4 squad leader. The squad leader's name was Mason. I was interested in finding out what type of squad leader he was. I had heard from day one in basic training that if your squad leader had his shit together, your chances of making it back home were good. My first impression of Mason wasn't good. Mason was a tall, thin, black man who came right out and said that he didn't care about anyone or anything but his own ass. Taylor from Denver, Mann from New York, and Henry Clark from someplace in Alabama were all new in-country. Mann and I had been in the same AIT company at Fort Polk. He managed to make it to the field a day or so before I did.

For the next few days, the company conducted what was called "search and destroy" operations. We would move several klicks (a klick is 1000 meters) from our night laager position to a new location. A CP (command post) would be setup with one platoon left behind to provide security while the other two platoons went to predetermined areas to search for Charlie. If contact had not been made by mid-afternoon, the two platoons would return to the CP, and then the company would retreat to the top of a nearby hill and set up a defensive perimeter for the night.

On my first patrol, our squad was ordered to check out an area a couple of hundred meters down a small, secondary trail. As we moved down the trail, I realized that I didn't know what I was doing. I remembered my training and all, but I still didn't know if I was supposed to study each step looking for booby traps, or if I was to challenge each bush and tree as a potential enemy hiding place or what? Clark acted like he knew what he was doing, so I started to follow his lead, and then I remembered that he had only been in-country a few days longer than I had. We took the conservative approach and checked out everything. We cautiously inspected every rock and twig on the trail and left no tree unchallenged. It took us over an hour to cover a short section of trail. Mason let us go about our business without saying anything. I figured his silence meant that we were doing a good job. I know now that we must have looked ridiculous, and I'm sure Mason was silently laughing his ass off as he watched a bunch of greens make fools of themselves.

As it turned out, Mason was a good squad leader who did have his act together, but like many of the more hardcore veterans, he felt that ten greens weren't worth one experienced grunt, and he treated us that way.

The war began for me sometime during that first week in the field. Off in the distance, I listened to the point man of the Third Platoon swap rounds with the Viet Cong. I felt a chill as I listened to the sounds echo through the valley and realized that I was really at war. I realized that they were trying to kill us, and we were trying to kill them.

First Firefight

The Third Platoon returned to the company that day with a VC prisoner. Upon hearing of the Thirds' success, I moseyed over to where the prisoner was being held to see just what the enemy looked like. The prisoner appeared to be quite a bit older than most of us, maybe even in his thirties, and wore nothing but a pair of black shorts. He was slim but had a mature chest and well-toned muscles. The man's dark skin was made darker by the mud that was unevenly spread about his body. His callused feet were tied tightly together at the ankles, and his wrists were bound together behind his back. The thin rope pressed deeply into his wrist, causing his hands to take on a dark, purplish-red color. When I made eye contact with the prisoner, the sympathetic look on my face quickly disappeared when he growled at me like a mad dog. He gritted his teeth, and his neck muscles were taut as he snarled and pulled at his bindings as if trying to escape. He let me know without saying a word that he would rip my heart out with his bare hands in front of God and everybody if only he could get loose. He scared the shit out of me, and he knew it. I turned my head to hide the fear on my face and got the hell out of there. The thought of me being a prisoner at the mercy of someone like him terrified me. It took some time to shake the edgy feeling that had overcome me after that first encounter with the enemy.

There were a lot of small villages tucked away in the mountain jungles we were working. Only the very old and the very young populated the villages. It was always a tense moment when we moved into a village or slipped up on a lone hooch. It was tense for us not knowing what we would find, and tense for the Vietnamese peasants who were unsure of our intentions. The old papa-sans and mama-sans normally showed little emotion, but the children were terrified, and it showed on their faces. I always felt bad for scaring them, and after the village had been secured, I would use a wide smile and some gum or candy to try and ease their fear.

Once again, it was the First Platoon's turn to provide security for the CP. All I had to do was to prepare a position and then take it easy for the rest of the day. To make things even better, it looked like the weather was going to cooperate at least for a while. My feet and back were sore, and I was ready for some rest.

My letter writing was interrupted when Sergeant Hanna began yelling for everyone to saddle up. The Second Platoon had trapped a squad of Viet Cong in a wooded area, and their only way out was across a large, wide-open rice paddy. The First Platoon and CP were to position ourselves across on the far side of the rice paddy in a wood line, and then the Second and Third Platoons were to move in and force the VC out into the paddy.

It didn't take long to reach the location at the pace Sergeant Hanna set. Each squad was assigned a section of the wood line, and the squad leader positioned his men. I didn't like where Mason put me, but he insisted I stay there, so I did. I worked my way down as deep as I could into the rocks and brush and then took aim. I looked down the barrel of my weapon toward the wood line on the far side of the paddy. Everything had happened so fast that I really didn't have time to think about what was about to happen. Moments later, the word was passed that the VC were headed toward the rice paddy. I can't explain the feelings I had at that moment. I wasn't all that scared because I guess I just didn't know what to expect. Sergeant Hanna yelled, "FIRE!" Everyone started shooting – pop, pop, pop, pop, pop. I couldn't see anything, but I opened up with the rest of them. We shot the hell out of the wood line on the other side of the paddy. The chatter from all the M-16s and our M-60 sent chills through my body. It didn't take long to realize that it wasn't all outgoing. We were being shot at. I heard the

First Firefight

sound of incoming for the first time. As a bullet passes you, you hear a sharp crack because it is traveling faster than the speed of sound – a mini sonic boom. It sounds like a bullwhip being cracked next to your ear. I lowered my head even more. The only thing showing above the small pile of rocks I was behind was my right index finger and my M-16.

In a few minutes it was all over. Somehow the VC escaped the trap. Nobody ever figured out how or where they went, and I didn't really care. I was glad it was all over and that no one had been hurt. I had experienced my first firefight and never did see an enemy soldier.

That night after foxholes had been dug and claymores set out, we all sat around the holes talking about the firefight. I admitted not seeing anything and only shooting up the wood line. Nobody else saw anything either except for Clark. Supposedly, he saw a VC soldier run into the rice paddy about 300 meters away, and while on the run, Clark shot him between the eyes. No one saw Clark kill his first VC, but Clark stuck to his story, so maybe it was true.

Chapter Three

Field Stand-Down

It was late in the day when Mason returned from the squad leader meeting with good news. Starting the next day, the company was going to head back toward LZ Center. Mason told us that it should only take a day and a half or so to reach the base of Center. I hadn't been in the field long, but long enough to know that Center meant hot meals and a chance to get some rest.

Early the next morning in a light rain, we saddled up and prepared to move out. I looked up to see Sergeant Hanna staring in our direction with a scowl on his face, and I knew that we had bunched up too close together again. As if he knew what the day had in store, Sergeant Hanna yelled, "God damn it! Spread it out! One damn grenade would get you all!" He was making a point. His forceful tone meant that he intended for his words of wisdom to stay with us the rest of the day. We had a long, tough day ahead of us, and Sergeant Hanna knew he had his hands full with so many greens to watch over.

The company worked its way out of the night laager site and headed toward Center in single file, the only way possible to travel in the highlands. As I waited to take my

Field Stand-Down

place in line, I made some last-minute adjustments to my tied-together backpacks to make sure that my load rode as comfortable as possible on my shoulders. Mason had promised me that I would get a rucksack the next time we were re-supplied, but until then, I would have to make do with the packs I had been given. I fell in line behind Mann, and we were on our way.

We followed a trail that snaked its way along the base of a jungle-covered mountain ridge. The trail would occasionally meander away from the ridge out into the valley. The valley was filled with rice paddies bordered by ominous-looking hedge rows and patches of jungle that concealed the remnants of deserted villages. In places we were forced to walk the paddy dikes out into the open. We increased our spacing as we moved across the paddies to present the enemy with a less inviting target. I felt uneasy and played it over and over in my mind what I would do if the enemy opened up on us and tried to anticipate which side of the dike would provide cover.

Rain fell over the jungle and the paddies as we continued on toward Center. The rain was clean and fresh and had a unique odor to it. It may have been the rain blending with the smells of the jungle and the paddies that gave the moist air a pleasant, sort of sweet smell. The rain had a way of making me feel alone. The sound of the rain beating the jungle would drown out everything except for the sounds I was making myself. I could hear my boots splashing through the water and mud on the trail, the rain hitting my poncho, and my own moans and groans as I struggled with the load I was carrying. At times I looked down at the trail, concentrating and trying to find some inner strength, but then I would be forced to look up to make sure that I wasn't alone.

We humped until about noon, and then stopped and spread out on the trail for lunch. C-rations don't really taste all that bad if you're hungry. As a matter of fact, if you know how to prepare them, C's can be quite tasty. For instance, suppose you're in the mood for chocolate pudding. Looking over your four-day supply of C's, nothing even remotely related to chocolate pudding can be found. Mason showed me this trick. First, you place three crushed Oreo type cookies into a canteen cup, add two packages of hot chocolate powder and four packages of coffee creamer, along with a half cup of water. Stir well and boil until the mixture thickens, and presto – chocolate pudding.

"Saddle up!" It was humping time again. After a few moans and groans, we were on our way. The march had begun to get tough. My leg muscles and back ached, and my shoulders were killing me. The backpack straps seemed to work deeper into my shoulders with each step, and with each step, the pain grew more intense. Sometimes I felt like the straps had sunken six inches deep. Momentary relief was available by making a quick upward movement with my body, followed by an instant downward jerk. This would leave my load in the air for a split second and momentarily relieve the torture and allow me to reposition the straps. With the straps repositioned on top of my shoulders and the pain lessened, the cycle would start all over. With each adjustment of the backpack, the duration between adjustments grew shorter. We pushed on. At times the accordion effect of the column had us moving at a snail's pace, and at other times we had to run to keep up. We would hump until about half the company was mumbling something about the long-legged SOB up front setting the pace, and then finally the word would be passed to take ten. After five minutes or so, we were saddled up and moving again.

What light was available under the overcast sky had begun to disappear, and I figured it was about time that we started looking for a night laager site. It had been a long day, and every muscle in my body ached, and the pain in my

Field Stand-Down

shoulders had become almost unbearable. I needed some rest.

Word was passed, "Hold up, spread out, and break out the C's." Captain Yurchak wanted to reach the base of Center by morning, so we were going to break for supper and then hump on toward LZ Center. I couldn't believe that we were going to move at night, but we were. I was standing there miserably wet and exhausted and had just learned that our journey was only half over – the easy half.

Darkness came soon after we had hit the trail. It was a long, hairy night. I quit worrying so much about the pain in my shoulders and began concentrating on following Mann in front of me. The last thing I wanted to do was to lose track of him. As I watched Mann pick up the pace and then pull back a bit and then head off again in another direction, I knew we were in trouble. It hadn't taken long for Mann, who never seemed to be able to keep up, even back in AIT, to lose track of the man in front of him. "Oh shit!" I thought. Fear began to grip me as I realized that we were separated from the rest of the company. Come to find out, Alpha was broken into five or six groups, with only the CP knowing their location. I guess Captain Yurchak decided it was impossible to travel at night with so many greens.

The captain gave orders by radio to meet on top of the hill located to the south of where we supposedly were located. Thirty minutes later, we were on top of a small hill. I guess it was a hill. It was so dark you couldn't be sure of anything. Our squad couldn't even decide on which direction the front of the foxholes should be facing. I wasn't even sure where the positions on our flanks were located. If Charlie had fired one shot at us that night, I'm sure there would have been a chain reaction, and we would have probably had one hell of a firefight among ourselves. The long day had left my body totally drained and my shoulders

My Story, Vietnam 1968, 196th Light Infantry Brigade

numb. The cold rain gently fell as I lie down in the wet grass and soon fell asleep.

Somehow or another, we made it through the night, and the sun began to appear over the ridge to the east. The sun was a welcome sight, but I knew it meant humping time again.

About noon that day, we rounded a hill, and LZ Center came into view. At a distance I could see the familiar green mountain with the small, brown bald spot on top. An hour or so later, we broke for lunch at the base of a mountain ridge across the narrow valley from Center. While we were eating, a chopper came down from Center, picked up the CO, and took him back to the top. We all knew something was up.

After lunch we were given the good news. The entire company was going to have a field stand-down. For the rest of that day and all of the next day, one platoon would provide a defensive perimeter while the other two platoons literally had a picnic. Hot food, beer and soda, clean clothes, a football, ball and gloves, and even a volleyball and net were all sent down by chopper from Center.

I'm sure the small pool formed by a crystal clear mountain steam was one of the reasons the spot was chosen. The steam started high up on the mountain ridge and trickled down a rocky ravine to gently feed a deep pool of clear water which was about fifteen feet wide and maybe twenty-five feet long. The large rocks surrounding the pool stair stepped down several feet to the water's edge. The entire area was beautiful. I thought of how great it would be to have some place like this back in the world where you could enjoy the beauty nature was offering and not have to worry about the war. The pool wasn't really large enough for swimming, but it made one hell of a bathtub.

Learning that the First Platoon had been given first shot at the pool, several guys quickly stripped down and headed

Field Stand-Down

down to the water. The first couple of guys in made a quick exit. One of the guys was making a hell of a fuss as I watched him pulling at the short, fat, blackish-gray leeches the size of my thumb that were busy sucking his blood. There were five or six leeches attached to his chest, and others on his back and arms. One of the veteran grunts said, "Hold it, hold it, hold it," as he calmly pulled a small, white plastic bottle of mosquito repellent from the elastic band on his helmet. One squirt from the bottle on each leech forced them to turn loose, leaving water-diluted blood flowing from the small wounds they had made. From the way the guy carried on, you would have thought he had been mortally wounded.

Although most of the guys had gotten used to finding small leeches attached to various parts of their body, many of the guys elected to bathe out of their steel pots rather than brave the pool leeches that were quite a bit larger. I had lived in the Canal Zone in Panama for almost three years as a kid, and I spent a good part of that time in the jungle. I was always bringing home some sort of critter and have the scars on my hands to prove it. After the iguanas, boas, caimans, tarantulas, and even a small bushmaster, the leeches and stuff in Vietnam didn't bother me. I stripped down butt naked and headed for the pool with my M-16 in one hand and a bandoleer of ammo in the other. After laying my weapon and ammo down next to the pool, I slid off into the cool mountain water. It felt great. It took a few minutes for the leeches to home in on me. An inch or so below the surface of the water I could see three or four leeches moving toward me. Their stretched-out bodies rippled as they moved like little heat-seeking missiles in my direction. I proceeded to enjoy the refreshing water, but after a few minutes, was forced to move to another location in the pool to avoid the masses of leeches moving in my direction. Although I had to move from time to time to escape the

My Story, Vietnam 1968, 196th Light Infantry Brigade

leeches and keep some of my blood, I enjoyed a good long bath. Afterwards, I washed the leeches off with mosquito repellent and then took a final quick dip to rinse off the blood and mosquito repellent.

There were clean, dry fatigue tops and bottoms waiting for me after my bath. There wasn't any underwear. I had learned that the grunts in the field don't wear underwear, green or white. Underwear would just hinder the air from getting where it needed to go to keep the jungle rot in check. I welcomed the feel of the clean clothes, and the dry wool socks soothed my tired feet.

The weather had mostly cooperated and gave us a chance to dry out and enjoy our break from the war. I played a little pitch, but mostly I just lay around in the sun shooting the bull with some of the guys.

At noon the next day, services were held for the boys killed in Que Son Valley. A chaplain from Chu Lai was choppered in to conduct the services. A special prayer was said for those still missing in action. I didn't know anyone on the long list of names read by the chaplain, but it was hard to believe that they were young boys like the rest of us. It wasn't like the war movies at all. We were not war-hardened soldiers with thick beards and a wad of tobacco in our mouth. Alpha Company was mostly young boys, with Sergeant Hanna being the only one I can remember able to grow much of a beard. Hey! Come to think of it, he even chewed tobacco!

We played like the kids we were until late that second day, then it was time to grow up and become soldiers again.

Chapter Four

Long Range Observation Post

We received more good news. It was Alpha's turn to provide defense for LZ Center. I did dread the climb to the top, but Center meant hot meals and no humping.

After reaching the top, I had just settled into a bunker when I learned that I had been volunteered by Sp-4 Mason to be one of a five-man Observation Post (OP). Mason had been chosen to lead the OP, and he picked me and three others to go along with him. A chopper was to take us, food for seven days, radio, spare batteries, and ammo to the top of Hill 408 about three klicks or so to the east of Center. Mason explained that our job would be to watch the hills around 408 and the flatlands to the east to detect enemy movement. I knew from the stories handed down that not everyone who went out on an OP made it back, so I wasn't looking forward to the trip.

An hour and a half later, the five of us were jumping off a chopper on top of Hill 408. The sight of the thick jungle that lay between us and the safety of LZ Center terrified me. I've got to hand it to Mason; he had his act together. He wasted no time establishing our position. Radio contact was established, defcons (pre-determined artillery coordinates)

My Story, Vietnam 1968, 196th Light Infantry Brigade

called in, and claymores and trip flares were set out. With our position prepared, Mason explained to us again what was expected. He said that if we were to get hit, it would probably be at night, and the first thing to do would be to fire the claymores and then start throwing hand grenades. Meanwhile, Mason would be calling in artillery. "DO NOT FIRE YOUR WEAPON!" he stressed. "The flash will give our position away, and then it will be over for all of us." Mason said that if things got worse, we were to leave the mountain down the west side, the only side not being shelled. From that point on, each man would be on his own to make it back to Center. Mason went over in detail where all the minefields were located around Center and suggested several routes up the mountain to the fire support base.

    The days were long. Most of my time was spent just doing nothing, and that is tough to do for seven days. I did get caught up on my letter writing though. I remember almost overdosing on chocolate. One of the earlier OPs had left a bunch of chocolate bars on the hill. Some were still in the box, and others were scattered about. I searched the grass and collected my share. The bars were so old that the wrappers had faded, and the candy inside had turned whitish brown. They didn't taste very good, but I ate them anyhow because it was something to do. Mason was relieved to find the candy because to him, it meant no booby traps. The VC apparently hadn't visited the hill prior to our arrival.

    The view from the mountain was beautiful. A thousand shades of green blended together flawlessly to create a breathtaking view. To the west I could see the rolling hills and ridges that melted into the grayish, green outline of much larger and higher mountains in the distance. The flat terrain to the east was a checkerboard of open paddies and hedge rows that captured patches of jungle as it stretched out toward the horizon. Just beyond the horizon was the ocean, and beyond that, my home. It seemed as though I could see that far from our position on Hill 408.

The nights were even longer – terribly long. I tried not to think about our situation because when I did, I felt like I was about to be overcome by the suffocating fear. Mason seemed certain that we would be hit. Over and over in my mind I practiced what I would do if things got bad. Charlie knew we were there, and he could take us anytime he wanted to. The only thing keeping him from sending us home early was the hell he would catch from our artillery as he made his retreat. Several times at night, sounds in the brush made me brace for the inevitable. I knew that the moment had come. "This was it, it was fixin' to happen." But it never did. We watched the hills and the flatlands around Hill 408 for a week and reported two fires and called artillery in twice, both times sending a lone VC running for cover.

My anxiety reached its peak when I saw the chopper coming to pick us up. I figured that the chopper might make it worth the risk for the VC. Charlie could want the chopper and us. I hopped aboard the chopper and held my breath the whole time the chopper was on the ground, praying that the enemy would leave us alone. The chopper lifted into the air, and the anxious moments passed as we cleared the danger area and headed back toward the safety of LZ Center.

Chapter Five

LZ Colt

Back on Center, the first thing in order was a hot meal and a carton of fresh milk. After eating, I reported to the chopper pad to be resupplied. I couldn't believe it; brand new M-16s, magazines, rucksacks, poncho liners, and anything else I wanted. I felt like a kid that was being given his Christmas presents. I surely didn't mind trading the piece of junk in my hand for a new, never-been-fired M-16.[1] My new weapon had the redesigned flash suppressor, which I liked. My old weapon had the open style flash suppressor, which seemed to have a way of hanging up on every vine or bush I passed. I didn't plan on killing anybody with my new weapon; I just needed it to make sure I got back home.

The rest of the company was packed and ready to move. Word had it that Alpha Company was moving back to the flatlands, back closer to Chu Lai and Da Nang. At the time I

---

[1] Although I didn't know it at the time, I was very fortunate that I didn't have to rely on my first weapon. Due to numerous design flaws, the early model M-16 had proved to be unreliable. Apparently the problems that plagued my first weapon had been corrected because my new weapon served me well.

knew nothing of the Tet offensive, but I'm sure the events of January 31 prompted our move.

It wasn't long until I was on a chopper in route to a fire support base called LZ Colt. As LZ Colt came into view, I could see a circular perimeter of bunkers and concertina with the artillery, medical bunker, and command post in the center. There was nothing heavy – just 105s and four-deuce and 81 millimeter mortars. As I stepped off the chopper, my first impressions of Colt were good. The surrounding area was nice and flat with wide-open fields of fire. Colt looked defendable to me.

We were assigned bunkers, and our first task was to clean them up. The hand grenades were to be inspected and replaced if necessary, new trip flares and claymores set out, and more sandbags filled and positioned. An hour or so later, the last of Alpha had arrived at Colt. By that time the two bunkers assigned to our squad had started looking pretty good. "BOOM!" An explosion sounded on the opposite side of the perimeter. I went down on one knee, undecided on what to do next. We were all green. No one knew what to do. Then I heard someone yelling, "MEDIC! MEDIC! WE NEED A MEDIC OVER HERE!" A hand grenade had just killed a soldier in the Third Platoon. Nobody knew exactly what had happened. He was cleaning his bunker when an old grenade somehow went off. The war was over for him. An accident had taken his life.

I liked Colt and the area around it. In my mind the flatlands just didn't pose the threat that the highlands did, plus we were closer to the larger bases on the coast.

Although the area around Colt was relatively open, the company still sent out LPs (listening post) at night to provide early warning in the event of an enemy attack. I liked Colt, but I didn't like the LPs. The idea of four men spending the night 100 to 125 meters out in front of the perimeter just didn't seem healthy to me. I had no choice; everyone had to go when it was their turn; that is, except for the officers and members of the CP.

I pulled my first LP at Colt on our third night at the base. That night it would be Mason, Mann, Clark, and I providing early warning for LZ Colt should the enemy attack. After the evening meal, it was time to prepare for the LP. We traveled light when we went out on LPs. I took only my webbing with two ammo pouches, a canteen attached, a bandoleer of M-16 magazines, and my weapon. To make sure I would be able to move quietly and unseen, I kept my dog tags taped together on the inside of my fatigues, and I buckled my watch to my breast pocket flap and let it hang down into the pocket to keep it from showing. After replacing my steel pot with a camouflaged jungle cap, I was ready to go. Mason did all the squad leader things, like establish radio frequency, and made sure everyone on the perimeter, especially those on the side that we would be on, knew where we would be located. He took a quick look at us to ensure that dog tags were taped up, nothing shiny was exposed, and there were no rattles.

After the sun set, it was time to go. In a single file we followed Mason through the wire. The exit path was a maze. We had to crisscross back-and-forth to make our way to the outside of the wire. Working through the maze, I thought to myself how difficult it would be to have to make it back to the safety of the perimeter in a hurry. I just hoped I wouldn't have to do it.

After clearing the concertina wire and crossing the open field, we entered a wooded area. Mason picked a spot about 25 meters into the woods. I didn't feel good about the location because you just couldn't see anything but the heavy brush around us. I believe that was Mason's point – if we couldn't see them, they couldn't see us. Mason had selected the location as more of a hiding place rather than a place for us to do our job. I felt that if Charlie were to come our way, he would be right on top of us before we knew what was happening.

We settled in and set up guard shifts for the night. Mann was to sleep next to the guard because he snored. One of the duties of the guard was to shake Mann every time he started to snore. Snoring was a life or death deal in the field. "Do you snore?" was often the first question a new man was asked. If the answer was yes, the squad leader's response was usually, "We don't want him!" I was surprised to find out that guard shifts were even used on LPs and ambushes; after all, no one ever slept in the movies. And besides that, your life was in danger every second you were outside the perimeter. With experience, I learned that a man needs sleep. The one on guard duty must be alert; more alert than he would be if he had stayed awake all night.

Like most of the LPs and ambushes I went on early in my tour, I planned on staying awake all night, but I must have dozed off and was awakened in the early AM for the start of my shift. For a second after being woke up, my mind was at peace, but then suddenly the realization of where I was and what I was doing struck home. Instead of waking up and being relieved that it was only a nightmare, I woke up and realized that I was living the nightmare. I was in the jungle thirteen thousand miles from home hiding from someone who wanted to kill me. The sweat slowly rolled down my face, and I could feel the tension build as I watched the blackness, listened for the enemy, and responded to the hourly SITREPs (situation reports). Breaking squelch twice (depress the button on the radio handset twice) informed the CP RTO that everything was okay. Although the volume was turned down as low as possible, the squelch still seemed too loud. I prayed Charlie wouldn't hear it.

"Z-Z-Z!... Z-Z-Z!... Z-Z-Z!" Mann started to snore again. The racket coming from his nostrils sounded like a chain saw in the silence of the night. A quick poke in the ribs would stop the saw – at least for a few minutes. We used Mason's watch. It had illuminated dials that seemed too bright and hands that moved too slow; painfully slow. I studied every sound. Could that be Charlie? Or maybe, and I prayed, it was just a lizard or something.

Daylight eventually came, and it was time to go back. Charlie had left us alone. No one can explain the intense feelings experienced by a soldier while on a LP or the total relief that is felt the next morning after it is all over and time to go back.

The next two or three weeks brought more "search and destroy" missions during the day, which included several air assaults, and LPs and ambushes at night. Our efforts around Colt were mostly unproductive except for the four VC killed by the Second Platoon. An occasional sniper provided the only excitement for the First Platoon. Clark almost got his tail shot off – literally. We were taking a break in a lightly wooded area on the edge of an open rice paddy when the snapping sounds of a burst of AK bullets filled the air, sending us to the ground and scrambling for cover. Clark had been sitting on his helmet, and a round put a hole clean through it. Nobody got hit, but it scared the hell out of all of us. After the danger had passed, Clark humorously played it for everything it was worth. He started, "He almost shot my ass off! I almost got my ass shot off!" He had us rolling on the ground with laughter as he raised his arm and looked around toward his butt and said, "Somebody check and see if he hit me in the ass!" The laughter helped us forget the danger.

Other than the snipers, the war had started to get easy. I hated every LP, but I was getting to the point that I didn't mind the patrols. We always traveled light (no rucksack), and the humping was easy. The monsoon weather was behind us, and we were being treated to some beautiful days. The AO (Area of Operation) around Colt was populated, and a number of small villages were in the area. When a patrol moved into a village, the suspicious-looking young men, and sometimes women, were detained and sent back to Colt or Chu Lai for interrogation.

Vietnam was beautiful, and I enjoyed moving from village to village. They were always neat and uncomplicated and had a way of making me somewhat envious of the simple life the people appeared to be living. Then I remembered the war. The war had everything screwed up. I remember thinking that maybe the war was about over. I had been in the field for over a month and had not seen any significant action.

I was on another squad size patrol no different than any other one we had been on during the past several weeks. We came upon a single hooch. As we approached the hooch, we stopped to listen before we cleared the cover of the trail. Hearing male voices, I immediately moved out to cover the back of the hooch. Clark positioned himself in front, and Mason motioned for Mann, Taylor, and Baugh, the new guy, to check out the hooch. We surprised an old mama-san, a young woman, several kids, an old man and a young man who was in his early twenties. Taylor ordered the two men out of the hooch and for the women and children to stay inside. Both men were trying to tell us something. Of course, we didn't know what, and apparently Mason didn't care. Mason shoved them around a bit. The whole time both of them kept jabbering about something, but he wasn't interested. Mason told us that we were going to take them in. He believed they were VC. Their hands were too smooth to be farmers, and the younger VC appeared to have marks on his shoulders, probably made by the straps of a backpack.

We moved away from the hooch and down the trail about 25 to 30 meters and then stopped. Mason got on the horn and reported that we had two detainees. A second later, he turned to us and said, "They don't want them. They've got too many now, and they don't want us to let them go either." Mason turned to me and said, "Shoot the dinks." At first I thought he was joking, but when I saw the look on his face, I knew he wasn't. Mason was dead serious. I told him that I wouldn't do it and tried pleading with him to check back with the CP to make sure that's what they wanted. Mason then turned to Baugh, who was on his very first patrol, and ordered him to shoot the prisoners. Baugh refused.

It was then when Mann said, "Well shit, I'll do it." He raised his weapon and pulled the trigger, "POP!" The young man fell. His body was totally void of life as it fell straight down to the ground and hit with a thud. I can't explain the feeling. I had never fainted before in my life, but I felt my eyeballs rollback. I thought I was going to go. A rush of emotions overwhelmed me. I physically couldn't say or do anything. Taylor broke open his M-79 grenade launcher, removed the grenade round, and then reloaded with a canister round (buckshot charge). The old man dropped to his knees, and without saying anything, was begging for mercy. Taylor shot him. He fell beside the young man. I hated them all. I hated Mason, I hated Mann, and I hated Taylor. And most of all, I hated myself for not stopping them.

We walked away. Just as we moved out of sight, I heard a woman scream. Her scream touched every nerve in my body. She screamed again, and then began a loud mournful cry. The rest of the family joined her when they arrived to see Mason's handiwork. I was sick. I felt like crying, and I may have. The emotions were strong, and they hurt. Taylor and Mann were not war-hardened soldiers. They had not seen any more action than I had.

After that day I didn't have much to do with Mason. I even asked around a bit to see if there was some way I could be transferred to Sergeant Stone's squad in the Second

Platoon. Stoney, as he was called, had the reputation for being one of the best, and I wanted to be in his squad. It didn't work out; I was stuck with Mason. Most of the guys seemed to side with Mann and Taylor. They had killed their first Viet Cong. Alpha's body count had dropped off after moving out of the mountains, and I'm sure whoever gave Mason orders to kill our prisoners didn't want to see McNamara's numbers drop any farther.

Mason received some bad news from home. I'm not sure what – family death or something. He left on emergency leave and was replaced with a new in-country buck sergeant named Rodgers. I liked him. Although he was new in-country, he seemed to know his stuff, or at least he talked a good story. Others joined the platoon. All were new recruits, basic, AIT, and Nam. Alpha Company's strength had increased significantly while at Colt.

There were more "search and destroy" missions, more LPs and ambushes, but no contact. The days spent at Colt weren't bad. It seemed like there was always something going on. The guys in Artillery had some pretty neat bunkers. They were more permanent than our perimeter bunkers, and I liked to go visit just to look at all the pin-ups, lots of centerfolds, and just plain rough, girly pictures hanging on the sandbag walls. You could get high just getting too close to some of the bunkers. I really wasn't interested in getting my head all messed up, but some of those guys sure seemed to be having a good time. I figured that some of them liked it better in Vietnam than they did in the State-side Army.

From time to time, children from a nearby village would come up to the first roll of wire and yell, "GI, chop chop!" They wanted us to throw them food and candy. The outside roll of wire was a pretty good throw, but if you had a good arm, you could get a tin of peanut butter or can of cookies out to them. Most of the guys liked the kids and enjoyed throwing them things, but several weren't nearly as thoughtful. They tried to see who could be the first to knock one of the kids down, hopefully with a heavy can of beanie weenies. The kids knew what the GIs were doing and always seemed to stay a step ahead of them. The more that was thrown at them, the better they liked it.

During one patrol in late February, we escorted a group of doctors and medics to a nearby village. They set up a clinic and provided medical services to those who needed it. It seemed ironic. One group of Americans would pass through and burn a hooch, and the next would pass out food. The next group would kill somebody, and the one after that would provide medical services... CRAZY!

Chapter Six

The NVA

We were told to pack it up. The company was leaving Colt, and there seemed to be some urgency about it. I hurriedly packed my rucksack, making sure I put everything where it belonged. Everything I carried had a place. I started by putting the twelve meals of C-rations inside the sack, followed by my toothbrush, toothpaste, shaving cream, razor, mirror, spare socks, jungle cap, soap, letters from home, gun grease, cleaning kit, and a bar of C-4 (plastic explosive) one of my buddies in artillery had given me. The C-4 worked great for heating C's. The outside pockets of the rucksack were reserved for things I wanted easy access to, like my writing paper and pen, matches, heat tabs, SP pack, toilet paper, mosquito repellent, and a collection of twine and string I could use for one thing or another.

I had learned how to fold and roll up my poncho and liner to the exact dimensions needed to fit snugly under the rucksack sack and be neatly tied in place along with my entrenching tool. Using my less-than-sharp bayonet, I cut out a section of cardboard from a C-ration box and secured it between the sack and the aluminum frame of the rucksack. The cardboard would provide a cushion between the load and my back. I filled my four canteens, snapped them in their pouches, and attached one on each side of my rucksack and two to my pistol belt.

Inside the bunker, I disconnected the claymore detonator from the wire, traded my three hand grenades for three fresh ones, and picked up a smoke grenade. I attached hand grenades to the sides of my right ammo pouch and a hand grenade and the smoke to the sides of the left pouch. I walked to the front of the bunker and pulled the loose claymore wire from the bunker opening, and then proceeded to wrap the wire around my left elbow and hand as I walked out to retrieve the mine. I unscrewed the blasting cap from the mine and carried the claymore back to the bunker where I put it, the wire and cap, and the detonator in the carrying bag. I tied the bag to the bottom of the rucksack over my poncho and entrenching tool.

After obtaining twenty-five new magazines from Sergeant Hanna, I loaded each with eighteen rounds and verified that the spring of each felt stiff enough to deliver the rounds. I filled my ammo pouches and the bandoleers with the magazines. The ammo pouches were designed to hold two M-14 magazines, but would hold five M-16 magazines, three turned down side by side, one turned down in front, and one magazine could be laid on top. Each bandoleer had seven pockets for a total of fourteen magazines in the two bandoleers. I carried a total of twenty-five magazines; ten in my ammo pouches, fourteen in my bandoleers, and one in my weapon.

Just as I finished getting my gear together, we began to saddle up. I put my webbing over my shoulders and fastened my pistol belt. My bayonet and scabbard hung from the belt, along with the ammo pouches and canteens. A first aide pouch was attached high up on the left shoulder strap of my webbing. The pouch was positioned upside down to provide easier access to the field dressing inside. I then put one M-16 bandoleer around my neck and under my right arm and the second one around my neck and under my left arm. They were positioned so the magazines crisscrossed on my chest. I picked up my steel pot and placed it on my head and draped an olive green towel around my neck and over my shoulders. I turned my rucksack around and propped it up against the bunker wall, and then sat down on the ground and scooted my back up against it. I put my arms through the straps and then worked the towel in between the straps and my shoulders. I had learned that the extra padding the towel provided would lessen the pain of the straps, and the loose end of the towel could be used to wipe the sweat from my face. The problem came after securing the rucksack to my back. How in the hell do you get to your feet? The buddy system worked best. I reached out, and one of my buddies helped pull me to my feet.

Sergeant Rodgers inspected each of us to see that we had all of our gear and that the squad had enough claymores and LAWs (light antitank weapons). Alpha Company was saddled up and ready to move out.

I didn't feel good about it. The war thus far had just been too easy on me. As Alpha made its way out through Colt's perimeter wire for the last time, the guys were unusually quiet. I believe we all felt the same way.

We left Colt and moved a half klick or so to a large open area where we waited for choppers to come and pick us up. Just as the company finished spreading out around the open area, the sky filled with Hueys slapping the air as they made their approach. Smoke was popped to give and verify our position to the chopper pilots. The area was large enough for four or five Hueys to set down at a time. Within minutes the entire company was airborne. We were airlifted

My Story, Vietnam 1968, 196th Light Infantry Brigade

to a small base camp someplace south of LZ Colt, which I believe was Hawk Hill.[2]

Our stay at the base was to be short. Word of our mission eventually filtered down to us grunts. The NVA had moved out of the mountains into the flat lands and was on the offensive. While Captain Yurchak talked strategy with the 1st Armored Cavalry, Sergeant Hanna was turning over command of the First Platoon to Lieutenant Gilbert, who was new in-country. Lieutenant Gilbert didn't strike me as the leader type. He was heavyset for a field soldier. Compared to us, he looked fat. At a glance you could tell he was about as green as they came. He still had a sling on his weapon, only carried two canteens, his dog tags rattled, his boots were black, and he didn't use an elastic band to secure his crispy green helmet cover. I hoped that our new platoon leader would let Sergeant Hanna continue to call the shots, at least until he could get it together.

We spent the night at the base, and the next morning moved out on foot, marching to the southwest. We spent several days searching for NVA patrols that were reported operating in the area, but the enemy eluded us. Early one morning the entire company moved into position for an attack on a village where enemy troops had been observed the day before. Our assault fizzled out when we found the village abandoned. As we moved through the village, I felt a little edgy because it was obvious that the village had very recently been evacuated. Some of the cooking fires were still smoldering, and there was fresh drinking water in the hooches. We heard reports of enemy sightings several times during the day; however, no contact was made.

---

[2] Early in my tour before I was given the privilege of carrying a map, I didn't have a clue where we were at or where we were going. These writings provide my best guess.

The NVA

The foxholes were deeper than usual that night. Everyone was a little uneasy, and if the reports on enemy strength in the area were accurate, it was for a good reason. "BOOM!" I was jolted awake about midnight when a mortar round exploded inside the perimeter. The blast sent me instinctively scrambling to my foxhole. I was scared. I wasn't sure what was happening and didn't know what to expect next, that is, until I heard a series of thuds from mortar tubes off in the distance. I knew what was coming. I stayed low in my foxhole with my face pressed against the fresh dirt. "BOOM! BOOM! BOOM! BOOM!" Explosions sounded on the far side of the perimeter. The explosions were followed by silence. Fortunately, nobody had been hit. Word was relayed from foxhole to foxhole, "Keep your eyes open – the CO is expecting an attack." With my weapon ready and scared to death, I watched my section of black jungle and listened for the enemy. A few minutes later, one of the LPs reported some movement and fired their claymore. I'm not sure if the enemy was probing our position or if the guys were just nervous. Anyhow, I spent most of the night in the foxhole and got very little sleep.

The fatigue showed on our faces as we started the next day at dusk. After a short march from our night laager site, Alpha Company rendezvoused with the 1st Armored Cavalry. There was a tank and a number of APCs (armored personnel carriers). I didn't know what the strategy was or what was to happen next. The only thing we grunts knew was that things seemed to be getting serious.

We were told to climb aboard the tracks. The tracks were going to transport us grunts to meet the enemy. I handed my rucksack up to one of the guys and then climbed up on the APC. Getting to ride for a change was a real treat for us grunts. The armor moved out in single file with us grunts riding on top. There was still enough kid left in me that I enjoyed the ride. It excited me to hear the powerful engines groan as the tracks navigated the terrain. I held on as the APC pulled its way out of a rice paddy, up a bank, into the jungle, and then continue on. I hoped for more banks and dikes, and maybe a ditch or two.

The closer we got to our destination, wherever that was, the more cautious the officers seemed to be. At one relatively small rice paddy, we were given the word to dismount and drop our rucksacks. The knee-deep rice paddy was 40 to 50 meters across and kind of in an "L" shape. I don't think any of us grunts had a clue to what was happening. The tracks spread out evenly along our side of the paddy, and we fell in behind the tracks. We were apparently going to assault the wood line on the far side. We slowly moved across the open paddy and then made our way into the woods on the other side. I figured it was just another one of those "practice your training" type assaults, but then suddenly, after we had moved about 25 meters up the slight incline into the woods, all hell broke loose. Boom! Boom! Pop! Boom! Pop! Pop! Sharp, bullwhip cracks filled the air, and rockets and mortars were exploding everywhere. I immediately hit the ground and opened up firing blindly into the thicket in front of me.

As the tank on my right began to advance, I prepared to move out and take cover behind it. Just as I raised up to make my move, "BOOM!" I thought that the tank and I had both been hit. I hit the ground again – my heart pounding. It took me a second to realize that the tank had not been hit but had just fired a round. I had never heard a tank fire before, and it sure sounded like incoming to me. I froze – I didn't know what to do.

The small arms and machine gun fire was intense. I stayed low and began firing my weapon in the direction of the enemy. I couldn't see him, but I knew he was there, and I could hear the snap of his bullets as they passed overhead. I saw a soldier to my right run forward and at point blank range fire several bursts from his M-16 down into some grass that apparently covered a spider-hole. He pulled an RPG launcher (anti-tank weapon) from the hole. An NVA soldier had held his position in an attempt to get a shot off at the tank. He apparently missed and was detected. He paid for his mistake with his life.

I kept my M-16 hot, chewing up the woods in search of an invisible enemy. Thomas, who was on my left, got up and advanced his position about 20 feet. As he hit the ground, he dropped his weapon and grabbed his chest. His boots dug into the dirt as he pushed and squirmed in pain and rolled over onto his back. I knew immediately that he had been hit and began low-crawling toward him.

When I reached Thomas, I was momentarily relieved to find only a small spot of blood on the front of his fatigues. I didn't believe it was serious until I saw the agonizing look on his face and heard his groans. I knew Thomas was in trouble. I yelled, "Medic! Medic! Medic!" I tried to comfort Thomas, telling him that he was going to be okay, but I could tell he was too busy fighting for his life to hear me.

Our medic and another soldier wasted no time in getting to Thomas. The battle raged around us as the medic ripped open Thomas' fatigues. He had a small hole in his chest. When the blood was wiped away, I could see that it wasn't a bullet hole. It looked to me like it had been made by a small wire fragment from a hand grenade or something. When I saw the blood bubbles coming from the hole, I knew he had a serious, sucking chest wound. I held the position and turned my weapon back toward the enemy while the medic and another soldier pulled Thomas toward the rice paddy and safety.

The fighting went on for another five or ten minutes. Mortars, grenades, and rockets exploded, and the snapping sound of an invisible bullwhip filled the air around us. I remember seeing Clark jump up on a tank, apparently to

My Story, Vietnam 1968, 196th Light Infantry Brigade

help somebody who had been hit. I never did find out exactly what had happened, but Clark showed me that he had what it took.

I soon realized that the tracks were retreating. We were pulling back across the paddy. I turned and low-crawled as fast as I could go toward the rice paddy. As I neared the paddy, I got to my feet and began running in a low crouch. When I hit the rice paddy, I made an all-out run for my life, taking care to stay out of the way of the retreating tracks. I sloshed through the deep mud and water, headed for the far side and safety. I climbed out of the paddy and took cover in a small ditch. I was safe.

There was a lot of confusion. I heard Sergeant Hanna and several of the officers yelling, but I wasn't sure about what. I was safe in my ditch and didn't want to move. Something had everyone's attention. Charlie had zeroed in on a couple of stragglers. The two GIs had taken cover in the middle of the rice paddy behind a dike only eight to twelve inches high. I could see rounds hitting the mud and water around them. One of the boys was apparently hit where he lay. The other got up to run, but he was immediately hit and fell back into the mud and water of the paddy.

Things eventually quieted down. After retrieving the fallen soldiers from the rice paddy, Alpha pulled back a couple hundred meters to regroup and care for the wounded. I was shaken from the experience. I was covered from head to toe with mud, water, dirt, and sweat. I had been in one hell of a firefight and never did see an enemy soldier. Sergeant Rogers had seen me attempt to help Thomas. He walked up to me and told me that I did good.

I never learned whether Thomas, or any of the others that were hit that day, lived or died. They were all medevac'd out of the field, and I never heard anything else about them.

We never got much feedback in the field about our fallen buddies.

At a safe distance, I listened to our artillery pound the woods on the far side of the paddy. Barrage after barrage of our artillery sent clouds of dirt and smoke high into the air. When the guns finally fell silent, the wood line was left in a million splinters.

We moved back across the paddy into the woods again, but this time we met no resistance. I counted a total of five dead NVA soldiers in the area I went through. I remember looking at one dead soldier who was face down in a trench and seeing a small shovel about fifteen inches long or so attached to his backpack. It looked like a child's toy shovel used to play in the sand. It was hard to believe that he had used it to dig the trench he was in. The corners were perfectly square and walls straight and deep. It was obvious that he had been a man with lots of patience.

The NVA had been a step ahead of us. They apparently knew we were coming, waited for us, kicked our ass, and then ran.

We were soon in a column headed west again and were later joined by another column of tracks led by three tanks. It was an impressive force moving to engage the enemy. We traveled along in single file, with the tanks first, followed by the APCs. As the lead tank approached a large, wide-open rice paddy, it stopped. The other tanks moved up on line. The wood line on the far side was studied closely, and then the tanks opened up with probing fire. The sudden burst of hell caught several of us grunts off guard. An M-16 popped. I instinctively jumped off the track along with several others. Someone was hit and yelling for a medic. Baugh was rolling around on the ground holding his foot. I soon figured out that there was no incoming. The tanks startled Baugh when they opened up. He was sitting on the side of the APC with the barrel of his M-16 resting on his foot, and he apparently had the safety off. When the tanks opened up, he jerked and pulled the trigger. He was fortunate. He wasn't hurt. The bullet either went between his toes or beside the foot or something, 'cause he still had all five toes. Baugh did, however, learn a lesson. He learned why there is a safety on his weapon.[3]

The probing fire received no response. I was back in the column a ways and couldn't see what was going on up front, but I could tell something was up. The word spread fast that several bunkers had been spotted on the far side of the paddy.

We took cover, and artillery was called in on what was believed to be enemy positions. We nervously waited for our turn as we listened to the whistling roar of the incoming artillery shells and the tremendous explosions that followed. The big guns pounded the hell out of the woods on the other side of the paddy.

---

[3] I received a phone call from Barry Baugh in December 1997. Barry wasn't sure that I remembered him until I mentioned the incident where he almost shot his foot off by accident. Barry knew I remembered. "Accident hell," he yelled, "I was trying to shoot myself in the foot and missed!" Barry said that he was convinced he was going to be killed and had decided to do whatever it took to get out of the field. He and Trammel had discussed various ways to do it. At one point Barry had propped his leg up on a stump and Trammel was going to jump on it and break it. Barry said he chickened out at the last moment. They both decided that it would be a lot cleaner if Barry just shot himself. The perfect opportunity came when the tracks opened fire. Barry said he didn't want to wound himself too bad, just serious enough to get out of the field. When he pulled the trigger, he was sure he had done it. One of the NCOs came to Barry's rescue and cut the lace of Barry's boot with a bayonet to get the boot off in a hurry. Barry was just as surprised as everyone else to find that he had missed. His boot had a hole in the side and bottom of it, but his foot was unharmed. Barry had to put his boot back on, tie it up with a bunch of short pieces of lace, and then climb back up on the APC.

The NVA

When the artillery stopped, we knew it was our turn. The 20 or so APCs moved up on line with the tanks, and we grunts fell in behind them. When I walked into the paddy to take my place behind one of the APCs, I could feel the adrenaline begin to build and the sweat pop out on my face. The engines roared, and the smell of diesel exhaust filled the air as the tracks began to move forward. We ground troops followed behind at a slow walk. My emotions ran wild when the tracks began to open up with their 50 calibers.

The smell of diesel exhaust and spent gun powder was strong. A tremendous rush of adrenaline prepared my body for what was to come. The sound from the 50 calibers was unbelievably loud. When the sound seemed as if it couldn't get any louder, others would join in and it got even louder. The tanks were spear heading the attack, flanked by APCs, and we grunts followed at a distance.

Our military force was evenly spread out along the wide-open rice paddy, headed for the wood line on the far side a good 300 meters or more away. I remember thinking that it looked like a classic, picture-perfect assault. Only one thing was missing – incoming – but that changed. When the first tank approached the wood line, it stopped, the hatch opened, and smoke rolled out. It had been hit. The crew scrambled out of the opening. One of the boys was covered with blood and was being helped by his buddy. They jumped from the burning tank into the knee-deep mud and started running for their lives.

The NVA opened up on us – cracks everywhere. We continued our advance. Although I was forced into the mud several times by the snapping sounds overhead, it was obvious that the enemy was targeting the tracks and apparently weren't as concerned about us ground troops behind them. Several of the APCs were hit in quick succession, and our forward movement stopped. An APC adjacent to one that had just taken a hit put it in reverse and began to retreat.

Others quickly followed, and soon all the tracks were moving backwards and firing there 50s to cover their retreat. As I turned to run, I saw one of the APCs stop and partially lowered the rear troop door. Buddies of the wounded soldier from the tank were trying to put him in the track when the track started moving backwards again. The APC ran halfway upon the wounded soldier before his buddies could get the driver's attention. The body of the APC had pushed the soldier down into the mud. With the boy's buddies yelling at the driver, the track pulled forward. The guys pulled their friend from the mud. He was still conscious and alive. A mixture of blood and mud covered his entire body. His buddies struggled to get him up and into the APC. I thought, "Oh God, how can this be happening." I couldn't believe what I was seeing.

The NVA hadn't let up. They had us on the run. The tracks were in reverse, and we ground troops were running for our lives. I was just as concerned about being run down by a track as I was about the enemy fire. In reverse, the track drivers couldn't see what was behind them, and apparently they didn't care. They were more concerned about getting their asses out of range more than they were about us ground pounders behind them. The tracks were continually changing direction in an effort to avoid enemy fire. I kept looking back over my shoulder trying to anticipate which direction the tracks would go. I sloshed through the mud in one direction and then back in the other. It's tough to run in knee deep mud, but you can when you are running for your life. Our classic, picture-perfect assault had turned into an "every man for himself, run for your life" operation.

We eventually regrouped on the safe side of the paddy and medevac's were called in for the dead and wounded. Charlie had concentrated his fire power on the armor. A tank and several APCs were left burning in the paddy. The guys in the tracks had taken much heavier causalities than we grunts had.

We spent what was left of that day watching artillery level the woods. Charlie took one hell of a pounding. Huey gunships circled the area to insure any attempted withdrawal by the enemy would be costly.

Just before sunset, we moved a klick or so to an area where, along with the tracks, we established a defensive perimeter for the night. The long day had taken a toll on me both physically and mentally. I was exhausted. Although we had the tracks with us, I still felt uneasy being so close to the NVA. These guys were hardcore North Vietnamese Regulars. Lieutenant Gilbert and Sergeant Hanna appeared to be working close together, so I began to feel somewhat better about our new platoon leader. They made their rounds to all of the foxholes and talked with each of us a bit. They knew that those of us still in the field had made it through the day physically, but were checking to make sure that we still had it all together mentally.

Like always, an LP was sent out that night. I remember being glad that it was the other guy's turn to go. They went out on the east side because it was heavily wooded. We would need some early warning if an attack came from that direction, and our four-man LP would provide it for us.

When I bedded down, I positioned my weapon and ammo in easy reach and took a mind-set on what I would do should Charlie suddenly awaken me. Mind-sets worked well for me. Without having to think, I just automatically did what I planned to do. It worked again that night. Sometime in the early morning hours, I found myself in the foxhole with my weapon in hand. I had been awakened by a mortar round. "BOOM! BOOM!" Several more hit inside the perimeter, and a series of tube thuds off in the distance meant that more were on the way. The tracks opened up with their 50 calibers. NVA mortars pounded the perimeter.

My Story, Vietnam 1968, 196th Light Infantry Brigade

At first I thought we were under a ground attack, but when the mortar barrage stopped, the only fire was from the tracks' 50 calibers. I couldn't figure out what was going on. We ground troops never opened up at night unless we had no other choice. If you pull the trigger on your M-16 at night, you're in deep trouble. Then I thought, "I don't guess it matters if you are sitting in a tank."

I heard Sergeant Hanna shouting behind me as he ran toward the APC on my left. He was screaming at the soldier on the 50 caliber. He wanted him to stop shooting. "CEASE FIRING YOU SON-OF-A-BITCH!! CEASE FIRING!!" Sergeant Hanna yelled. The gunner either didn't understand him, or didn't hear him, because he stayed heavy on the 50 caliber. Sergeant Hanna climbed up on the track, grabbed one of his grenades, and made a gesture like he was going to pull the pin. I thought for a second he was going to throw the grenade into the track. He managed to get the gunner's attention this time. He stopped firing. I couldn't figure out what in the hell was going on. Then it hit me; the LP was still out there. Sergeant Hanna jumped off the track and headed out of the perimeter toward the LP. All the tracks soon stopped firing. A few minutes later, three members of the LP came running back toward the perimeter. Sergeant Hanna followed behind carrying the forth. Back inside the perimeter, Sergeant Hanna laid the bloody body of the young boy down. He looked dead to me. A 50 caliber round had ripped him open.

Some of the NVA mortar frag found its mark, wounding a number of soldiers. The medics scurried around attending to the wounded as others worked to prepare a LZ. The casualties were medevac'd out.

We all learned a lesson that night. Armored units don't send out LPs at night. If they feel threatened, they just open up with searching fire. I hoped the officers had learned the lesson. A stupid mistake had cost a young man his life.[4]

The next morning we found that the enemy had pulled out, leaving behind the price for making a stand. I saw nine or ten dead NVA soldiers spread out over the landscape and another one partially buried in his collapsed fighting position. The vegetation had been shredded. It looked as if the area had been run over by a giant lawn mower with a dull blade set at about four feet high. The smell of burnt vegetation, spent powder, and death was strong. The entire area, including the dead soldiers, was covered with a layer of dirt and dust. We searched the battlefield and collected the weapons the NVA left behind.

The retreating enemy allowed us to continue our journey west without any more resistance, and eventually Alpha arrived at our objective. The main force of the NVA was reportedly dug in on several rolling hills at the base of the mountains. A large, wide-open area stretched out between us and the hills. It wasn't a wet rice paddy this time, just an open field between us and the NVA bunkers off in the distance. I could tell from the number of choppers circling the area that the coming battle had everyone's attention.

We spread out in a defensive posture in a lightly vegetated area within sight of the hills and waited for word on what was to happen next. Choppers brought in one load of officers after another. I had never seen any of them before, and judging from their unsoiled appearance, it was obvious that they didn't plan on doing any of the fighting. Some journalists and cameraman arrived, followed by more officers. Apparently the loss of a number of tracks and our mounting casualties had gotten somebody's attention. Other choppers brought more supplies and ammo and more

---

[4] In August of 1997 at a reunion of the 196th Light Infantry Brigade held in Washington, DC, I learned that this man survived.

officers. One of the commanders came around shaking everyone's hand and telling us what a good job we were doing. He made the rounds like a politician with polished talk that meant nothing. Like everyone else, I smiled and politely shook his hand. "Where you from soldier?" he asked.

"Tennessee sir!" I responded.

"Keep up the good work," he added as he walked off toward the next man. I guess he hadn't heard that the NVA had kicked our ass twice the day before, and there was a good chance he was going to do it again. The officer, followed by his entourage, got back aboard his chopper and flew off toward the east and the safety of the rear. I later learned that there was an article in one of the Americal Division's newsletters, or some publication, about this turkey being presented a Silver Star for leading us in battle.

Lieutenant Gilbert came around and told us that an air strike had been called, and that the planes were on their way. The Air Force was going to attempt to soften the enemy's position before we began our assault. Lieutenant Gilbert ordered Sergeant Rodgers to take our squad to a small village at the edge of the open area about fifty meters away and make sure that the Vietnamese civilians knew to take cover. The only inhabitants of the village were three or four mama-sans and some children. We went to the hooches and tried to convince them to leave and to take cover in a shallow ditch at the edge of their village. They were scared and didn't know what we were trying to say. We tried to explain, but they didn't understand. They didn't understand, that is, until the first Phantom began to make its approach, and then it all of a sudden became perfectly clear. The mama-sans herded the kids to the ditch, and we followed. I took cover next to a little girl about five or six years old and several young boys. I didn't have to tell them to stay down. They knew what was going to happen. I had never seen an air strike before and didn't know quite what to expect, so I kept my head up so I could see.

As the first Phantom made its thunderous approach, the little girl scooted up close to me and put her arm around my waist as if to hold on.[5] I looked down and saw the fear on her face. The Phantom released its bombs, and they sailed down toward the hills and the NVA. The scream of the Phantom was enough to scare anybody, and then the bombs hit and their TREMENDOUS EXPLOSIONS followed. BOOM! BOOM! The little girl squeezed tight. I could literally see the shock waves radiate out from the explosions and feel the ground tremble as clouds of dirt and smoke rolled hundreds of feet into the air. I was scared. A second Phantom started its dive, followed by another. Explosions shook the earth. I lowered my head into the ditch, overwhelmed by the awesome display of power. I wondered how the NVA soldiers felt. The Air Force put on a real show that continued for quite some time. I couldn't imagine how any of the NVA could have survived.

I knew the time was getting close when all of our visitors began leaving. I believe that most of them were there just to watch the air strike, and apparently none wanted to stay around for what was to follow. It was time to go to war. The Air Force had done what they could, and now it was time for the Army to do its job.

The engines roared and exhaust filled the air as the tracks moved out into the open flat and maneuvered into position. I left the ditch and took my place in the field. For the third time in two days, Alpha Company had lined up behind the 1st Cav' preparing to assault a bunker line. I knew more what to expect this time and had good reason to

---

[5] Even though they were scared, young children were often "extra" friendly toward the GI. I often wondered if they had be instructed to act that way toward us just to help keep us friendly.

My Story, Vietnam 1968, 196th Light Infantry Brigade

be scared. We began our advance evenly spread out across the open flat. It was hard to believe that the NVA was going to make a stand on the small, sparsely-covered hills to our front, especially with the cover of the rugged mountains only a few klicks away. The tracks began opening up with their fifties. The familiar smell of spent powder and the powerful sound of the fifties caused my adrenaline to flow. My fatigues were wet with sweat, and my heart was beating hard as I moved toward the enemy. I worked my way over in behind one of the tanks to provide me with some cover. I walked to one side so I could peer around the edge of the tank to see our objective. "Crack! Crack! Crack! Crack!" They opened up on us. I made a quick step in behind the tank and kept moving. The machine gun fire from the hill was intense.

As we continued our advance, their machine guns were joined by small arms. The snapping sounds of incoming filled the air. The tracks were attracting a lot of fire, and I knew I was in the wrong place. I hit the ground and began low-crawling toward some cover. I took refuge behind a small, dried-up rice paddy dike. I opened up, firing blindly at the hills.

There was plenty of cover in the field; a ditch here, one over there, and the remains of paddy dikes from place to place. Our advance was slowed, but we didn't stop. The APCs were heavy on the fifty calibers. Back from behind us, a Huey Cobra gunship made his approach. He opened up, firing over our heads toward the enemy positions. As the rounds from his cannons passed overhead with powerful cracks, I felt a rush of adrenaline flow down my legs and through my arms, leaving a tingling sensation in my toes and fingers – devastating firepower.

The Cobra was followed by a number of Huey gunships providing support for us. The slow rat-tat-tat of their M-60s was continuous. I saw several choppers working the backside

The NVA

of the hill toward the mountain and figured that some of the NVA were trying to withdraw. Some of the guys stayed behind the tracks, and others advanced their position by moving from cover to cover. I stayed low and waited until the enemy fire seemed to be concentrated someplace else, and then I would make my move. I knew the enemy was on the hill, but I couldn't see him. Thus far I had just been shooting at the hill in front of me. And then I spotted one, an enemy bunker about halfway up the side of the hill. It only stuck above the ground a foot or so and looked more like an elongated clump of shrubs, but it wasn't. It definitely was a bunker; the squared off edges on the sides gave it away. I looked to the left of the bunker and saw another, and then a third and a fourth. I took aim and emptied a magazine into the clump of shrubs. I could tell the gunners on the APCs had also located the bunkers. They turned the heat up. Fifty caliber rounds ripped at the bunkers. We were no longer just shooting up the hill; we were concentrating our fire power on the enemy bunkers.

The intensity of the enemy fire dropped dramatically, and we began moving toward our objective much faster. Lieutenant Gilbert was walking fully erect with his RTO behind him. Every once in a while he would kneel down on one knee, but he never got on the ground like the rest of us. I spotted my next position, a small ditch at the base of the hill. The bunkers were located about 50 or 60 meters up the gradual incline of the hill and were still sporadically spitting lead. Apparently Valdes had the same idea because we hit the shallow ditch at the same time. A burst of rounds from the bunker just ahead kept us down. Valdes looked at me wide-eyed and with a grin on his face and yelled, "Do you believe this!"

I shouted, "It's almost like a real war!"

One of the APCs passed us on our left and moved up the hill toward the bunker. The track pulled right up beside the enemy position and stopped. A GI jumped off the track and at point blank range fired his AR-15 on full automatic into an opening on the side of the bunker. He was followed by his buddy who tossed a grenade into the opening. They hit the ground, and the grenade went off with a quick, muffled explosion. Dirt and dust belched from the bunker opening. The Cav' soldiers proceeded to pull three dead enemy soldiers from the bunker. By that time Valdes and I had moved up to the bunker. Dead soldiers just don't look like they had been real people, especially if they had been killed in an explosion. The uniform coating of dust makes the soldiers skin, uniform, and equipment appear to be all a single color, a light, yellowish brown. And it's not all bloody like what you would expect. The heart stops immediately, so you don't have anything pumping the blood out, and the dirt and heat from the explosion seems to stop what blood there is.

Valdes and I turned our attention to the bunker on our right. I had not seen any activity in the bunker and wasn't sure if it was occupied or not. I pulled a grenade from the side of my ammo pouch, pulled the pin, and Valdes opened up on the bunker with his M-16. I jumped to my feet and ran toward the bunker, crouched low, and chucked the grenade in the bunker opening. I took a few quick steps back toward Valdes and then dived for cover. "Boom!" The grenade exploded. Valdes and I immediately moved to the bunker prepared to finish the job, but as the dust settled, found that the bunker had been abandoned. We took cover in front of the blown bunker to protect ourselves from the occasional fire we were receiving from farther up the hill.

There were lots of heroes running around mopping up the last of the enemy positions, but I liked it where I was and took advantage of the cover to catch my breath. Most of the bunkers were silenced before the grenades were dropped in. I believe we put so much heat on the enemy positions that most of the enemy soldiers just hunkered down in the bottom and waited for the grenade that they knew would be coming. We didn't disappoint them.

The gunships off in the distance were apparently giving the retreating NVA hell. I believe that the NVA had left enough front-line bunkers manned to slow us down so the main force could retreat to the mountains. Valdes reached over and touched me to get my attention, and then pointed to Lieutenant Gilbert. He was standing fully erect and didn't seem to be concerned about the enemy still shooting at us. "Crack! Crack! Crack!" We received another burst of incoming from the top of the hill. Those of us that weren't on the ground hit it. Those of us on the ground got closer to it, except for Lieutenant Gilbert. I'm not sure what his problem was. He wasn't the leader type, and I think he was trying to prove something, plus it may have been a little hard for him physically to get up and down so much because of his size. A moment later, Lieutenant Gilbert collapsed straight down to the ground like a limp ragdoll. He had been shot in the chest, and it was serious. Valdes and I crawled over and helped the RTO pull Gilbert back to some cover. Several guys and the medic dragged Gilbert over to one of the tracks. He looked dead to me. I never did hear whether he lived or died.

As we began to withdraw, the shooting stopped, except for the gunships off in the distance still chasing the enemy. My confidence, which had been shattered the day before, had been restored – we had defeated the NVA. We moved back across the flats to the staging area to regroup and evacuate our casualties. Some of the guys were showing off their war trophies they had taken from the bunkers and the dead NVA soldiers. Our causalities were relatively light considering what had just happened. We put a real hurtin' on the NVA. They were licking their wounds as they ran for the safety of the mountains to the west. Their losses that day were enormous. The NVA may have had the will to fight, but they didn't have the firepower or support necessary to counter what we had thrown at them.

I left the battlefield that day feeling better about our abilities and had also developed a healthy respect for the NVA. It takes a hard-core soldier to hold his position in a small hole while 500 pound bombs hit all around him and then to look out across the field and see a large ground force reinforced with armor coming toward him, not to mention the sky full of Cobras and Huey gunships. He could have surrendered or run for his life, but he didn't. He stayed, fought, and died.

Riding on the tracks, we pulled back several klicks or so and set up in a defensive position on a small hill for the night. I still felt a little uneasy. We weren't that far away from the enemy, and their willingness to die frightened me. My uneasiness slowly subsided as an almost festive mood swept over the perimeter. Maybe it was our youth that gave us the ability to put the deaths of our buddies behind us and allowed us to celebrate our victory. We were proud and our spirits were high. We had kicked the NVA's ass, and we all knew it. We had a good time that night. For starters, we didn't send out an LP – the officers had learned their lesson. The guys on the tracks broke out their beer and shared it with us. The soldiers of the 1st Cavalry had earned my respect, and I'm sure they felt the same toward us. We joked and laughed and enjoyed one another as we drank the hot beer. We were all Americans, and we loved one another. The normal friction one sees in a group of young boys just wasn't there. There were no bullies, and there were no wimps. There is a certain understanding that comes with the realization of learning just how fragile human life is.

Morning came and we waited to see what the day was to bring. Sergeant Rodgers came back from the morning squad leader meeting and told us that we were going to stay with the tracks. The company was going to ride back to the armored unit's base camp, and the Cav' was going to treat us to a hot meal. We were soon on our way back to safety and a hot meal. It was a long journey, but I didn't mind the ride. I'm not sure why, but the countryside didn't seem to be as threatening to me. I had more confidence now, and anything less than the NVA we had faced just wasn't a threat.

One thing that amazed me was just how effortlessly the tracks moved across the water and mud of the paddies, especially the APCs. They seemed to slide over the top of everything. One of the tanks did get stuck, however. It mired down deep in the mud of a rice paddy. The tank had found a hole or something in the paddy because it was up to its turret in mud. Attempts by the tank to free itself only made things worse. Another tank and several APCs stayed behind to help while the rest of us moved on toward the base camp. The guys were connecting tow cables to the trapped tank when the rest of us moved on out of sight.

The closer we got to the base camp, the more familiar the track drivers became with the area. I could tell they knew where they were going, but there didn't seem to be any logic to why they went around this way instead of going that way. When I asked the APC gunner, he said that the trick was to miss the land mines. He said the guy in the lead track had his shit together and knew the area around the base. He knew where he could go and where it would be best not to. We passed a demolished APC along the way. It was covered with rust and had apparently been part of the landscape for a long while. The whole left side of the thing was gone. I was told that the APC had hit a booby trapped 500 pound bomb. The more I talked to the gunner about tracks and land mines, the more I began to appreciate not being on the lead track. We talked some more, and I decided that being a foot soldier wasn't all that bad.

My Story, Vietnam 1968, 196th Light Infantry Brigade

As we approached the base camp, the surrounding area became more populated. During the last half a klick or so, children would run up alongside the tracks wanting a handout. "GI chop chop!" they would yell. I liked the Vietnamese children. Most of the guys were good to the kids and tossed them a tin of jelly or peanut butter, or maybe a candy bar. The kids scrambled to be the first to reach the treat. A few of the guys weren't nearly as thoughtful. Our APC gunner was one of them. "Watch this," he said. He peeled the foil back on a heat tab, lit it, and threw it to the kids. Heat tabs are used for heating C's and burn hot with an almost invisible flame. The group of kids stopped short of the tab. They recognized what it was. I'm sure they knew from experience, and they also knew the GI.

We finally reached the base camp and were treated to the hot meal we had been promised. Our stay on the Hill was short. The company used the break as an opportunity to be re-supplied and add a few new greens to our numbers.

Chapter Seven

Stand-Down in Chu Lai

Alpha left the base camp by chopper in route to our AO in the mountains around LZ Center. The mountains and the valleys were beautiful from the air. Some of the mountains and ridges were covered in thick jungle while others supported only green grass. Rice paddies filled most of the valley floors, and terraced paddies stair stepped up the sides of the surrounding mountains. The mountains were beautiful, but it scared me when I thought of the dangers they held. It wasn't long before the choppers were putting us down in an open area at the base of a small, grass-covered hill. It wasn't a hot LZ, but we scrabbled around as if it were. An hour or so later, we were digging in on the hill. Plans were to spend the remainder of the day and that night on the hill before starting "search and destroy" missions the next day.

Sergeant Hanna had again assumed the platoon leader's duties, and I felt much better with him calling the shots. It was an easy afternoon for us, and everyone seemed to be in a good mood. Mail was choppered in, and promotions were handed out. All of us Private E-3s were promoted to SP-4 and presented Combat Infantryman Badges. I guess it was kind of a reward for the previous couple of weeks. Rumors of a stand-down in Chu Lai made things even better.

The next several weeks were spent conducting "search and destroy" operations. There was plenty of light action; mostly the point-man for one of the patrols spotting several VC crossing a paddy or walking up on a hooch and surprising one or two of them. Whether you were on point or back in the column a ways, it was nerve-racking. It was a life-or-death situation for the man on point, and for those back in the column, it meant suffocating tension until the magnitude of the confrontation was known. I walked point a lot, mostly because I could read a map better than most of the guys. I was given several opportunities to empty a clip or two at fleeing VC. The patrols were physically, as well as emotionally, demanding; however, I always felt like we were in control of the area. The company had not encountered any NVA regulars, and we seemed to have the Viet Cong pretty much on the run, at least during the day. They did screw with us a lot at night, which made for some long, sleepless nights and some terrifying LP and night ambush experiences.

The rumor of a stand-down in Chu Lai finally came true in early April. The entire company was air-lifted out of the field and flown to Chu Lai. We climbed aboard the "deuce and a halfs" that were waiting for us and were trucked to a place that we called the Charger Hotel. I believe the complex was specifically built for field troop stand-downs. A large building, which housed a mess hall and a lounge complete with a bar and a stage for live shows, sat inside the front gates. A series of Quonset huts were located behind the main building to provide quarters for the troops. The lounge was less than fancy with its unpainted interior wood floors and walls showing the scars of past beer busts. The booze-soaked bar was also constructed of unpainted wood and was the primary source of the sour beer smell that filled the

Stand-Down in Chu Lai

room. The large party room was furnished with folding chairs and tables, but nothing else. Each two-man room out back in the Quonset huts was furnished with two cots and a blanket for each. Duffle bags full of clean fatigues and socks waited for us in the large bath-house located to the rear of the Quonset huts. I'm sure the fence that surrounded the complex wasn't to keep others out. They needed some way of protecting the rear echelon troops from the uncivilized grunts they had let out of the jungle. We were told that we had to stay on the compound and that at the Charger Hotel, the only rule was "There Are No Rules." We were just thrilled to be out of the field, and as far as we were concerned, the Charger Hotel was as luxurious as you could get.

Once inside the gates, there was a race to the showers. I found the first room that didn't already have two rucksacks in it, threw my gear in, and then headed for the showers. We normally bathed out of our steel pot, and on occasions, were treated to a bath in a river or creek. I was looking forward to a hot shower and a chance to take a crap without having to worry about Charlie catching me with my pants down.

The party had already started by the time I got cleaned up and made my way to the lounge. There were garbage cans full of iced-down beer, and the bar was stocked with all the hard stuff you could stand. Things began slowly with everyone relishing our break from the war. We drank beer, talked, and enjoyed one another's company. The evening started with a live band complete with a little Vietnamese gal shaking her bootie. By that time no one was feeling any pain. We were having a hell of a good time, and it wasn't long until the wolf calls and whistles drowned out the music the band was attempting to play. An assault on the stage soon followed when several drunken GIs made an attempt to get to the shapely singer. The show ended shortly after the two GIs were thrown off the stage. We had gotten so rowdy

My Story, Vietnam 1968, 196th Light Infantry Brigade

that the show had to be cut short – but we were too drunk to care! Several of the garbage cans had been emptied, but there was still plenty to go.

I walked outside to take another leak and saw Sergeant Arzola sitting alone. He was crying. I stumbled over and sat down beside him. We were both dog drunk. Arzola wept as he told me that his daddy had recently died, and because of the shittin' war, he didn't get a chance to tell his daddy how much he loved him. With tears running down my face, I tried to provide some comforting words. We talked some more about the guys who were no longer with us and the misery the war had caused. The alcohol had washed away whatever it is that holds back a young man's tears in war, and we both had a good, hard cry.

I went back inside to get another beer. The party had really gotten wild. I saw Jamison sitting in one of the garbage cans trying to get out as several of the guys poured beer on his head, and others were pushing him down into the beer and ice water mixture. He looked to me like he was about to drown, but he had a smile on his face, so I went on about my business of getting shit-faced drunk.

I'm not sure when the night ended, but I remember having to work my way past Max, our big, ugly machine gunner. He had arms the size of my legs and was stronger than a bull. Max was drunk out of his mind and was lying on his back in the narrow hall of the Quonset hut. He was punching the walls with his fist – the right wall with the left fist and then the left wall with the right fist. I wasn't in any shape to help him, and besides, there was a good chance he would kill anyone who tried.

For some reason I wanted to take another shower before I hit the cot and wound up falling in the shower and cutting my knee open. I was too drunk to worry about my injury, so I just let it bleed and went to bed.

Stand-Down in Chu Lai

I had one hell of a hangover the next morning and didn't feel much like eating, but I sure wasn't going to pass up a hot meal. I was surprised to see Jamison standing in the chow line – I was sure he had drowned. The night had been hard on us, but we hadn't suffered any KIAs; however, I still wasn't sure I was going to make it.

After blowing off all our bottled-up steam, our remaining two days were easy and relaxing, at least for some of us. Others continued to raise hell. The company commander allowed us off the compound the second and third day during the daylight hours to go to the PX and downtown Chu Lai. I made several leisurely trips downtown to sightsee and buy souvenirs for the family. I bought a Vietnamese doll for my sister, Wanda Lynn, toy tigers for Timmy and R.D., and a jacket for Rydell, my youngest brother.

Shortly after the morning formation on the fourth day, our transportation arrived. With a lot of moans and groans, we climbed on back of the "deuce and a halfs" and went back to war.

A few days later, Sergeant Rodgers received word that his transfer had come through. He had landed the job back in the rear he was looking for. I was glad for him. Sergeant Hanna appointed me acting squad leader. The idea didn't really set well with some of the more experienced guys, several of who had transferred to the First Platoon from the other platoons. I had only been in-country for four months, and some of them had nine and ten months. On one hand it was kind of scary knowing that I was responsible for the lives of the men in the squad, but on the other, I knew I could perform a squad leader's duties, and I wasn't so sure about some of the other guys.

Sergeant Hanna made sure he assigned two experienced men to go with me on the first LP that I led. They didn't like it. They didn't like the idea of following someone who had been in-country only half as long as they had, and they let

My Story, Vietnam 1968, 196th Light Infantry Brigade

me know it. I appointed a RTO, made commo checks, and made a quick check of the guys. It was dark when we moved out. I put Johnson on point, and then I followed with the RTO and the other two behind me.

After traveling 50 meters or so, Johnson stopped and pointed to a small opening in the brush indicating that the opening was where we were going to position ourselves. Selecting the LP location was my job, and I had been ordered to position the LP close to a trail junction about another 50 meters or so down the hill. I whispered to Johnson that we needed to move on down the trail. He informed me that he wasn't going any farther, and at the same time, motioned to the others to move into the opening where Johnson wanted to setup. In an effort to keep things quiet, I had everyone to group up close together. I told Johnson that if he didn't want to be part of the LP to get his ass back to the perimeter. I told the rest of them that I was going to the trail junction even if I had to go alone, and they could follow me or go back with Johnson. I took over the point, and the rest followed me, with Johnson falling in behind. We sat up in the position I selected, and the remainder of the night was uneventful.

I returned to the perimeter the next morning, relieved and feeling a little more confident. It wasn't until later that I began to realize that sometimes it was just plain stupid to go where you were ordered to go, and that Johnson had probably been right. I had been just as green and dumb as Johnson believed me to be.

Although there had been a lot of contact, the war had gotten easy for us. We were always shooting at them, and they were always running. We had the upper hand, and with that came a certain amount of complacency. I began to wonder if the VC could do much more than just shoot a few sniper rounds from time to time and shake the bushes at night. After all, the only real trouble we had experienced was with the NVA. The foxholes had gotten shallow, and the guys weren't even doing a good job of cupping their cigarettes with their hand at night to keep the glow from showing. Mann did, however, learn a lesson about this time. Vaughn had just finished telling Mann to get the hell away from him if he wasn't going to cup his cigarette when a burst of automatic fire sprayed their position. It was obvious the glow from Mann's cigarette had been the target. Charlie missed Mann but did teach him a lesson; the glow from a cigarette can be seen from a long ways off, and Charlie was always watching.

A grunt held his cigarette between the thumb and index finger, with the burning end being cupped in the palm and fingers to hide the glow. The smoke and heat from the tobacco permanently stain the inside of a smoker's hand a brownish-yellow, or at least it looked permanent to me. If you smoked and wanted to stay alive, cupping your cigarette quickly became a habit.[6]

The second week in April, the company headed back toward LZ Center. It was Alpha's turn again to provide security for the fire support base. I was ready for the break. I was tired of humping and tired of digging foxholes, and I needed some rest; we all did.

---

[6] Several years after the war, I watched this guy smoking a cigarette in the Student Center at Memphis State University and knew that he was a grunt. I walked up and asked, "What unit were you with?" He acted surprised until I pointed to the cigarette he had cupped in his hand. He simply said, "Habit." He had been a grunt like I had suspected.

Chapter Eight

NCO School

On Center it wasn't long until we were enjoying hot meals and packages from home. Everyone was always a little nosy about what was in the other guy's package because we knew that he would soon be sharing it. We leisurely worked that afternoon preparing our positions. We cleaned bunkers and set out claymores and trip flairs. The bunks in the bunkers were constructed of empty ammo boxes, with empty sandbags being used as padding. After sleeping on the ground for months at a time, a pile of sandbags can look pretty damn inviting.

Sergeant Hanna made the rounds introducing us to our new platoon leader, Lieutenant Harrison. Lieutenant Harrison had replaced SSG Hanna as the platoon leader of the First Platoon, and Hanna was being transferred. Lieutenant Harrison was a soft-spoken, likeable fellow, not much older that the rest of us.

The second day on Center I was called to Lieutenant Harrison's bunker. The lieutenant told me that I had been selected to attend the Americal Division's NCO school. He asked me if I was interested. My reply was immediate, "HELL YES!" It wasn't that I wanted to go to NCO school;

NCO School

it was that it meant two weeks out of the field; it meant no humping, no patrols, and no damn LPs or ambushes for two whole weeks.

The next day I boarded a ship headed for Chu Lai, and the day after that I was in school. Most of the units in the Americal Division had sent someone, so it was a pretty big deal. The school consisted of playing army part of the day and attending classes the remainder. I could play army with the best of them. I could spit shine my boots, make a bunk, and snap to attention like a lifer. The classes were easy. I already had considerable experience with claymores, M-16s, M-60s, LPs, and ambushes. A lot of the guys were from units in the rear and didn't know much about anything except where the PX and the EM club were located.

In the second week of school, a NCO from the 196th rear headquarters interrupted one of my classes. He asked me to step outside; he had something to tell me. At first I thought something was wrong back home, but then he started talking about the company. Alpha had left Center and split into platoon-size units. Each platoon had laagered alone the night of April 13. My platoon had laagered at the east end of a valley that we called "AK Valley." I could see it in his face and hear it in his voice that something was dreadfully wrong, and it was. My platoon had been overrun the night before. The sergeant told me that everyone in the platoon had been killed or wounded and left for dead, except for Benjamin Dabis. The sergeant believed that Dabis had played dead or something.

I was taken to the 196th rear headquarters in Chu Lai to see Dabis, or Pineapple as everyone called him. He had been hit in the arm and several places in the back. He had been treated and released. I walked into the tent, and without saying anything, walked back and sat on the cot next to Pineapple. I asked him what had happened. His account of that night scared me. The story he told produced a string of

My Story, Vietnam 1968, 196th Light Infantry Brigade

nightmares that tormented me for years.[7] What would I have done if I had been there that night? I wasn't, but I knew the boys that were, I knew the enemy, I knew the place, and the war had acquainted me with the sights, sounds, and smells that were present that night. I had all the ingredients necessary in my mind to create some really hairy nightmares.

Our 30-man-plus platoon had linked up with Echo Company, a small reconnaissance unit, and had established a defensive perimeter in a village at the base of a ridge at the east end of AK Valley. The platoon didn't dig-in because the ground in the village was as hard as concrete. Generations of activity in the village had packed the soil down solid, making it impossible to dig in. I had dug a foxhole every night I had spent in the boonies, without exception. I was shocked at what I was being told. Establishing a night laager site on the low ground in an area where you could not dig-in was an inexcusable mistake. Lieutenant Harrison and the men knew it. The lieutenant voiced his concern to the recon captain, but the captain pulled rank. He didn't believe they faced any real danger

---

[7] Most of what I thought I knew about April 13 came from stories I was told while I was in Chu Lai. In later years I learned details about that night that didn't quite mesh with what I thought I knew. I talked to several of my buddies who were present that night and others who had knowledge of the battle. I had bits and pieces of the picture but was still unsure how it all fit together. As I put the story to paper, I had a hard time turning loose of what I thought were facts for many years, and a harder time yet trying to incorporate the newer information and firsthand accounts. I did my best, and if I didn't get things quite right, I apologized to the men of my platoon and those from Echo Company who were there that night. The one thing that I am sure about, and Gene Tilson, Toney Valdes, Ronnie Vaughn, and Barry Baugh all agree, is that the blame rests squarely on the shoulders of the recon captain. Thirteen young men lost their life, and over thirty others were wounded because the recon captain wanted to sleep in his hammock.

and wanted to take advantage of the shelter in the village. The captain had tied up his hammock in one of the hooches and wanted to use it. The captain used his rank to brush off the concerns of Lieutenant Harrison and the soldiers under his command.

As Pineapple described the place, I knew exactly where he was talking about. I had patrolled the area several times before.

A patrol was sent out after dark to make sure the area around the village was clear. I'm sure the patrol was mostly to justify laagering in the village rather than on top of the adjacent ridge where they should have been. The patrol came in late and reported seeing bookoo Viet Cong moving toward the perimeter. A fatal mistake had been made, and the enemy was watching. You don't make mistakes in war without paying for them.

At midnight it started; an explosion inside the perimeter, and then another, and another, followed by dozens more. Mortars rained down on the perimeter. The VC took advantage of the high ground to target the GIs. Other VC slipped up on the perimeter to within grenade-throwing distance and started throwing their grenades. There was no small arms fire. There was nothing to give away the enemy's position. A storm of mortars, hand grenades, and concussion charges rained down on the guys. They had virtually no cover to speak of. One of the hooches was set afire, which served to light up the area and make the Americans an even easier target. The initial barrage of grenades and mortars left a bunch of young American boys screaming for help. The VC began moving in for the kill with automatic weapons. The Americans that were able opened up with their M-16s. The VC worked to eliminate the positions with small arms, grenades, and RPGs. As the enemy began moving toward the perimeter, a Viet Cong soldier yelled out, "GI you die tonight!" Mullins, the soldier manning Alpha's M-60, lost it. He left his weapon and ran to the cover of a bunker inside one of the hooches. Seeing that the M-60 had been abandoned, Sergeant Lesure quickly made his way over to the position and manned the weapon himself. He opened up with the machine gun, firing at the advancing enemy. Other VC yelled, "You die tonight GI!"

Sergeant Lesure responded, "Come and get me you son of a bitch! Come and get me!" as he continued firing the M-60.

Sergeant Lesure held the enemy at bay until they finally silenced his position. He was hit with an RPG, blowing the lower portion of both legs off. After he was hit, he was heard yelling, "Somebody kill me, my legs are gone... somebody kill me, my legs are gone!" Baugh was in a position near Sergeant Lesure and wanted to help, but could do nothing because he was pinned down. Sergeant Lesure died where he lay.[8]

The defensive perimeter broke down, and it was every man for himself. There was an open rice paddy on the south side of the village. The snapping sound of AK bullets filled the air as GIs ran and crawled toward the cover of a small creek bed out in the rice paddy. The Viet Cong moved into the perimeter. Baugh, Trammel, and several other GIs, including Mullins who had left his hiding place in the bunker, took cover behind some heavy bushes on the rice paddy side of the village. An enemy soldier sprayed the bushes with his AK. Mullins was hit in both legs. "Ping!" One of the bullets hit Baugh's helmet.[9] The round penetrated

---

[8] At the 2013 196th Light Infantry Brigade reunion held in Washington D.C., I talked to Barry Baugh about Sergeant Lesure. He told me that Sergeant Lesure was a hero in every sense of the word. Barry said he didn't know whether or not Sergeant Lesure had been decorated, but if not, he should have been. He was a real hero.
[9] "Ping" is how Barry described it. Barry Baugh still has this helmet. He brought it with him to one of the 196th Light Infantry Brigade reunions.

the top of the helmet and exited on the side over his ear, only creasing Baugh's scalp. And then a grenade sailed in over the bushes and landed in the middle of the GIs. One GI was killed; several others were severely wounded. The wounded soldiers crawled toward the paddy. Baugh crawled backwards, firing his weapon to provide cover for the wounded soldiers behind him trying to escape.

As Valdes ran across the village toward the rice paddy, a wounded soldier yelled for help. It was Tilson. Tilson had grenade frag, mortar frag, and an AK round in his body. He lay on the ground in the village dying when Valdes passed him. Tilson yelled out with the last of his breath, "Valdes... help... me! I've... been... shot!" Even though Tilson was dying, he still spoke extremely slow as he always did. Valdes answered Tilson's plea for help. Valdes pulled Tilson out of the village into the paddy. They crossed a section of the paddy and then slid down into the creek bed. The enemy was working the creek bed and rice paddy with automatic weapons. The trapped soldiers knew that they had to get across the paddy to the cover of the hills on the far side. Pineapple, who had made it to the creek bed, saw Valdes struggling with Tilson trying to pull him up the far bank of the creek. Pineapple immediately moved to helped Valdes. They pulled Tilson up the bank into the paddy, and then the three headed for the hills on the far side. Valdes, Pineapple, and Tilson made it up out of the rice paddy, across the trail at the base of the hill, and then up the thickly covered hill. About halfway up, Pineapple and Tilson took refuge in some heavy brush. Valdes found cover nearby.

A number of GIs were pinned down in the middle of the paddy. Lieutenant Harrison was seen lying dead in one of the artillery craters. It is believed that he had called artillery on his own position hoping to give his troops a chance to escape across the paddy while the VC had their heads down.

My Story, Vietnam 1968, 196th Light Infantry Brigade

Vaughn, who had been hit with mortar frag and shot twice, managed to make it across the paddy but didn't have the strength to pull himself up out of the paddy. He attempted to climb out several times, but rolled back down into the paddy. He eventually made it out of the paddy and crawled across the trail into some cover at the base of the hill, where he passed out.

The artillery and shooting finally stopped. From their hiding places and aided by the light of the burning hooches, many of the soldiers that escaped the village could see the VC move in for the kill. The enemy met no resistance from the wounded GIs still in the village. The VC moved from boy to boy, shooting him whether he needed it or not. They saw Perez, who had just joined the company while on LZ Center, on his knees, pleading for his life with enemy soldiers standing over him with fixed bayonets. Perez begged for his life, but there is no mercy in war. Perez was run through with bayonets, and then he was shot.[10]

The VC were soon going through packs and belongings of the GIs. They were having a victory party, laughing, hollering, and having a good time. A squad of VC moved slowly along the trail at the base of the hill where Pineapple and others were hidden. "Surrender GI! Surrender GI!" they called. They never did come up on the hill. Pineapple tried

---

[10] I was told by a 196th rear echelon NCO that the enemy used bayonets on the wounded and those begging for their life. I even remember the particular soldier that I was told was begging for his life before he was bayoneted. I also have a letter that I wrote home. In the envelope there was a second sealed envelope addressed to my dad only. I didn't want my mama to read it. In that letter I told my dad that the VC used bayonets on several of my best friends. I wrote that I wasn't coming home until I got even for each and every one of my buddies. In later years I talked to several of the guys who were present that night but was unable to confirm the use of bayonets by the enemy. The only thing Barry Baugh would say was, "Well, they weren't taking prisoners."

to comfort Tilson to keep him quiet as they waited through the night for the help they knew would be coming the next morning. When Vaughn regained consciousness, several VC soldiers were standing on the trail having a conversation only a few feet away from him. Vaughn stayed perfectly still until they moved on. At some point during the night, as gunships circled overhead, Vaughn began to get concerned about being mistaken for the enemy because he was so far outside the perimeter. Not thinking very clear, he crawled back into the rice paddy and headed toward the perimeter. Vaughn spent the remainder of the night lying in the rice paddy.

At daybreak the rest of Alpha Company arrived. Pineapple said he knew that they were the Americans he had been waiting for, but still could not convince himself to move. He knew Tilson needed help, so he forced himself to stand up, expose himself, and yell for help. After walking off the hill, Pineapple told the CO that he knew others were still hiding. The guys were just too scared to expose themselves. Pineapple said it took some time to talk the other survivors out of their hiding places. Baugh had held on to an exposed tree root on the side of the bank at the edge of the paddy all night long. After being helped off the root and up the bank, Baugh could not stand on his own. At first he and his rescuers thought he had been wounded, but finally realized that the blood circulation to his legs had been cut off by his position on the root. Baugh was able to stand again once blood was allowed to return to his legs.

Thirteen American boys from Alpha and Echo companies lay dead that morning. Over thirty others were wounded, many of them seriously. Pineapple wasn't real sure when he got hit, but he believed it was during the initial grenade barrage. He showed me his watch. It had been hit by a piece of frag and had stopped at midnight. I sat there staring at Pineapple in disbelief. I couldn't believe that all those guys were gone, but they were. For many of them, it was their first trip to the boonies. For that matter, for many of them, it was their first time away from home. Pineapple and Mann were the only soldiers from the First Platoon to return to the field. I was never told the fate of the others. I didn't know who lived and who died. All I knew was that Gene Tilson, Barry Baugh, Ronnie Vaughn, Tony Valdes, Jim Trammel, and other friends were just gone.

Lieutenant Gibbs, Alpha's executive officer, made it his personal mission to go after the recon captain to make sure the captain paid for his incompetence. Before becoming the company's executive officer, Lieutenant Gibbs was the well-liked, very capable platoon leader of the Second Platoon. He had proven himself during the fighting in Que Son Valley in January. He had a love for the men in Alpha Company and blamed the recon captain for the loss of so many good men.

After listening to Pineapple's story, I promised myself that I would never let my guard down, and I took a mindset, "If things ever get bad, run.... Don't think about it, just run.... Don't expect any mercy, just run...."[11]

I returned to NCO school, completed the course, and graduated first in the class. I was the Americal Combat Leadership course's honor graduate. The top three of us received a promotion. The commanding general of the Americal Division presented me a plaque, a cigarette lighter, and my buck sergeant's stripes. I had only been SP-4 for a month, and now I was a buck Sergeant, E-5. I have always suspected that the situation with the company gave me an advantage in the ranking – Alpha Company needed NCOs.

---

[11] One last thing about April 13, 1968: Even today, after all these years, I still feel guilty for not being with my buddies on that night.

NCO School

After the graduation ceremony was over, I reported to the company's rear headquarters in Chu Lai. I was told that the battalion commander was extremely pleased with me and had granted me a 3-day R&R in Vung Tau just outside Saigon. After visiting the PX to pick up some civies, I hopped a plane to Tunsun Nuk, an air strip just outside Vung Tau. On board I met Rudy Shotts, who was from the artillery unit on LZ Center. We had the Mud Monster in common, and we both needed a friend. By the time we arrived in Tunsun Nuk, we were both hungrier than hell and started looking for a mess hall. A friendly airman gave us directions to an Air Force mess hall if we didn't mind the walk. Hey, that was no problem. The one thing I knew I could do was walk.

As Shotts and I strolled toward the mess hall, I began to feel like I had entered a time warp to the future or something. I had left a world of mountains and jungles, a world where I slept on the ground and shit in the rice paddies, and I had just entered a world of paved streets, sidewalks, movie theaters, and swimming pools. We were both amazed at the modern conveniences available to the airmen. The Air Force definitely impressed us – these guys had it made.

We finally found the mess hall and were in awe at what we saw inside. A large selection of mouth-watering hot food was waiting for us. The one thing that impressed me the most was the milk machines – all the fresh milk you wanted at the touch of a lever.

A few minutes later, Shotts and I were sitting at a mess table stuffing our faces. Between the two of us, we had five glasses of milk sitting in front us. We were definitely uptown.

While we were enjoying our meal, I began to notice a loud-mouthed airman sitting at a table behind us. We both began to listen to him. He was complaining about this and then about that. We learned just how bad he had it in Nam.

He had to fill sandbags, pull KP and everything. "And this slop stinks!" the airman grunted, referring to the tray of food in front of him.

That was it, I couldn't take it anymore. I had friends dying in the field, and this guy was complaining about his fuckin' food. As I got up, I told Shotts, "I am fixin' to kick this guy's ASS!" Shotts grabbed me by the back of the pants and pulled me back down and tried to calm me down. After a few more smart-ass comments from the airman, I was pulling Shotts down. Our restlessness caught the attention of the group of airmen. They didn't have the foggiest idea why we were upset and seemed amused at our apparent irritation. Shotts and I decided that we didn't want to spend our three days in jail, so we drank our milk and left.

The three days in Vung Tau were filled with a lot of new experiences, and at times, I almost forgot about the war. Three days can seem like a lifetime in the boonies, but they were gone in a flash in Vung Tau. Before I knew it, I was back in Chu Lai reporting in to the 196th.

Chapter Nine

The DMZ

Just before I left for Vung Tau, I learned that the 196th had moved up north to Camp Evans, a rear supply base near the city of Phu Bai. I had hoped that they would be headed back south by the time I got back to Chu Lai, but they weren't. Camp Evans was too close to the DMZ for me. I knew we would be facing hardcore NVA regulars, and I had already gained a healthy respect for them.

The trip to the DMZ was an interesting journey. On the first stretch, I caught a ride on a "deuce and a half," which provided a shuttle service between Chu Lai and LZ Baldy, where I hoped to catch a flight headed north. After climbing into the back of the truck and talking to some guys who had made the trip before, I knew I was in trouble. The driver was a certified wild man. He had a reputation for keeping the pedal to the metal and for running down Vietnamese civilians. His specialty was Vietnamese on bicycles. He wasn't trying to run over them or anything; he just wanted to get close enough to run them off the road. He traveled the road every day and kept a running tally in the cab of his truck that proved he was an ACE. Although he made several attempts, he only added one to the count that trip. I thought

My Story, Vietnam 1968, 196th Light Infantry Brigade

for sure he had run over an old papa-san riding a bicycle when we ran him off the road. As we moved on down the road with everyone cheering for the driver, I watched the old man slowly get to his feet and inspect his bike. We didn't need an interpreter to translate the meaning of the gestures that followed.

As we were passing through a populated area, the "deuce and a half" took a sharp left off the road, barreled up a side street, and screeched to a stop in front of a building. "What are we stopping for?" I thought. My question was answered when I saw two girls walk out of the door dressed in a manner that gave me an instant clue as to what their profession was. As our driver slammed the truck door, he was greeted by the girls. With a girl under each arm, he turned to us and said, "This will only take a minute." I was told that our driver made the stop twice a day every day. He stopped once on his way north, and again on the return trip. A couple more girls came out and walked up to the tailgate of the "deuce and a half" and greeted us, "Hey GI, GI boom – boom." They enticed several of the guys to go inside. I passed. I was still a little green when it came to that part of the war. A few minutes later, we were on the road again headed north.

I boarded a chopper at LZ Baldy, and after a bumpy ride, arrived at Camp Evans. Rather than report to somebody and take a chance of being put on some kind of duty, I decided to find a place on my own to spend the night. It was no problem. After four and a half months in the field, I had learned how to plop down on the ground anywhere, get comfortable, and go to sleep.

The next day I found a supply ship headed for the company. Captain Yurchak was now Major Yurchak, the battalion's operations officer, and Captain Oxford had taken over Alpha Company. Captain Oxford used the call sign "Cherokee." When I stepped off the chopper, I was congratulated for my promotion and then introduced to a new First Platoon. Several soldiers from the Second and Third platoons were transferred to the First to provide some experience to an otherwise all green outfit. Lieutenant Simpson, or Watchdog as he was called, was the new platoon leader. I liked him right away.

Watchdog was the fourth platoon leader for the First Platoon in five months. He told me that he was assigning me to Sergeant Huff's squad as a team leader. Sergeant Huff had originally been with the Third Platoon and was a short-timer. I was to be given the squad when he left. "Team leader?" I questioned. The First Platoon had never used team leaders before, at least not while I had been with the company. There had never before been enough men in a squad to split into teams, but while I was away, the company's strength had increased significantly.

Sergeant Gary was the other team leader. He was a ninety day wonder straight from a State-side NCO school. He didn't look like the NCO type to me. He was somewhat short and maybe a little bit on the chubby side, and his helmet always seemed to be cocked to one side or the other, which made him look somewhat goofy. Sergeant Gary was a likeable guy, but a leader? I didn't think so. I would soon learn that my first impressions of him were wrong. Sergeant Gary proved to be as good as they came.

Sergeant Huff wasted no time before informing me that he was a short-timer and wasn't going to take any more chances. He had pulled his last LP and wasn't going on another ambush or squad-size patrol. He had talked to Watchdog, and they both thought it would be best if Sergeant Gary and I handled that part. I knew that Sergeant Huff had a good reputation and was supposed to know his stuff, but I didn't like his short-timer attitude.

I was introduced to the rest of the squad. Buckney was from the Second Platoon and Green from the Third. The rest

My Story, Vietnam 1968, 196th Light Infantry Brigade

of them were greens. Kirk, Alverson, Phillips, Baker, and several other guys were among the new boys to join the company. Buckney was easy-going, and from what I had heard, could be counted on. Green was the gung-ho type. He often volunteered to walk point and given the chance, would leave a patrol behind and slip up on a village by himself. He carried the high body count for the Third Platoon most of the time.

We spent the next several days patrolling an area of thickly-covered rolling hills. There weren't any trees, just thick brush seven to eight feet high with no greenery whatsoever.[12] It was hard to navigate through the stuff because you couldn't see anything but the sticks around you, and the route more often than not was determined by the density of the vegetation. Although we were up north to fight the NVA, I didn't feel threatened because there was no way in hell anybody could have slipped up on us in that mess.

Late the second day Alpha Company moved out of the thicket to the top of a small, sparsely-covered hill, dug in, and spent the night. The next day, after being re-supplied, we moved down off the hill a short distance to a large open area where we were to wait for the choppers that were apparently going to transport us farther north. Off in the distance I looked to see several Chinooks (CH-47, twin rotor transport helicopters) headed our direction. I had never flown in a Chinook before, so the trip was going to be a new experience for me – one I wasn't looking forward to. I had watched Chinooks deliver supplies to LZ Center before, and as far as I was concerned, the "shit hook," as we called it, was too big and too slow, making it an easy target, but of course I didn't have anything to say about it.

---

[12] At the time I didn't think anything about the lack of foliage in April, but of course, back then I didn't know anything about Agent Orange.

The DMZ

I looked around again for Green. It was my responsibility to account for my men before we boarded the choppers, and I hadn't seen Green for a while. I began to get worried and asked around, but nobody had seen him. About the time I decided I better say something to Sergeant Huff, I saw Green walking toward me with this big shit-eatin' grin on his face. Green always had a grin on his face, but this one meant something – I could tell.

"Where you been?" I asked. Green told me that he had gone back to the night laager site alone and set a booby trap. "You did what?" I questioned in a soft, hush-hush tone because I had already decided that I didn't want anyone else to hear our conversation. Green explained that he had pulled the pin on a hand grenade and had placed the grenade under a flak jacket one of the new guys had thrown away. The new man had brought a flak jacket to the field but learned real quickly that it was too damn heavy to hump. Green decided to take advantage of the discarded jacket and set a trap for Charlie. "Hell Green, anybody could pick the shittin' thing up!" I growled, still attempting to keep it quiet.

Green smiled and said, "Don't worry about it. I just gave them some of their own medicine. We'll get one of them, and maybe more." I tried to be serious, but the grin on his face made that impossible. He never took anything real serious, and besides that, he was one hell of a soldier. As he walked off, he gave me a friendly punch in the arm and said, "Lighten up."

I knew I should tell Sergeant Huff, but I knew that if I did, Green would get in trouble. As the chinooks approached the field, I knew nobody had time to do anything about it, even if I did say something. Green was right; we would probably surprise the NVA. An American would never pick up something just lying there like that without first checking it out. "What the shit," I thought, "this is war, and war is awful damn dangerous." I put the

My Story, Vietnam 1968, 196th Light Infantry Brigade

situation behind me and prepared to board the waiting Chinook.

Just boarding the Chinook turned out to be an experience. The turbine engines were running, and their exhaust was being directed back toward the boarding ramp. As I approached the ramp, I began to feel the hot gases flowing around me. The blowing air became hotter with each step, and as I made my way up the long ramp, I began wondering if it was supposed to be this hot. Maybe something was wrong. About the time I decided that I was being cooked and it was time to turn back, I cleared the rear of the chopper and the hot exhaust. The temperature dropped sharply, but by that time I was well done. I made my way on into the chopper and strapped myself in one of the canvas seats that lined the wall. The turbine engines began to scream, and I thought the damn thing was going to shake apart before it lifted into the air.

We were flown to an open field north of Dong Ha, and after a short hump, established a defensive perimeter for the night in a lightly wooded area on the east bank of what I believe was Jones Creek. The foxholes were deep. Our surroundings were unfamiliar, and everyone was a little jumpy. Nobody seemed to know exactly what was going on, and there was a lot of confusion. We had left our home in the mountains and had been thrust into this conventional war, and none of us really knew what to expect. My foxhole was located on the bank of the creek and faced the water. Down south I would have felt good about my position because the enemy couldn't slip up on me, but up north, it only meant that I didn't have any place to run.

As I watched the water, a thought struck me. I wondered if there were any fish in it. Water and fishing had always excited me, and I wanted to catch a fish. I hurriedly dug through my rucksack looking for something to make a hook out of. I had momentarily forgotten about the war. I

The DMZ

tied several pieces of string together and attached a safety pin to one end. With my tackle in hand, I had second thoughts. To get to the water, I had to walk outside the perimeter and climb down the bank three or four feet to the water's edge. Better judgment prevailed, and I decided to postpone my fishing trip until I got back to the world.

The next day we moved out on foot headed north, and after humping four or five klicks, Alpha spread out in a defensive posture in a lightly wooded area. We were now within a stone throw of the DMZ. Word of our mission began to spread. We were now working for the Marines. The 3rd Battalion, 21st Infantry of the 196th was OPCON to the 3rd Marines. Lieutenant Colonel Snyder, our battalion commander, now reported to the commander of the third Marines. The NVA had dug in at Nhi Ha Village just this side of the DMZ. They were well armed and had support from artillery positions in the north and from NVA armored units operating in the area. The battalion of Marines responsible for the area had been virtually wiped out by the NVA. The Marines were spread thin along the DMZ, and the Army had been requested to supply reinforcements. The 196th's mission was to take and hold Nhi Ha Village.

The sound of a distant firefight erupted. Charlie Company had pushed on ahead of us and had apparently run into a strong resistance as they advanced on Nhi Ha. There was a lot of activity around the company CP, and then word was passed for the Second and Third Platoons to saddle up. They were going in to help Charlie Company to withdraw. The First Platoon had lucked out. We laid back in reserve and waited. I'm sure we got to stay behind because our platoon was so green.

By mid-day Charlie Company had pulled back with the assistance of Alpha. We soon learned from Watchdog that we were going to launch another attack on Nhi Ha that afternoon.

My Story, Vietnam 1968, 196th Light Infantry Brigade

We grunts waited as the officers put the final pieces of the battle plan together. When Watchdog returned from the CP, I knew it wouldn't be long. It was a sobering moment when I looked across the large, wide-open, dry rice paddy to see the wood line on the far side that concealed Nhi Ha Village and the NVA, who were waiting.

The shelling of Nhi Ha increased. I waited and watched the thunderous explosions of our artillery send clouds of dirt and smoke rolling into the air over the wood line. Word had it that a lot of the artillery was coming from the Navy's Seventh Fleet sitting off the coast. They pounded the woods for over an hour as we waited our turn. The display of power astonished the greens. Sergeant Gary looked over at me and said, "Hell, they keep this up, there won't be anything left for us!" I knew better. I had learned the hard way that if the enemy is dug in, the only way to get him out is with a hand grenade, and only grunts carry grenades.

Alpha moved out of the woods into the field and staged for an attack on Nhi Ha. Spread out evenly, Alpha began to advance on the woods on the far side of the wide-open rice paddy. To my surprise, we crossed the open terrain without a shot being fired. Alpha Company had pushed a hundred meters or so into the woods before all hell broke loose. I heard the terrifying scream of a 152 mm artillery shell sent from North Vietnam for the first time, followed by an immediate explosion, "BOOM!" It was followed by several more. "BOOM! BOOM! BOOM!" The initial round of incoming was followed by an intense barrage of artillery, rocket, and mortars fire. Our assault was stopped immediately. I hit the ground and low-crawled to a small artillery crater and buried my face in the bottom. Fortunately, there was an abundance of cover, fallen trees, artillery and bomb craters, and ditches. Nobody moved. I just kept my head down and hoped for the best as artillery shells exploded around us. The troops on our left flank attempted to advance, but ran into strong small arms fire and were stopped. I could hear the snapping sound of small arms fire up ahead and knew I needed to stay right where I was. Most of us just hunkered down and waited for NVA to let up. There seemed to be a lot of confusion. I don't know if Cherokee ordered us to retreat or if the majority of us just took advantage of a lull in the shelling and ran, and the rest followed. Anyhow, it was obvious to me that the NVA needed to be softened up some more, and it was time to retreat.

As I made my way out of the woods, I was forced to take cover several times because of incoming mortars. At one point Green and I had taken cover behind an old, abandoned well when he looked at me and said, "I've been looking for a place to get rid of this thing." He was referring to the white phosphorus grenade he was holding in his hand. Sergeant Huff wanted the squad to carry one or two of them and had given one to Green to hump. The grenade was heavy, and Green could lighten his load if he could find a use for it, and he just did. He pulled the pin on the white phosphorus grenade, dropped it over into the well opening, and then ran. By the time I realized what was going on, the grenade exploded. The well opening directed the white hot pieces of burning phosphorus vertically upward high into the air. I made an attempt to get out of the way, but as I watched the white smoke trails arch up and over and then follow the burning pieces of phosphorus as they fell toward the ground, I knew I hadn't cleared the danger. Rather than run and hope not to get hit, I elected to stay put and attempt to dodge the pieces as they fell. I managed to sidestep several pieces of phosphorus that came my way. I apparently looked pretty comical in doing so because Green, who was watching, cracked up laughing. At first I was furious. I was running for my life hoping to avoid the NVA rockets and mortars, and now Green tried to burn me alive with Willie Pete. Green was doubled over with laughter. After seeing how tickled he was, my anger quickly subsided, and I couldn't help it. The frown on my face turned to a grin, and then I began to laugh. Green and I ran for the paddy still giggling and hoping not to be killed. I finally made it out of the woods and across the dry paddy to safety. We regrouped, and medevac's were called in.

Things could have been much worse if it hadn't been for the abundance of cover in the woods. I didn't realize how serious the situation had gotten because I didn't see anybody get hit. I later learned that Alpha had suffered two KIAs and over twenty wounded.

Alpha saddled up, moved a short distance, and set up a defensive perimeter for the night. Our perimeter was located out in the open, due east, and in sight of Nhi Ha. The sandy soil was easy to dig in, and the foxholes were deep. I believe they would have been deep even if we had been on rock. We were all uneasy. There was a lot of talk about Soviet-built tanks and human wave assaults coming from across the border. Normally the LAW (light anti-tank weapon) was just something heavy to hump, but that night we were glad to have them. With our positions prepared, I sat at the foxhole staring north. Looking out over the flat terrain, I envisioned a NVA human wave coming at me. My thoughts scared the shit out of me. I had fought the NVA before and knew killing a few of them wouldn't stop the attack. They would keep coming until we killed all of them or they overran us.

I was glad when Watchdog stopped to talk. His confidence helped me shake the uneasy feeling that had gripped me. Watchdog seemed to know his stuff when it came to the military. We talked about the Marine's efforts in the area, and I began to understand why the Marines took such a beating. When the Army assaults a position, they move in until the incoming starts to get heavy and then will pull back

The DMZ

and call in artillery or an airstrike. The Army will keep attacking, retreating, and calling support until the resistance is reduced to an acceptable level. According to Watchdog, when the Marines hit resistance, they just keep on pushing until they take their objective or don't have any men left. I thought the tactics used by the Marines to fight the war were stupid when they had the artillery and air support options. We lost two men, and the Marines lost a battalion. But according to military strategists, the Marines will more often carry things to a definite conclusion, whereas Army engagements are not nearly as decisive. When the Army finally moves in for the kill, they usually find that the enemy has escaped. When the Marines move in, they are often rewarded with a chance to poke Charlie with their bayonets.

After reviving my spirits, Watchdog reminded me that it was my night to lead the LP. I smiled and knew I had a job to do. That night I led the guys out about 75 meters or so to the north of the perimeter and established a position inside the two and a half foot high, ten foot by ten foot, walls surrounding a small pagoda. Although I signed guard shifts, I don't believe anyone planned on sleeping much. I positioned the guard next to an opening on the north wall, the side facing North Vietnam and the NVA.

Sometime during the early morning hours, I was leaning back against the west wall falling in and out of sleep when I thought I heard a sound to my rear on the west side of our position. I looked at Baker, who was on guard duty, and I could tell that he had heard it too. I immediately turned and peered over the wall and was shocked to see a lone NVA soldier within ten feet of the pagoda, walking toward the perimeter. I apparently startled him, and he took off running straight toward the perimeter. He had either walked into us by mistake, or found us before he expected to. I had no options. I couldn't take a chance and throw a grenade back toward the perimeter. I grabbed the horn and

My Story, Vietnam 1968, 196th Light Infantry Brigade

immediately informed the CP. Somehow the enemy soldier slipped away. The guys in the foxholes never did see him, and he didn't come back our way. Needless to say, we stayed more alert the rest of the night. I was sure he had been sent to probe our position in advance of an attack. I knew that if I let the enemy get that close again, we would all be killed. I placed a guard on each wall, and we all stayed awake the rest of the night. There was a lot of activity during the night with several other LPs reporting contact. I was relieved to see the sun peering over the horizon the next morning.

After returning to the perimeter, we packed it up but were told to hold our positions. We soon received the word that we knew was coming. Alpha Company was going to attack the NVA at Nhi Ha again. This time the Air Force was going to attempt to soften the enemy's position before we began our assault. Positioned just across the flats, 500 to 600 meters from Nhi ha, our foxholes were going to provide us with front row seats for the air show. I knew from experience that the Air Force might soften the enemy's position, but they wouldn't eliminate it.

Before long I could hear the roaring scream of approaching Phantoms. Flying low over Nhi Ha, the first Phantom released its bombs. Tremendous explosions sent clouds of smoke and dirt rolling high into the air. The jet was followed by another. The Phantoms were impressive and the 1000 pound bombs awesome. Out in the field, I saw several puffs of dust, followed by several more closer to our position, and then my eye caught a piece of metal as it kicked up some dust just outside the perimeter. It was damn shrapnel from the bombs. As several pieces of the bomb skipped through the perimeter, somebody yelled, "Get your head down!" The shrapnel that reached us skipped across the dry ground to our front, much like a flat stone does when it is skipped across the water.

The DMZ

I watched each tremendous explosion and the visible shock wave that radiated outward, and then would be on guard for any shrapnel that was sent our direction. One explosion delivered a sizzling hot piece of shrapnel to within a few feet of my foxhole. As the air strike continued, more pieces came skipping our way. One ragged piece about 18" long whizzed by as it turned end-over-end. The piece forced Green and me down deeper into the foxhole we were sharing. Green jokingly said, "Do you know what you are going to have to tell your friends back home if you get hit by a piece of this shit? Do you think they will believe you when you tell them you were blown up by a 1000 pound bomb?" One of the Phantoms released a shiny canister that tumbled end-over-end as it fell toward Nhi Ha. It exploded into a huge fireball – napalm. The Air Force gave the NVA hell. Several more canisters of napalm were dropped, and then more bombs.

As the scream of the Phantoms faded, the sky began to fill with helicopter gunships. The choppers attacked Nhi Ha, pounding the enemy positions. I watched a chopper make an extended low pass. At first I thought he was trying to be a hero, but as the chopper disappeared into the woods south of Nhi Ha, I realized he had just been shot down.

The gunships continued to pour lead on Nhi Ha as we left our foxholes and moved into the open field in preparation for our assault. The grand scale of the morning's events had my adrenaline pumping. A nervous excitement filled the air as we began to advance. Like our first assault from the southeast, we crossed the open flats and moved into the wood line before they opened up. "Boom! Boom! Boom!" Artillery and mortar shells started falling into the wood around us. I hit the ground and began low-crawling toward our objective. The intensity of the enemy fire wasn't nearly as strong as it had been the day before. I took advantage of the short lulls between mortar barrages to advance my position on foot.

Alpha continued moving toward Nhi Ha. Enemy fire had been sporadic enough that by the time we reached the edge of the wood line and Nhi Ha came into view, most of us were on our feet moving at a slow walk, firing our M-16s toward the village. I could see the remains of what used to be Nhi Ha. Only the batter walls of several buildings stood above the rubble that littered the landscape. Mounds of dirt that appeared to be enemy bunkers were randomly positioned among the ruins. The open terrain between the bunkers and us was dotted with bomb and artillery craters. The hedge rows and sparse vegetation had been shredded, and no greenery whatsoever remained. The few trees that were standing had been totally stripped of branches. A yellowish brown blanket of dust and dirt covered Nhi Ha and everything in it.

As we moved into the open, rockets and artillery sent from North Vietnam began exploding around us. Just as I cleared the cover of the woods, "BOOM!" A tremendous explosion sounded, and I felt the slap of the blast. The next thing I knew I was on the ground. I'm not sure what happened, but I found myself lying on the ground face down. A rocket or mortar had hit close, and the blast had knocked me to the ground. Somebody leaned over me and asked if I was hurt. I didn't know. I had been stunned. As I regained control, I began to realize that I didn't feel any pain and had somehow escaped injury. I can't explain how or why, or for sure what even happened. I got to my feet with the help of a friend and ran to the nearest bomb crater and took cover. By that time most of the guys had taken cover in the bomb and artillery craters and in an irrigation ditch that ran diagonally across the field. I kept my head down as enemy rockets and artillery fell.

A few minutes later NVA artillery and rocket fire began to slack up, and then it totally quit. The small arms fire from the enemy bunkers seemed weak. In the absence of enemy artillery, Alpha Company was able to significantly increase the heat being put on the bunkers. I stayed low in the bomb crater and emptied one magazine after another as I fired into a hedge row at the edge of the village. I was sure that the dark spot visible through the shredded hedge row was a bunker and the source of the incoming that had halted the First Platoon's advance. The soldiers on our left flank were having more success. From my vantage point I could see that they had taken several bunkers and moved into the enemy's perimeter. Several of the soldiers had moved up into position where they had an open view of the bunker behind the hedge row to our front. The intense heat put on the bunker forced the enemy fire coming from the bunker to become more sporadic and allowed us to move.

I left the crater, sprinted across the field, and dived into a shallow ditch only about thirty meters from the hedge row. I peered over the edge of the ditch and opened up with my M-16, firing bursts of three and four rounds at the dark spot in the hedge row. We put so much heat on the bunker that the enemy weapons were silenced. Our fire slacked up as a soldier casually walked up to the bunker and chucked a hand grenade in the opening on the side. "Boom!" the grenade sounded. We had taken the position. The muffled sound of grenade explosions could be heard as soldiers moved across Nhi Ha. It was just like down south; they just quit shooting and waited for us to throw in the grenade. Alpha Company soon had control of what was left of Nhi Ha village.

We found that only a handful of the bunkers had been manned, and the rest had been abandoned when the NVA main force retreated north, apparently sometime during the night before.

My Story, Vietnam 1968, 196th Light Infantry Brigade

Our assault had been successful; however, it came at a price. We paid for our success with the lives of several more American boys and the limbs of a bunch more.

A fresh battle field has its own unique set of smells. Maybe it's the sulfur mixed with scorched vegetation and blood, I'm not sure, but if you have ever smelled it, you won't forget it. No matter where you are or what you are doing, certain smells can put you right back on the battlefield.

We helped several of the soldiers, who had been on our left, pull three dead enemy soldiers and their weapons from the bunker hidden behind the hedge row. We helped ourselves to the abundance of war trophies. I picked up a NVA gas mask and several other trophies that I thought would make good conversation pieces. Some of the guys roamed the battlefield scarfing up as much stuff as they could because word had it that it would bring a premium price from the rear echelon troops.

Although I had a close call, I never did get trembling scared like I had in the rice paddies down south. I knew more what to expect, and I knew what I should and shouldn't do. Down south I thought every bullet had my name on it, and now I could tell from the intensity of the crack whether or not the round was meant for me. I had gained considerable experience during March and April and felt much more confident.

Sitting in a shallow ditch leaning back against my rucksack, I realized for the first time that day just how damn hot it was. There was no shade in Nhi Ha; it had all been blown way. The searing sun beat down on me as if it had sided with the enemy. I kept my helmet on to at least provide shade for my head. The yellowish brown dust had penetrated every thread of my fatigues and had caked up where it had mixed with my sweat. The pattern on my soiled fatigues resulting from several cycles of being wet with sweat and then being dried by the hot sun attested to the hardship I had endured. I not only looked like a grunt, I smelled like one too.

Alpha soon moved in and set up a joint defensive perimeter with Charlie Company around Nhi Ha village. There was a lot of activity going on; choppers in and out, and visits by a number of senior officers. Watchdog came back from one of the meetings and gave us the official word. Alpha and Charlie Companies were going to hold Nhi Ha. Normally, words like that were music to a ground pounders ears because his feet were going to get a rest, but this time was different. We were within range of artillery and rockets sitting in North Vietnam, and word had it that 8,000 or more NVA regulars had moved in to the area. We were in deep shit. I was ready to give this place back to the Marines and go back to the mountains. At least in the mountains I felt that if things got desperate, I could always find a place to hide. On the DMZ it was all just too open. The rice paddies had long since dried up and were just open, dusty fields, and in this part of Vietnam, the enemy had the numbers. Besides that, if things got too bad for Charlie, he just had to run back across the border. He knew the Americans wouldn't follow because Mary Jane Fonda would get upset. We were told that we were being used as a blocking force, but most of us believed that we were just part of an early warning system should the enemy attempt to launch a major offensive against Dong Ha. When they rolled over our two-hundred-man outfit, our cry for help would provide an early warning.

The only thing left of Nhi Ha Village was the ruins of an old French-built church, two standing walls of another structure, and a bunch of rubble. The church stood in the middle of our perimeter, and its battered walls supported several roof trusses that had survived the battle.

One supply chopper after another brought in empty sandbags, food, ammo, claymores, trip flares, and concertina wire. After a meeting with Watchdog, Sergeant Huff gave Sergeant Gary and me our orders. Our squad was to build two bunkers. Sergeant Gary would be in charge of one and me the other. The bunkers were to be built to withstand enemy rockets and artillery fire. Sergeant Huff said that there was a real possibility that we could be overrun by the NVA, so we were to build the bunkers to defend three hundred and sixty degrees around the position – we didn't want to make it easy for them. Grenade sumps were to be dug into the bottom of the bunkers and each was to be stocked with plenty of ammo and grenades.

I stripped down to my waist, picked up my entrenching tool, and went to work in the hot sun. I dug an eight by ten foot outline in the ground to start our bunker, and then two of us at a time took turns digging. One used the entrenching tool configured as a pick to loosen the dirt, and the other would shovel it out. The hard work and the stifling heat helped take our minds off the danger we faced. We sweated profusely as we worked on our bunker in the hot sun. The soil was a sandy-clay mixture that held its shape and was easy to dig in.

Our bunker took shape fast. After the hole was about three and a half feet deep, we filled sandbags and began positioning them around the perimeter of the hole, leaving openings for our weapons. This was one time that nobody bitched about filling sandbags – the more the better. The thick sandbag walls were built up eighteen to twenty inches high and were used to support the logs and timber we scavenged from the ruins of Nhi Ha to build the roof. Three or four layers of sandbags were placed on the roof to provide extra shielding. As the guys put the finishing touches on our bunker, I cut a flap off a C-ration carton and used it to make a sign. I hung the sign at the entrance of our bunker identifying it as the "Quan Tri Hilton."

The DMZ

We spent the next day fortifying our perimeter. Waist-deep fighting trenches were dug between the bunkers, and the entire perimeter was circled with triple rolls of concertina wire. We laced the wire with trip flares and set out the boxes of claymores that had been delivered to us.

I began to feel good about our defensive perimeter. The bunkers were well built, not too far apart, and stocked with plenty of ammo, and an elaborate network of trenches connected our positions. I felt better, but I was still concerned about enemy tanks. There had been some talk about a Marine base called Lang Vei located to the west of us that had been overrun by NVA tanks. My concerns were eased when I watched reinforcements roll in. The Marines had sent us some help to counter the armor threat. The perimeter was reinforced with three M-48 Marine battle tanks, a mortar team, and several 3.5 millimeter rocket launcher (bazooka) teams.

Hale and Shiver, one of the rocket launcher teams, were assigned to our squad. Shiver was a little older than the rest of us. He was a likeable fellow, but not very sociable and stayed pretty much to himself. Hale was about my age and was friendly enough, but his serious disposition left no room for anything but business. They were both all Marine, and as far as they were concerned, their job was simple: stop the enemy tanks.

With the Marines at our side, we were ready for the NVA.

Chapter Ten

Defending Nhi Ha

Alpha Company began sending out platoon-size patrols to ensure the area around Nhi Ha was secure. Watchdog led the First Platoon on a sweep south of the perimeter. He was extremely cautious. We moved slowly. Prior to crossing one open paddy, he studied the hedge row on the far side with binoculars for thirty minutes or longer before deciding to move out into the open.

We were all nervous, but not nearly as much so as Sergeant Huff. During one of our breaks, Sergeant Huff jumped all over Sergeant Gary and me for not positioning men to provide security. We were spread out, and I didn't feel they were necessary. There was open paddy on three sides, and we had just finished patrolling the woods on the fourth. Visibility into the woods was good, and there was no way the enemy could have slipped up on us. Sergeant Huff began to get on my nerves, but he was the squad leader, so I did what he said. My real problem with him was that he didn't seem to mind asking us to do things that he wouldn't do himself, and that short-timer bullshit just didn't wash with me.

We completed our sweep south and reported the area clear. Like everyone, I was glad to get back inside the perimeter wire.

The next day Alpha Company was sent north of the perimeter. Sergeant Huff and several of us from the squad were left behind to man Alpha's side of the perimeter. About noon that day a bull session at my bunker was broken up when the crackling sound of a distant firefight erupted. I knew immediately that Alpha was in trouble. I scrabbled to the roof of my bunker to see if I could see anything out across the paddy. I couldn't make out much, but it was obvious that they were in one hell of a firefight.

Sergeant Huff began yelling for us to saddle up. In a few minutes we were on our way out to join the company. The Second and Third Platoons, followed by the First Platoon, which was being held in reserve, had almost crossed the open flats to the north of the perimeter when the NVA, who were waiting in ambush, opened up on them.

We joined the rest of the First Platoon, which was spread out in the dry paddy moving toward the ambush site. Before we had advanced far enough to provide any help, the sound of an automatic weapon cracked over our heads. "Crack, crack, crack." I dived to the ground and crawled to the cover of a six inch high dried up paddy dike. The dike didn't provide much protection, but it was all that was available. Watchdog got to his feet in an attempt to rally us and get us moving across the paddy, but a burst of automatic weapon fire forced him back to the ground. The NVA had apparently anticipated our movement and had positioned an automatic weapon to prevent us from reinforcing the Second and Third Platoons.

The enemy was giving the guys hell, and we were pinned down and could do little to help. I heard the whistling sound of our incoming artillery and watched powerful explosions rip the wood line that concealed the NVA. The stuff looked

My Story, Vietnam 1968, 196th Light Infantry Brigade

to be almost on top of the Second and Third. The exploding shells sent pieces of shrapnel skipping across the flats in our direction. Artillery continued to fall on the enemy, and I watched the stray pieces of shrapnel kick up dust out in the paddy. I looked up and saw a puff of dust straight out in front of me, and then actually saw a small piece of metal coming my direction. As I attempted to roll out of the way, the piece hit the ground a few feet in front of me, bounced, and hit me on the left arm just above the elbow. I felt a sharp sting. "Shit!" I barked as I looked down to see a small tear in my fatigue sleeve and a dab of blood. I thought for a moment that I had won a ticket to the rear, but the joy was short-lived when I raised my sleeve to see only a small cut. The piece of artillery frag had hit me and bounced off, leaving only a minor wound. I reached over and picked up the small piece of metal lying on the ground beside me. "Damn!" I muttered as I immediately threw it back to the ground and licked my fingers to sooth the burn. The thing was still sizzling hot. With a smile on my face, I yelled at Sergeant Huff, who was 20 feet or so to my left, to show him how close I had come to getting that ticket to the rear. He didn't crack a smile. His attention was on the Second and Third Platoons and the NVA. When I saw the look on Sergeant Huff's face, I realized just how serious the situation had become for the trapped American soldiers. Sergeant Huff had a radio and could hear Lieutenant Kimball from the Third Platoon and Lieutenant Smith from the Second desperately crying for help.

With our artillery pounding the woods and under what limited cover we could provide from our position, the Second and Third Platoons pulled back, dragging the wounded with them. Fourteen soldiers were left behind, including a boy who had apparently cracked, jumped up, and charged the NVA with only a 45 pistol. Several guys had been seen making a run for the cover of the woods just

Defending Nhi Ha

to the left of the enemy's position, and others were known to still be alive, but had been trapped in their positions. No one knew the fate of the guys left behind.

Artillery pounded the woods to the north of the perimeter off and on the rest of the day. Apparently Cherokee had reason to believe that the NVA had held their position and had finally decided against sending anyone else back out into the paddy to retrieve the bodies and look for survivors. I heard that a group of volunteers had approached Cherokee about going back out, but he refused. As night fell, we knew that if any of the guys were still alive, the NVA would make sure that they wouldn't survive the night.

The NVA probed our perimeter that night. Several of the LPs made contact with enemy soldiers. It was a long, hairy night for all of us.

Early the next morning just after sunrise, I heard some hollering and yelling on the north side of the perimeter. A lone soldier had been spotted in the middle of the paddy running toward the perimeter. Several guys made their way out through the wire and ran to meet him. I never did get the whole story, but somehow he made it out of the paddy into the cover of woods and hedge rows that lined the banks of a small creek. He hid in some heavy brush on the bank of the creek the rest of that day and on into the night. Several times during the night, columns of NVA troops had moved down the creek bed only a few feet from him. He stayed motionless most of the night, but finally found the courage to slowly work himself up the side of the creek bank and though the woods to the open paddy, where he began low-crawling toward the perimeter.

Later that morning, Buckney was sitting on top of our bunker with his steel pot full of water, a mirror in one hand, and a razor in the other. I heard the terrible scream of an incoming rocket, followed by an immediate explosion, "BOOM!" It hit to the front of our bunker as Buckney belly flopped to the ground. I quickly ran over to help him. When Buckney looked up at me, his eyes were as big as saucers. He shouted, "I could have touched it! The damn thing passed so close, I could have reached out and touched it!" Other than having the breath knocked out of him, Buckney was unharmed.

The bodies of eleven American boys were recovered the next day after it was somehow determined that the NVA had pulled back. Two of the guys couldn't be found, and their names were added to the growing list of MIAs. Lieutenant Kimball was found lying among his fallen men. The guys who went out to get the bodies were forced to wear gas masks because of the sickening odor. The bodies had lain in 100-degree-plus heat for too long, and the stench was awful. Not wanting to spend any more time out in the open than they had to, the guys stacked the corpses like firewood in the back of Marine tracks. I hated the enemy.

That was the last patrol Alpha Company sent out while we were at Nhi Ha. We had learned the hard way that the area around Nhi Ha wasn't secure. The only thing that belonged to us was the land inside our perimeter wire, and we knew the rest belonged to the NVA.

We continued to receive reports of increasing enemy strength in the area. Sometimes Watchdog would tell us grunts what was happening, and other times we would hear it from our buddies in the CP. There were progressively more enemy sightings right from the perimeter wire. Off in the distance, I watched a group of ten or fifteen of them casually cross an open area to the northeast of the perimeter. Normally a single dink brought a barrage of our artillery, but now if there were less than a platoon of them, we just let them go about their business. It was frightening. You didn't have to be a general to figure out that the NVA was preparing for an all-out attack on Nhi Ha. The word was that

Defending Nhi Ha

they wouldn't attack until the odds were ten or fifteen to one.

Watchdog normally stopped to talk with us when he made his rounds. His confidence was always reassuring. I didn't understand the situation. I didn't understand why we weren't being reinforced and why Nhi Ha was so damn important anyhow.[13] An Army position sitting just off the DMZ was an inviting target for the NVA, especially since the majority of Army units had little experience with the conventional tactics used on the DMZ. Our position probably looked like easy pickin's to the NVA. I wondered why we didn't just pull out and leave. Then I remembered that we were working for the Marines, and they were not known for having a lot of smarts when it came to situations like this.

The siege of Nhi Ha continued. Off and on artillery, rockets, and mortars hit inside the perimeter, sending us scrambling to the cover of the trenches and bunkers.[14] Although we took casualties, it could have been much worse if we hadn't put so much work into our fortifications. The NVA never let us rest.

The nights were worse. Every couple of hours they would drop a mortar or spray the perimeter with automatic fire. From time to time they would boldly open up with an automatic weapon firing tracers. The tracers weren't fired into the perimeter; they were sprayed just over the top to give everyone the full effect of the harassment.

---

[13] I later learned that the Paris peace talks were scheduled to open on May 10. North Vietnam wanted an impressive victory to open the talks with, and Hanoi had ordered the NVA to over-run our position at Nhi Ha.

[14] There is a photograph in the February 1997 issue of "Vietnam" magazine showing nine NVA artillery rounds hitting our position at Nhi Ha simultaneously.

My Story, Vietnam 1968, 196th Light Infantry Brigade

Several of the LPs were pulled back during the night of May 8th after they had detected enemy movement. One of the LPs killed an NVA soldier when they detonated their claymore. The soldier had crawled up to their mine and had started to disarm it when he was discovered.

May 9, 1968 started slow for us. A morning sweep just outside the perimeter proved just how active the enemy had been the night before. The ripped-up body of the NVA soldier killed by the claymore blast was found, and blood trails proved that he had not been alone. Everyone was exhausted, and we desperately needed sleep. We were just plain worn out. I tried my best to get some sleep between artillery barrages, but I couldn't rest. I knew that when night came, it would be my turn to lead one of the LPs, and I couldn't shake the uneasy feeling. My insides would retch when I thought about leaving the safety of the perimeter wire.

Late that day, Watchdog returned from a meeting with the CO. Cherokee felt that tonight was the night. Reports from spotter planes and recon teams were frightening. The NVA had moved a large force into position and was staged for an attack. The NVA was using classic military strategy – they had us worn down, their probing gave them the information they needed about our defenses, and now it was time to launch their ground assault.

I didn't have to be reminded that it was my turn to lead the LP. That night Green, Phillip, Baker, Hale, and myself were to establish a position approximately 200 meters out in front of the perimeter on the east side. Hale, the Marine, had volunteered to go with us. At first Watchdog wasn't going to let him go because there might be a need for his rocket launcher, but Hale convinced Watchdog that one of our guys could assist his buddy. And besides that, we would be back inside before the rocket launcher would be needed. It was then that I began to realize that all that gung ho stuff the two

Marines talked wasn't just to impress us Army grunts. Those guys were for real.

I was scared. I knew this was it. I felt that they would attack from the east, the same side we hit them from, and the side offering the most cover.

As the sun set and the last of the C's were finished off, I tried not to let my fear show as I began preparing for the LP. I remember watching other LPs preparing to leave when things were tough and being glad that I wasn't going, but this time I was, and things had never been so bad. Watchdog gave me final instructions, radio frequency and all, and told me that he wished he could go in my place, and I really think he meant it. The instructions from Watchdog were clear. He kept emphasizing to me that we were to haul ass just as soon as the first dink was spotted.

It was soon dark and time to go. I lead the LP out through the concertina wire, across the open flat, and through a splintered wood line to the edge of a wide-open, dry paddy. I established radio contact and had the guys set out claymores to guard our flanks. We all agreed to forget about the normal guard schedule. I was planning to stay awake all night, and so was everyone else.

It wasn't long until we started receiving reports detailing enemy troop movements. Spotter planes were reporting a large troop concentration moving our direction. The reports were relayed to me by a nervous CP RTO. Sometime in the early morning hours, the CO gave orders to start probing M-79 and mortar fire. Reports of enemy movement came closer and closer together. That night the Vietnam War was transforming from a guerilla war to a conventional war, and I was scared.

It started. "Boom!" A round exploded close enough to our position that we were sprinkled with dirt. Relating the thud of the friendly mortar tube to the recent explosion, I was sure that the fire was ours. I grabbed the horn and

My Story, Vietnam 1968, 196th Light Infantry Brigade

reported that friendly fire was within 20 meters of our position. The captain was manning the radio now. I was told in no uncertain terms that the friendly fire was nowhere close and to keep my head. I desperately tried to explain that the damn stuff was closer, but Cherokee wouldn't listen. He was preparing for battle.

"BOOM!" One hit real close. Green screamed, "Damn! I've been hit!" Green was holding his right forearm. A piece of shrapnel from an exploding mortar shell had found his arm. The wound didn't appear to be serious, but it was hard to tell with the limited light. Hale helped Green apply the bandage from his first aid pouch to stop the bleeding.

I yelled into the radio handset, "Green's hit. The fuckin' stuff is on top of us. We're coming in."

"You stay out there soldier! You watch for the enemy! I want to know when he is coming!" cracked Cherokee's voice.

"You stop those fuckin' mortars or I'm coming in!" I responded.

After a heated discussion, Cherokee compromised. He ordered me to establish a new position back closer to the perimeter and hold it until I spotted the enemy.

After I had time to calm down and think about it, I believed that our position on the edge of the paddy had been detected by the NVA on the far side. It was probably NVA mortars and not friendly fire that forced us to move. After the initial shock of being hit, Green remained calm. I told Green that when we moved back closer to the perimeter that I would let the CO know that he was coming in. Green said that he wanted to stay with us. I reported to the CP that Green's wound wasn't that serious and that he was going to stay with the LP.

I moved the guys back to within sight of the perimeter and found a bomb crater that accommodated all five of us with ease. I felt much better because I knew now that it

Defending Nhi Ha

would be a lot harder for the enemy to get between us and the safety of the perimeter. I was concerned, however, that the enemy could get a lot closer to us before we could see him. I re-established radio contact and had Hale set one of the claymores back out to the front of our position.

I monitored a radio conversation between the Cherokee and the LP that was sent out to the south of the perimeter. Apparently the guys didn't go out as far as they were told to go, and Cherokee had just caught on. "Just where in the hell are you soldier?" screamed Cherokee. "You get out there! You know the location!" The LP leader never did say exactly where he was, and I'm not sure he ever moved.

I listened to our artillery pounding the distant woods. It would get heavy to the north of the perimeter, and then the intense shelling would be shifted to the east. If there were NVA everywhere our artillery was landing, they were everywhere. Spotter planes reported more enemy movement. We were in serious trouble. The 76th Regiment of the 304th NVA Division had crossed the DMZ with orders to overrun the Army troops dug in at Nhi Ha.[15]

Sometime in the early morning hours, artillery and mortar shells began to fall to the front of our position. The incoming wasn't ours. I requested permission to return to the perimeter, but Cherokee refused. There was one explosion, then three, and then more, and then a wall of explosions began moving our direction. I knew that the NVA would be advancing behind the barrage of artillery fire. Years of experience had given the NVA the ability to walk artillery in toward their objective with the ground troops following extraordinarily close behind the exploding shells. The strategy was to weaken our positions and force us

---

[15] The NVA units involved were obtained from the book "The Magnificent Bastards" by Keith W. Nolan.

My Story, Vietnam 1968, 196th Light Infantry Brigade

to keep our heads down while they advanced. I desperately wanted to go back, but my request was denied.[16] Cherokee ordered me to hold my position until the enemy was in sight. The guys wanted to go back, but I refused. I don't think it was my orders that prevented them from leaving; I believe they were just too scared to move. Green started talking crazy. "We're all going to die tonight. This is it. This is the end of my life." Green pulled out his wallet, dug a small hole in the bottom of the crater, and buried it. I tried to keep my head up. I knew they were coming.

Cherokee knew the NVA would be right behind the artillery and wanted them to be on top of us rather than the entire company. He wanted the early warning to give the officers enough time to get everyone's head up ready to meet the NVA. I had heard horrifying stories about the NVA using this tactic with much success against American troops. An American will keep his head down if there is any possibility of being hit. Let somebody else take a chance and look. When the artillery is lifted, Charlie is jumping into the foxhole with you.

The artillery barrage was soon on top of us, and things got unbelievably loud. It now sounded like one continuous explosion. Strong vibrations from the exploding shells penetrated every fiber of my body. I believe the entire North Vietnamese Army was throwing everything they had at us. Artillery shells were exploding everywhere. I could no longer even manage a peek. We all huddled together in the bottom of the crater praying not to take a direct hit. "BOOM!" A powerful explosion sounded just to the front of

---

[16] I learned at a 196th Light Infantry Brigade reunion that a heated shouting match that almost turned physical was taking place in the CP at this time. Lieutenant Gibbs, who had returned to the field after the death of Lieutenant Kimball, was yelling at Cherokee, demanding that he pull my LP back in.

Defending Nhi Ha

our crater, and the blast covered us with dirt. The radio cracked, "Come on in! Get back here now!"

My reply was simple. "It's too late! It's just too damn late sir!!" I threw the handset to the ground. I began listening to the artillery explosions. I could tell that the barrage was slowly passing us and seemed to now be concentrated on the perimeter. I knew it was now or never. I had to get a look. As I peered up over the edge of the crater, my heart sank. "Oh God!" Literally hundreds of NVA soldiers had just cleared the wood line and were advancing at a slow walk. Artillery flares lit up the night sky and the battle field like a ball park on opening night. The flares swinging from the falling parachutes made the shadows of the advancing soldiers move in an eerie manner. They were uniformed soldiers camouflaged with leafed branches attached to their helmet, pistol belt, and webbing. They were moving in our direction with bayonets fixed.[17]

I grabbed the claymore detonator and squeezed it in an attempt to blast a storm of steel balls at the advancing enemy, but nothing happened. The claymore was gone. It had been hit by enemy artillery, leaving the detonator cord attached to nothing but a hole in the ground. It was time to go. I screamed at the top of my lungs, "MOVE IT, MOVE IT, MOVE IT!!!" But nobody moved except for the Marine. Hale prepared himself to run but apparently didn't want to be the first to leave the cover of the crater. The rest of them stayed huddled together in the bottom of the crater. I screamed at them, but nobody wanted to make the first move, so I did. Without hesitation, I jumped up out of the crater and started running toward the perimeter. Hale followed me, and the rest followed him. Green was the last to clear the hole, and just as he did, they opened up on us.

---

[17] This vision is seared into my brain. I had nightmares for years because of it.

Green, Phillips, and Baker hit the ground. I didn't. I set a weaving course back toward the perimeter with Hale right behind me. The cracks from the bullets were so intense and the moment so desperate that I wasn't sure if I was being hit or not. As we approached the perimeter, I began yelling at the top of my lungs, "LP! LP! LP! LP!"

I couldn't hear myself – the sounds were deafening. I saw flashes coming from our M-60 position and actually felt the immediate cracks. Our gunner had squeezed off a burst before he realized that it was us. The guys on the perimeter were nervous and were ready to shoot at anything. I didn't slow down. I kept heading toward the perimeter screaming "LP! LP! LP!" To this day, I don't remember how I cleared the concertina wire, but I know it didn't slow me down. I must have jumped over part of it and ran through the rest. Watchdog spotted us and began frantically waving his arms trying to help us run faster. I didn't let up until I was diving over the sandbag berm and sliding down into the trench head first. Hale was right behind me. Watchdog helped me to my feet. I'm sure the dirt on my face didn't hide the fear. I couldn't say anything. I had almost been killed. I was breathing hard, my heart was pounding, and sweat poured down my dirty face. My body had been pumped so full of adrenaline, I felt like I was about to explode. The reassuring sound of Watchdog's voice helped me collect my composure.

Watchdog asked me about the others. We had to yell just to hear one another over the sounds of the raging battle. I paused for a second to think, and then reported that they were dead. I didn't see any of them get hit, but I knew they couldn't be out there and still be alive. Watchdog grabbed the horn and reported to Cherokee that only two of LP made it back. The CO questioned, "Did they bring the radio?"

"No sir!" responded Watchdog.

"They shouldn't have come back without it!" snapped Cherokee.

Defending Nhi Ha

That did it. I had had enough. Cherokee had forced me to keep the guys out there too long, and now they were dead. I hated him, and I hated myself for obeying orders. My emotions exploded as I turned and started to climb out of the trench headed toward the CP. At that moment I had full intentions of blowing Cherokee's shit away. Watchdog grabbed me and pulled me back down and said, "We'll get him later." Watchdog skillfully redirected my anger toward the advancing enemy.

It didn't look good for any of us. I could hear Watchdog's PRC-25 cracking with the captain's voice, "I want to know when they penetrate the perimeter! I want to know when they're inside! I want to know immediately!" It would be impossible to describe the expression on everyone's face. It was more than a serious look; it was an expression that only the prospect of certain death can produce. There were hundreds of enemy soldiers now moving at a slow run toward the perimeter.

At that point I felt sure we were going to be overrun. I cried out, "Mama, please help me!" As a kid I had always called on my mama when I was in trouble, and I just instinctively blurted it out.

The sounds were deafening. There was their small arms and our small arms, their automatic weapons and our automatic weapons, their rockets, their artillery, our artillery, and naval guns from the 7th Fleet, all concentrated in an area not much larger than a football field.

As the NVA advanced on the perimeter, our firepower began forcing them to the ground. They began taking positions – craters, trees, ditches – just whatever was available. Flares kept the battlefield lit up as the fighting continued. The ground out in front of me looked to be alive as hundreds of enemy soldiers crawled toward the perimeter. I kept my M-16 hot, feeding it one magazine after another.

My Story, Vietnam 1968, 196th Light Infantry Brigade

The NVA human wave was stopped at the wire. Our firepower was too much. The NVA increased their artillery, if that was possible, and the small arms and automatic incoming remained strong.

Like everyone else, once we stopped their advance, I no longer even looked at where I was shooting. I exposed nothing but my M-16 and my right hand. Crouched down in the trench, I would reach up and stick my weapon over the top of the sandbags and empty the magazine, pull it down, shove in another, and do it again. Occasionally, I would sneak a quick peek to make sure that we were still winning.

I left my position in the trench next to Watchdog's bunker and moved along the trench line toward my bunker, stopping several times along the way to empty a magazine or two up over the edge of the trench. When I reached my bunker, the guys had the same terrified look on their faces. There was no time for a reunion. Our large stockpile of loaded magazines was almost gone, and the guys were feverishly collecting the scattered empties. I never imagined that we would ever use all the magazines we had filled, and I thought the stack of ammo boxes in the bunker was overkill, but I just found out that I was wrong. Several of the guys began the reloading effort. The loaded magazines were passed from position to position and along the trench to replenish our supplies as we continued to fight the NVA.

At first light of day, the fighting was still strong. I heard the thunder of approaching aircraft – low flying Phantoms. There was now enough light for an air strike, and the Air Force was coming to our rescue. The Phantoms approached from the west. Their flight path would take them just outside the wire, parallel to the front of my bunker. I was going to have a front row seat for the air show. I could feel the thundering roar of the first Phantom as it began its attack. The phantom came in so low you could clearly see the pilot. At the low point in its dive, the Phantom released a bright aluminum canister of napalm that tumbled toward the earth. It hit the ground, and I hit the bottom of the trench face down. Even in the trench I could feel the intense heat from the fire ball.

As the second fighter made its approach, a figure jumped up, and then another. Two soldiers were struggling to get through the concertina wire. It was Phillips and Baker. They were still alive. The roaring Phantom began its attack as they pulled free of the wire and began frantically running toward the perimeter. I screamed for them to run. Everyone was yelling and screaming for them to run. Baker was the first to reach the perimeter trench, and Phillips followed. Neither had their weapon, but Phillips had a hand grenade in his hand, and the pin had been pulled. He let out a blood curdling scream as two guys grabbed him and wrestled him down, trying to pry the grenade out of his hand. His limbs looked strangely stiff but forcibly strong as he fought to hold onto the grenade. He wouldn't or couldn't turn it loose. Phillips had totally lost it.

Two canisters of napalm hit just outside the perimeter wire, exploding into huge fireballs that sucked the air from our lungs. What air was left in the trench was incredibly hot.

After the explosions, I made my way over to them. One of the soldiers had secured the grenade, and Phillips had somewhat regained his composure. "Baker, where is Green?" I asked. Baker told me that when the NVA opened up on us after we had left the crater, he, Phillips, and Green hit the ground. He and Phillips started low-crawling toward the perimeter, and Green crawled back to the crater. Baker said he looked back to see the enemy soldiers throwing grenades at the crater. Several explosions went off beside the crater, and then one in the crater.

After losing his weapon somewhere along the way, Baker stayed face down in a small ditch just outside the wire all night long. Phillips said he had taken cover on the perimeter side of a fallen tree, and at times during the night, enemy soldiers had taken cover on the opposite side of the tree. Only inches above him, the barrels of several AK-47s, with their bayonets fixed, spit fire toward the perimeter. Phillips had somehow lost his weapon and only had a grenade. He pulled the pin and held the grenade all night long.

In the heat of the moment, I had forgotten about the radio. Phillips was the RTO and should have brought it with him, but it was my responsibility to make sure that he did. Green was a good soldier and may have been going back after the radio, but I am not sure that at the time he was in the right frame of mind to think about doing that. He may have just been looking for someplace to escape the hell the NVA was throwing at us. The heat from the napalm had been too much. Phillips and Baker had to make a move – they did, and it saved their lives.

Another Phantom began its approach. The thundering scream of the Phantom was frightening and sent chills through my adrenaline-filled body. This one released bombs. I watched the high-drag fins pop open as the bombs sailed down toward us. They were going to hit right at the wire – too damn close. I dived into the bunker, and a series of tremendous explosions followed. "BOOM!! BOOM!! BOOM!! BOOM!!" I could feel the sandy soil of the bunker walls shake. Dust and dirt filled the air. Still shaken from the experience, I emerged from the bunker to see another Phantom begin its run. I prayed that he wouldn't drop them any closer and dived back into the bunker, closed my eyes, and grabbed the earth to hold on. "BOOM!! BOOM!! BOOM!!" The bombs hit, and the ground shook like Jell-O. The air filled with more dirt and dust, and I could feel the grit in my mouth and eyes. Phantoms made several more passes, but dropped their bombs farther away from the perimeter.

Defending Nhi Ha

The Air Force had finished the job – the NVA was beat. The NVA soldiers that could ran for their lives, while others were trapped in their positions by the strength of our firepower. As visibility improved, we continued to fight, but now with the knowledge that we weren't going to be overrun. The tide of battle had turned. The NVA soldiers were now out in the field in front of us fighting for their lives. They no longer had artillery support from the North, and I'm sure their ammunition was running low. The enemy soldiers were at our mercy as they tried to break contact and run. That more-than-serious look began disappearing from the guys' faces. You could even see a few smiles and hear a cuss word or two. The incoming became sporadic. There was just enough to keep our heads down. When an enemy soldier exposed himself, the small arms fire would go from sporadic to intense, and then back to sporadic when his position was eliminated.

We knew now that we were going to survive and that our ammo was going to last. We let it all hang out. Lots of heroes were popping up, exposed from the waist up, firing on full automatic. We put a real hurtin' on the NVA. The bastards didn't show the Second and Third Platoons any mercy, and now it was payback time.

Sometime later things started to quiet down – a shot here and then one there. Straight out in front of my position almost out to the wood line, a lone NVA soldier, who had taken cover behind a well, began waving a piece of cloth. The word was passed around the perimeter to hold our fire. Watchdog ran over to my bunker and waived his arm, motioning the enemy soldier to come toward the perimeter. The soldier slowly stood up. He was scared shitless. I could see him shaking from where I stood. He slowly moved toward the perimeter with his hands held high into the air. The prisoner was met by several very unfriendly American GIs who went to work tying him up. Our Vietnamese interpreter immediately began to interrogate our guest. His questions were supplemented with plenty of kicks, slaps, and punches.

There was no more shooting. The battle was over.[18] There was a lot of activity going on inside the perimeter; medevac and supply choppers moved in and out, ammo counts, and so on. Bunkers were being restocked, and patrols were being organized to sweep the area around the perimeter.

Our casualties were unbelievably light considering the battle. Credit has to be given to our fortifications and to the officers who did a hell of a job that night.

Our M-60 gunner walked up to me and apologized for shooting at me. I simply responded, "It's not a problem."

Baker walked up to me visibly shaken and was almost to the point of tears when he told me that Cherokee had refused his request to be sent back to the rear for a few days so he could recuperate from his experience outside the wire. I was tired and exhausted and was not very sympathetic. I told him that there was nothing I could do and figured that he should be happy just to be alive.

I walked over to where the prisoner was being held. He had come with his bayonet fixed and prepared to kill me, and I wanted to see the bastard close up. With a cold stare, I looked the enemy soldier straight in the eye. I hated him. Green was dead, and I hated the dink. His hands were tied

---

[18] Over the years after hearing what others had said about the battle, I realized that there are as many different stories about the battle as there were soldiers. And it is understandable. On our section of the perimeter, we used virtually all of our ammo. There were other positions on the perimeter where the soldiers never emptied a whole magazine. Once the NVA started taking cover and because of their camouflage and the abundance of craters, ditches, and other hiding places, some GIs never realized just how many of the enemy was out in front of them. I knew. I had been out there nose to nose with them, and they followed me in with their bayonets fixed.

behind his back and his feet bound together. My stare was returned with a smile. He smiled at me. The asshole actually smiled at me. I couldn't handle it. I kicked him as hard as I could in his exposed gut. I kicked the shit out of him, again and again. I wanted to kick harder, but I just couldn't, so I raised the butt of my rifle. Someone grabbed my arm. I don't remember whom. I turned and walked away.

I walked back to my bunker, sat on the edge of the trench, and tried to get a handle on my emotions. Hale walked over and sat down beside me. We talked a little about our ordeal outside the wire, and then he made me feel much better when he said, "Lyles, you did one hell of a job out there," and then he added, "for a soldier." Hale told me that he would go out with me again if I were to ask. Coming from a Marine, I took it as a real compliment.

Watchdog approached and asked if I was going to be OK, and I nodded. Watchdog said he was leading one of the patrols and was looking for volunteers. He said he would understand if I didn't want to go. I knew it was time to go back to war. Besides that, Hale and his buddy had already volunteered, and I didn't want to be outdone by a couple of Marines. I was ready to go. I felt like the patrol wouldn't be much more than just a game considering what I had just experienced.

Watchdog led us out through the wire. Dead NVA soldiers were everywhere, and weapons were scattered. We started the sweep due south of the perimeter and worked our way toward the east, visually witnessing the high price the NVA had paid. I moved up on one large bomb crater and saw at least fifteen bodies lying around the sides and in the bottom. It looked as if our artillery had made a direct hit in the crater. I'm not sure why, but all the death didn't really bother me. I guess it was because the dead soldiers just didn't look like they had been real people.

My Story, Vietnam 1968, 196th Light Infantry Brigade

"POP! POP! POP!" Everyone hit the ground. A burst of automatic fire cracked over our heads. It appeared that the fire had come from a small crater only about 40 meters away. As I low-crawled to the cover of a small ditch, I couldn't shake the feeling. I wasn't scared at all, and it felt like I was playing a game. I could tell some of the other guys felt the same way by the way they were joking around. After the ordeal we had experienced the night before, one AK-47 just wasn't a threat. Someone yelled out, "What the shit is he tryin' to do. Doesn't he know that I am a short-timer!"

I saw the camouflaged helmet of a NVA soldier showing above the rim of a small crater. His AK appeared again, and he fired several more shots well over our heads. Hale hollered, "This is a job for the Marines!" Both Marines moved out toward the crater. Shriver opened up with his M-16 while Hale advanced his position, and then Hale put heat on the enemy position while Shriver moved up. When Hale got close, he low-crawled to within easy chunking distance, took a grenade from his pistol belt, pulled the pin, and threw it into the crater. "Boom!" The grenade sounded, and dust and dirt mushroomed from the crater. Before the dust had cleared, the soldier's AK appeared again and several more shots rang out, sending us back closer to the ground. I couldn't believe it; he was still alive, but it was obvious by the erratic movement of his helmet that he had been dazed. He must have had a hand grenade sump in the bottom of the crater or something. Hale tossed a second grenade that finished the job. I'm sure the soldier knew he could surrender, but apparently he preferred death instead.

Our patrol found my LP position. Green was at peace in the bottom of the crater.[19] He looked typical of somebody

---

[19] After the war I tried without success to contact Carl Green's family. I had taken several pictures of Carl just prior to his death, and I was sure

killed by an explosion. A light coat of dirt covered his body, and there was little blood. A small trail did make its way from his nose, through the dirt on his face, to his blond hair where it had stopped and dried. Watchdog had several of the guys carry Green's body back to the perimeter. The radio was found in the bottom of the crater, and Green's wallet was found right where it had been buried the night before.

We spent the next couple of days collecting weapons and burying the dead. The whole world had started to smell. The odor from the bodies baking in the hot sun was stomach-heaving awful. Many of the large craters had

---

that his family would like to have them. I finally decided to post one of the pictures on the Internet in hopes that the picture would find its way home. It worked. Almost a year after the picture had been posted, Carl's sister, Shirley Woodruff, stumbled on to the site. After the tears and the screaming, she called the rest of the family, who rushed to her house to see what she had found. She later contacted me by phone, and we had a long conversation. The story she told me about Carl was as unbelievable as the story I told her. Shirley sent me a package of letters, official documents, and newspaper clippings which confirmed her story. As it turned out, her brother's name was Carl F Burdick, not Carl F Green. Carl had gotten in trouble with the law and wanted a fresh start, so he tried to join the Army in July of 1967. The Army would not accept Carl because he was only seventeen at the time and would not turn eighteen until December of that year. Using his mother's maiden name, Carl changed his name to Carl Green, lied about his age, and then joined the Army. Before anybody was the wiser, Carl Burdick was in Vietnam as Carl Green. Carl went to Vietnam to prove something to himself and his father. After Carl's death, Herbert Burdick, Carl's father, struggled to convince the Department of the Army that Carl Green was really Carl Burdick and that his body belonged back home in Racine, Wisconsin. It took a lot of aggravation, sworn affidavits, and congressional help to resolve the insurance issues and get Carl's body back home where he was finally put to rest. Carl's sister sent me Carl's funeral memorial card showing Carl's birth date as December 15, 1949. Military records still show Carl as being born in 1947. Carl's name is on the Wall in Washington, DC engraved as "Carl F Green."

standing water in the bottom of them, and the bodies lying in the water had started to swell. I saw one that had swollen to the point that his eyeballs had bulged out of their sockets. His puffy cheeks and bulging eyes almost made him look comical, but there was nothing funny about the smell he emitted – god he stank. The only way to get rid of the smell was to bury it. We tried, but we didn't do a very good job of it. Most of the graves were so shallow that parts of the corpses remained exposed. I remember passing one grave that had two black tennis shoes sticking out the end of the mound.

The smell of death was everywhere. Like everyone else, I had lost my appetite to the stench. We had been getting our drinking water from the bottom of some of the larger craters, but now all the water was contaminated with death. What water we did have was choppered in in big plastic bottles. The water from the bottles tasted like plastic, which seemed to complement the smell in the air.

Although the hatred I felt toward Cherokee had been somewhat tempered because I knew he had a tough job to do, it was just too deeply rooted to forget. The stern look Cherokee always had on his face was intimidating, especially to us lowly grunts, but just the same, I wanted him to say something about the radio I left behind. When he did, I was going to use the opportunity to unload. I wasn't sure what I was going to do, but I was going to do something, and he wasn't going to like it.

The CO never did question me about the radio. He knew the mistake made that night was as much his fault as it was mine. He had kept us outside the perimeter too long, and I hadn't yet learned that some orders are bullshit.

I did get an opportunity to vent some of my anger. One afternoon Cherokee was standing at the perimeter wire target practicing with his forty-five. Like always, he was surrounded by a group of officers and RTOs from his CP. I walked out toward Cherokee. Fearful of what I was going to do, Sergeant Gary ran to catch up with me. I walked up to the wire and stood within hearing distance of the CO. Acting as if I was talking to Sergeant Gary, who was attempting to keep me calm, I yelled out, "He's pretty damn good with that forty-five. They ought to send him out on LP with it!" Upon hearing my remark, Cherokee quit pulling the trigger but continued to stare down the barrel of his weapon toward the target. Everyone was shocked at what I had said and waited for Cherokee's response. He stood there like a tiger being annoyed by a pesky mouse, and I waited for him to bite my head off. Cherokee just stood there looking down range for at least thirty seconds, and then began squeezing off rounds again. Without saying anything, he told me that he was giving me another chance. With the forceful help of Sergeant Gary, I walked away and nothing else was ever said. The hard feelings I had for the CO really bothered me, but I decided that it would be best to postpone his ass kickin' until the playing field was level. I nosed around enough to find out the name of his hometown in Texas, and with that knowledge, I was able to keep my anger in check.

Rumors about us going back south started to spread. I was ready to go. I was ready to give this place back to the Marines. The rumor came true a couple days later. Our deployment to the 3rd Marines had come to an end, and the Battle of Nhi Ha was officially over. During the battles to take and hold Nhi Ha, the 3rd Battalion, 21st Infantry, and 196th Light Infantry Brigade suffered 29 KIAs, 130 WIAs, 1 MIA, and 1 captured. 580 members of the 76th and 270th NVA regiments were killed.[20]

---

[20] The casualty figures were obtained from the book "The Magnificent Bastards" by Keith W. Nolan.

My Story, Vietnam 1968, 196th Light Infantry Brigade

We received word to pack it up. Alpha Company was leaving Nhi Ha. The Marines were staying behind and would be joined by our Marine replacements. I remember it feeling good to saddle up. I welcomed the feel of the rucksack straps on my shoulders. We were ground pounders, and we weren't happy unless we were humping. I was ready to leave Nhi Ha. Nhi Ha was a hell.

It was hard to say goodbye to Hale. I hated to see him have to stay. He talked like he knew what was in store for him when he told me that if a Marine unit got hit as hard as we did, there was no doubt in his mind that they would be overrun. He said the Marines never have as much ammo as we did, never call for as much support, and would have never used flares to the extent that we did, at least not until the NVA had penetrated the perimeter.

I only saw Hale step out of that hard Marine shell one time. Just before we left, he asked Watchdog if there was any way possible that he could go with us. Watchdog told him that he didn't believe so, and Hale said that he didn't think there was, but just thought he would ask. Hale immediately became a Marine again.

As we humped south, we passed a Marine outfit heading north to Nhi Ha. It was strange. Our parallel paths were within 10 meters of one another, and not a word was exchanged between the two columns. I felt like they were on a death march, and they apparently knew where they were going. I could tell by looking at their expressionless faces that they were an experienced outfit.

Rumor later had it that the NVA had overrun the Marines at Nhi Ha. I wasn't sure if it was true or not, but I said a prayer for Hale and his buddies anyhow.

Chapter Eleven

The Trail Junction

Alpha Company left the DMZ on foot, and after a short march, we were air-lifted by chopper to the Quang Tri Air Base (I think). We were loaded on C-130 transport planes and flown south. The C-130s didn't have seats, so we sat on the floor with each row of soldiers sharing a common seatbelt that anchored to rings in the floor between us as it stretched from one side of the plane to the other. The airplane was loud and rough looking, but I didn't care. I was glad to be riding anything headed south.

There was a lot of conversation about where we were going and what it would be like once we got there. The troops that joined the company in April and May had learned fast. In less than two months, they had learned what they were made of. They knew a lot about the DMZ and the NVA, but nothing about the mountains and the Viet Cong. They knew from our war stories that the First Platoon had been nearly wiped out by the Viet Cong back in April while patrolling the mountains, and from their questions, I could tell that some of them were worried. I explained that there had been some dumb mistakes made and that as long as we kept our shit together, we didn't have to sweat the VC. All we had to do was walk around the mountains kicking ass, and they couldn't do anything about it unless we screwed up and let our guard down.

Once back down south, choppers were waiting to take us to the mountains. I was soon jumping off a chopper in a grassy field at the base of the mountains someplace northeast of LZ Center. We soon learned that Alpha was being staged for an air assault on the hills and mountains southwest of Center. Watchdog explained to us that the 198th had moved in to take our place on LZ Center when we were moved up north to assist the Marines. Charlie immediately started giving the 198th hell. The local VC were assisting several NVA units that had moved into the area. The 198th was green when it came to the NVA. The 198th's normal area of operation was a populated area back closer to Chu Lai. They had primarily dealt with snipers and VC booby traps, and not the NVA. The 198th had allowed the NVA to place anti-aircraft guns on several of the mountains surrounding Center, and the enemy had halted all air traffic to the base. The 198th was short of supplies and ammo and needed help.

We patrolled the hills adjacent to the staging area while all the pieces where being put into place. The next morning we were told that Alpha was going to be choppered to a rice paddy at the base of LZ Center, and in all likelihood, it would be a hot LZ. The First Platoon was going in first. Once on the ground, we were to position ourselves south of the paddy and provide cover for the remaining choppers. After Alpha was on the ground, the First Platoon was to take point and follow a trail that would take us around to the backside of the mountain ridge across from LZ Center. I didn't know exactly what the plans were, but I believe we were trying to get into position to block the enemy's retreat off the mountain. Watchdog asked me to walk point since I was familiar with the area. I didn't mind, and for some reason I really wasn't all that scared. I guess it was because all the air assaults I had been on thus far had fizzled out when the enemy failed to show up, plus I knew exactly where I was going and had been there before.

The sky soon filled with Hueys making their approach to the grassy field where we waited. In a short time the entire company was airborne headed toward Center. I heard an "Oh SHIT!" from one of the guys as we rounded a large mountain and the rice paddy came into view. The paddy stretched out in the narrow, lush valley between the two mountain ridges. Center was on our left, and the enemy was someplace on the ridge to our right. Gunships were already working the high ground.

As we made our approach, the chopper dropped fast toward the paddy. The blades began to slap the air in an attempt to slow us down, and the Huey began to vibrate violently. Up until that point I had remained relatively calm, but now I felt my body begin to respond to the coming danger. Things had gotten serious, and the pilot was pushing the chopper to its limits. The chopper crew wanted to get down fast, get us off, and then get the hell up and out of range as fast as they could. As we neared the rice paddy, I could tell that it was a hot LZ. I could see the GIs, who hit the ground just ahead of us, scurrying around as if a swarm of hornets was after them. I could hear the fire from the gunships as they worked the high ground adjacent to the LZ, and I could hear the cracks of the incoming – Hot LZ big time!

As the chopper approached the rice paddy, the chopper crew began yelling, "Move it! Move it! Move it!" We were still 30 feet in the air, and these guys wanted us off their chopper, and they wanted us off now. I was sitting next to the door gunner, and he kept yelling at me to jump. Bullshit, I wasn't ready – we were still too high. I wasn't going to get off until the damn thing touched the ground, but the gunner

My Story, Vietnam 1968, 196th Light Infantry Brigade

had other ideas. We were still a good six or seven feet in the air when he reached over and grabbed my rucksack and helped me out. My arms moved wildly in a circular motion as I fought to maintain my balance and make a feet first landing. My boots disappeared as the load on my back drove me deep into the mud of the rice paddy. I struggled to work myself free from the mud, and then began scrambling for safety.

The NVA was working the paddy with automatic weapons. Cracks from the incoming filled the air as I sloshed through the deep mud and water toward the cover of the mountain ridge. With all the gear strapped to my chest and the over-filled rucksack on my back, I felt like a big clumsy elephant as I floundered through the mud of the paddy, struggling to get to the other side. I fell back into the mud several times, but my legs never stopped driving me forward. At the edge of the paddy, I climbed up a bank and took cover on the side of the trail that ran around the base of the ridge.

My heart began to beat a little easier as I tried to assess the situation. I had managed to keep the barrel of my M-16 out of the mud, but the rest of it was covered with thick, gooey, brown mud. I wiped the mud away from the bolt cover with my hand and then began looking for a target. I had no idea where the automatic weapon fire was coming from. We sprayed lead at the adjacent high ground, but didn't know whether or not we were even close. Our supporting fire had little effect on Charlie; he kept the heat on the incoming choppers.

As the last chopper cleared the area, the shooting stopped. A number of the Hueys had taken hits, but none of them were downed. A couple of guys from the Second Platoon had been hit and were put back aboard one of the departing choppers. As things started to quiet down, I double checked my map to make sure I knew where I was

The Trail Junction

going. I had the next move – I was the point man for the company. I moved out down the narrow foot path, with the rest of the company finding their place in line behind me. I cautiously followed the trail through the heavy jungle and up the narrow pass that divided the two adjacent high points on the mountain ridge. After reaching the far side of the ridge, the trail leveled out, and a short distance farther I broke into the open at a trail junction. The main trail went straight ahead, and the other branched off to the right and followed the base of the mountain ridge. The two trails bordered a large, green rice paddy that stretched out to the right-front of me. At the junction, tall posts on each side of the trail supported an overhead wooden sign with some Vietnamese words carved on it. I knew that I wanted to take the path to the right, but stopped to check the map and make sure. I guess I had been away from the mountains for too long because I made an almost fatal mistake. Rather than stepping to the side of the trail to get my bearing, I stopped directly underneath the sign, in full view from any place along the wood line and hedge rows that lined the far side of the rice paddy. I knew better. I just made a stupid mistake. "Crack! Crack! Crack! Crack! Crack!" Charlie opened up on me with a burst of automatic weapon fire. "Boom! Boom!" Two mortars followed.

The AK bullets were meant for me personally, and the mortars were dropped into the trees that covered the trail behind me in an attempt to get some of my buddies. Even when a bullet passes within 20 or 30 feet, a sharp, terrifying "crack" is heard. It's an unmistakable sound for anyone who has ever experienced combat. However, there are very few live combat veterans who can tell you what it is like to have a shower of bullets pass within inches. The cracks are so intense that you can actually feel the bullets pass. All the action is right there where you are. You don't hear the

My Story, Vietnam 1968, 196th Light Infantry Brigade

chatter of the enemy's guns. You don't hear anything but the snapping bullwhip around you.

I instinctively dived toward the ditch on the side of the trail. For a second after landing in the ditch, I couldn't move. The terror of the moment had paralyzed me. I lay there for a few seconds not knowing if I had been shot or not. I eventually regained control of my body and low-crawled the ditch back to the cover of the jungle.

The mortar rounds hit in the heavy jungle off to the side of the trail. One of the mortars exploded close to Jamison. He was sitting on the trail yelling, "I've been hit! I've been hit!" Scotty, our medic, helped Jamison shed his rucksack and open the front of his fatigues. I remember the wide-eyed look on Jamison's face when Scotty tried to explain to him that he was OK and hadn't been hit. The blast had slapped him down, but not the first piece of shrapnel found its mark.

With his RTO following, Watchdog and I cautiously low-crawled up the side of the trail to a position where we could see the wood line on the far side of the rice paddy. Watchdog pulled a compass from his leg pocket. It was tethered to a belt loop with a long, black bootlace to ensure it was available when needed. He flipped open the cover, raised the eye piece, and then aimed it toward the enemy to read an azimuth. With his map in one hand and the radio handset in the other, Watchdog proceeded to call a fire mission. He called for a first round of white phosphorus. The round hit short about 40 meters out into the paddy. He made the necessary adjustment and then ordered, "Hotel-Echo (high explosive) fire for effect." I listened to the whistling roar of the incoming shells and the explosions that followed. "Boom! Boom! Boom! Boom! Boom! Boom!" The barrage was right on target, shredding the wood line and sending dirt and smoke into the air. The powerful explosions sent rumbling echoes through the surrounding valleys. Before the last echo had faded, Watchdog spoke

The Trail Junction

calmly into the radio handset, "Repeat Hotel-Echo... fire for effect." Our artillery again pounded the wood line.

As the rumbling echoes of the last artillery barrage faded, Watchdog and I rejoined the rest of the guys, who had moved back up the trail to clear the danger. On the horn Watchdog explained the situation to Cherokee, who promptly ordered him to move out back down the trail toward our objective. That meant walking back out into the open at the trail junction and then proceeding along a path at the base of the mountain in full view of the wood line that I believed concealed the enemy. When Watchdog told me that Cherokee had ordered us to move out, my heart sank. The terror that I had experienced was fresh on my mind. I had lost my nerve. I knew I couldn't walk back out into the open.

Watchdog waited for my response. He didn't want to order me. There was a real possibility that the first one who walked out into the open would be killed. The RTO, talking to Watchdog, said, "Cherokee ordered us to move out again, sir. He wants to know what the holdup is." I didn't give a shit what Cherokee said, but I knew the situation put Watchdog in a real predicament.

We talked a few minutes, trying to convince one another that our artillery had chased Charlie away from the wood line. I knew from experience that the Viet Cong would have hauled ass after shooting at me because they knew that our artillery would follow, but I wasn't convinced that they were VC. If it was the NVA, they would still be there waiting for me, and I didn't want to die. I was the point man and still young and stupid, so I didn't want anyone else to take my place except for maybe the CO. It was then that the situation really got screwed up. Sergeant Gary walked up and volunteered to walk point. I wasn't sure if he realized just how dangerous the situation had become, so I explained it to him, and he still wanted to be a hero. I couldn't let him walk point. Without any more words, I saddled up and began walking toward the deadly trail junction, and Sergeant Gary fell in line right behind me.

Just prior to stepping out into the open at the overhead sign, I stopped for a moment to talk to myself. I had to be in the right frame of mind. I was going to walk out there, and Charlie was going to open up. If I hit the ground fast enough giving him only one chance, I would probably only be wounded, and if so, they would have to send me home. I was ready to go home.

I moved on toward the sign, the trail junction, and the enemy, with Sergeant Gary right behind me. As I walked under the sign and out into the open, I heard Sergeant Gary say in a low, soft voice, "Let's go get them Sergeant Lyles." I walked out into the open with my heart pounding, ready to hit the ground when Charlie opened up. I walked on past the trail sign, took a right, and proceeded down the trail at the base of the mountain ridge. I'm sure that I had almost turned purple by the time I took my next breath. Our artillery had apparently forced Charlie to retreat. I cautiously moved down the trail as it snaked its way along the base of the ridge. I rounded a bend and moved on along the trail with the company spread out in single file behind me. Up ahead I noted a ravine that ran down the side of the mountain and joined the trail. The ravine concerned me, but not any more so than the thousand other things I continually evaluated as I walked down the trail.

When I was within a few steps of where the ravine joined the trail, I heard noises coming from the ravine. A NVA soldier darted out of the ravine right in front of me. We had both reached the juncture at the same time. I could have reached out and touched him. It startled both of us. Everything went into slow motion at that point. At first I physically couldn't move. Then I sluggishly pointed my M-16 in his direction and in a single motion pulled the safety down with my thumb and squeezed the trigger with

The Trail Junction

my index finger. The NVA soldier started to raise his AK-47 but realized that I had beaten him, and in the same motion turned in an attempt to get back into the ravine. Two rounds from my M-16 knocked him down at the mouth of the ravine. All hell immediately broke loose.

I had walked into the point man of the NVA, who were retreating off the mountain. I couldn't see up the ravine, but from the sound of the clattering gear and all the commotion, I knew I was in big trouble. There were lots of them. I stuck my weapon round the edge and fired on fully automatic up into the ravine. I began receiving fire from one or two automatic weapons, and then three, and then four, and then some more. I knew I was in deep shit, and it was time to run. As I turned to run, Sergeant Gary yelled, "Let's get them in a cross fire," and darted toward the other side of the ravine opening. I couldn't believe what the fool was doing. The ravine was only about six or eight feet wide where it joined the trail, but there was a lot of lead coming out of it. As Sergeant Gary made his move, he was hit immediately. His momentum carried him to the other side of the ravine opening. He had been hit in the thigh of his right leg, and the blood flowed. He worked his way up against the bank to protect himself from the hell that was coming out of the ravine. The guys behind me turned and began running back up the trail. The whole company was in retreat except Sergeant Gary and me.

As the thought of running flashed through my mind, Sergeant Gary screamed, "Don't leave me, please don't leave me!" I dropped my rucksack, and the rest of the guys ran for their lives. I stuck my M-16 and my right index finger up over the bank, and on full automatic, emptied a magazine. I emptied the next around the corner and up into the ravine. I exhausted one magazine after another, alternating between throwing lead around the corner up into the ravine and then over the top of the bank toward the ravine.

My Story, Vietnam 1968, 196th Light Infantry Brigade

At times the incoming was so intense that I was afraid to stick my weapon out. Dust and dirt flew from the edge of the bank above me as the enemy worked it with automatic fire.

Watchdog and the guys from my squad had taken cover at the bend in the trail about 50 meters away. The remainder of the company had pulled back to the cover of the jungle. I frantically waived my arm signaling for help, but it was futile; no one came. Sergeant Gary continued pleading with me not to leave him. I kept as much heat on the NVA as I could to force them to hold their position. I expected any moment that a grenade would come rolling out of the ravine, or several blazing AK-47s would pop out, or maybe an NVA soldier would come charging over the top of the bank with his bayonet fixed. I didn't know what I was going to do next.

My supply of 25 magazines had dwindled down to 3. I grabbed a hand grenade from my pistol belt, pulled the pin, and threw it up over the bank, trying to drop it down into the ravine. Charlie's fire instantly stopped when the grenade hit the ground. "Boom!" It exploded, and then the NVA resumed the battle as strong as before. I tossed my other two grenades with the same results and then went back to my M-16. I was surprised that the NVA hadn't made a move. I only had 54 rounds left and knew I had to make my mind up. Sergeant Gary pleaded with me, "Please Lyles, don't leave me! Oh God, don't let him leave me!" The thought crossed my mind that I could expose more than just my hand up over the bank, and with as much shit as Charlie was throwing, I would surely be hit. Being unable to continue the fight, I would have to leave.

As I continued the fight, I made up my mind. I planned to use the rest of my ammo and then run for my life, leaving Sergeant Gary behind. I had done everything I could for him. I knew he faced certain death – but that's war. I turned

The Trail Junction

toward Watchdog one last time and yelled and signaled for help. This time Buckney started toward me and was followed by the rest of the squad that were there with Watchdog.[21] Watchdog yelled at them to get back, but they didn't listen. Scotty, our medic, followed the guys down the trail toward me. My last magazine was almost empty when Buckney handed me another one. We turned up the heat on Charlie. Scotty didn't hesitate. He jumped into the paddy and low-crawled across the ravine opening, using the paddy edge for cover. Scotty dragged Sergeant Gary back across. One of the guys helped Scotty pull Sergeant Gary up out of the paddy onto the trail. Sergeant Gary put his arms around their necks and used his good leg to assist them in carrying him down the trail to safety. As soon as Sergeant Gary cleared the bend, I secured my rucksack, and we all broke loose and ran. As I rounded the bend in the trail, I turned and fired another couple of bursts toward the ravine opening for good measure. We still had a ways to go before getting out of the open. "BOOM!" An explosion went off out in the rice paddy, and another one followed. The second one was a little closer. The NVA was trying to walk mortars in on us as we were retreating along the trail. We kept moving at a brisk pace. Charlie's mortars never did get very close.

---

[21] After this firefight the squad showed some resentment toward Watchdog. I didn't learn exactly what went on between the squad and Watchdog while I was begging for help until thirty-one years later. At a 196th Light Infantry Brigade reunion held in Washington, DC, I had a long conversation with John Buckney about the firefight. Watchdog had ordered the squad to pull back with the rest of the Company, but the squad jointly refused. Buckney quoted Watchdog as saying, "Leave them! They are gone!" (referring to me and Sergeant Gary) Buckney's response was, "Fuck you sir!" And then he came to my aid, and the rest of the squad followed. I have no ill feelings toward Watchdog. I understand his decision. He had men out in the open, and NVA were everywhere.

We soon moved out of the open into the cover of the jungle. In the calm surroundings of the protective jungle, I talked to Sergeant Gary as Scotty worked to stop his bleeding and get a field dressing in place. With a wide grin on his face, he said, "You got one of them, Lyles. Did you know that you got one of them?"

I answered, "I know. You and I kicked their butt."

I watched as Sergeant Gary was carried off to meet a medevac chopper. He was in good spirits. He knew he had that million dollar wound and a ticket that would take him to the rear, and maybe even as far as home. The war had been only one month long for him, but that month had been packed with experiences that he will talk about for the rest of his life.

Sergeant Gary's rucksack, with a LAW tied to the back of it, and his weapon was left on the trail. Sergeant Gary always carried an extra heavy rucksack. I would have liked to have seen the expression on the little guy's face who tried to pick it up. I'm sure it took two NVA soldiers to haul it off, and I'm also sure the enemy made good use of their find.

I'm not sure why, but I was ready to go back after the enemy. I believe I was actually becoming addicted to the massive doses of adrenaline my body had been receiving on a regular basis. I figured if we moved fast, we could get back, position ourselves on the far side of the rice paddy, and pick them off as they came off the mountain. Most of the time in the mountains, we were fighting an invisible enemy. This time I knew where they were at, and I wanted to go after them. I was actually disappointed when Watchdog told me that we were going to pull back and regroup. I tried to convince him that if we hurried, we could catch them in the open, but it wasn't his decision. The CO had ordered us to pull back. I'm sure Watchdog thought I was

The Trail Junction

crazy, and after I had a chance to calm down and think about it, I agreed.

I was later told that Watchdog planned to put me in for a Silver Star for my actions that day. It never came through. Medals were normally reserved for units that had time to push the paper and cut through the red tape. We were full-time grunts and didn't have time for that sort of thing.

Chapter Twelve

Home in the Mountains

After the hot LZ and the ordeal on the trail, Alpha Company moved several klicks to a grassy area on the valley floor and established a defensive perimeter. Supply choppers flew in and out while we grunts sat around freshly dug foxholes shooting the bull. The consensus was unanimous; thus far, the new guys didn't like this place any better than the DMZ.

That night I led a five-man LP out about 75 meters east of the perimeter to a small creek that divided an open rice paddy. I was instructed to position the LP on the far bank of the ten foot wide creek. The banks of the creek dropped down three or four feet to the clear water that trickled around the rocks in the bottom. I established the position, made a commo check, and then assigned guard duty for the night. After I pulled my shift, I retired to my "bed" for the remainder of the night. It was a large rock in the middle of the creek. Trees lined both sides of the creek, but I still felt a little too exposed up on the bank, so I decided to sleep in the creek. The rock was just big enough to accommodate me and my M-16. I lay down, moved around a bit to achieve the best possible fit between myself and the contour of the rock, and then fell asleep. I was tired and slept soundly, and apparently didn't move much because I was dry when I woke the next morning.

The day began early. The new guys were introduced to the pain involved in humping the mountain trails. I had learned not to fight it and took it in stride as our squad brought up the rear. About mid-day we were climbing a steep mountain trail. Most of the company had cleared the top and had started down the other side when I heard a single "pop." I half-heartedly hit the ground, not being sure if it was incoming or not. It lacked the sharp crack associated with an incoming bullet. A second "pop" confirmed that it was. I heard the bullet hit the brush and rocks ahead of me and off to the right. It apparently came from the ridge on the other side of the valley. We were out of range for even a high powered weapon, so the VC must have been lobbing the rounds in.

On the horn, Sergeant Huff reported the sniper to the CO. After hearing that the sniper was someplace on the other side of the valley, Cherokee ordered us to move out. A light weapon at that distance wasn't a threat. I had to agree with the CO. After battling the NVA for the past several months, a VC with a pop gun off in the distance just wasn't something to get excited about. I looked at the situation as more of an opportunity to take a break from the murderous climb than as a threat to my life. I think we all felt the same way, that is, except for Sergeant Huff. He had been on the edge, and I knew it wouldn't take much to push him over. The good reputation he once had was gone, and he had become a fanatic about not taking chances – the guys in his squad did that. Sergeant Huff was due to leave for home in a few days, and as far as he was concerned, the VC was trying to cancel his ticket.

Sergeant Huff pleaded with the CO to call a fire mission. Cherokee refused and again ordered Sergeant Huff to move out. After a heated verbal exchange, we resumed our climb up the mountain. "Pop!" Another shot sounded. Sergeant Huff immediately hit the ground, rolled over, and at the same time, violently slung his rucksack off. He reached around and felt his back and then looked at his hand as if he was expecting to see blood. He then reached out and grabbed his rucksack. One of his canteens attached to the back was leaking. He popped open the snaps and pulled the canteen from its pouch. It had a hole in it and was leaking water. He shook it. The sound of a rattling bullet grew louder as more water was ejected. He grabbed the horn and violently shook his canteen next to the handset. "Ya hear that? Do you know what it is? It's a fuckin' bullet in my canteen. I've been shot!" Sergeant Huff told Cherokee that he wasn't going anywhere until some god damn artillery started to hit the ground. Several direct orders later, we cautiously began moving up the trail again. The sniper apparently decided that he had enough fun for the day and let us move on over the mountain and out of sight.[22]

Sergeant Huff left for home a few days later, and I took over as squad leader. Although I did harbor some resentment toward him, I was happy for him when he climbed aboard a chopper headed for the world.

A day or so later, Alpha was choppered out of the highlands to the base of the mountains to meet the NVA, but again they had fled and refused to fight. We did find an abandoned enemy base camp, but no enemy.

---

[22] I was always cautious not to tell this story because who would believe it; a sniper at that distance, picking the one short-timer in the column, and then shooting him in the canteen. My memory was validated thirty-one years later at a 196th Light Infantry Brigade reunion when I sat drinking a Budweiser and listened to John Buckney tell the story just as I had remembered it.

Home in the Mountains

After the unsuccessful attempt to corner the NVA, Alpha pulled back to a low-lying, wooded area and dug in for the night. I remember not feeling good about the laager site. The woods weren't thick enough to hinder an assault but could provide plenty of cover for an advancing enemy. I knew from experience that the enemy was patient. They waited and watched for you to make a mistake, and when you did, they would take advantage of it. I figured that we had made that mistake when a mortar exploded inside the perimeter, sending everyone scrambling for the foxholes. Several hand grenades were thrown at sounds in the night, and one of the Second Platoon LPs came running back to the perimeter after firing their claymore when enemy soldiers were detected probing the perimeter. Upon learning that the LP had left a starlight scope at their LP position, our asshole of a leader, Cherokee, ordered them to go back out and get it. Sp-4 Larry McFaddin went back out to retrieve the starlight scope and was killed by the waiting Viet Cong.

The situation had all the makin's of something bad. Cherokee surprised everyone when he gave orders to saddle up. A few minutes later, we simply walked away from the coming battle. In the cover of darkness, each platoon took a separate route out of the woods and across a large rice paddy to a rendezvous point about a klick away. The move came off without a hitch. We settled into existing fox holes at our new laager site and left Charlie trying to figure out what in the hell happened.

We moved back into the mountains and spent the next couple weeks patrolling the area around LZ Center. We found several large, recently abandoned camps, but no NVA. I felt uneasy as we searched the camps. The heavy jungle canopy made the camps impossible to detect from the air. The limited light that shined through the tree cover made the place just down-right spooky. Just knowing that they had been there and not knowing how long they had

My Story, Vietnam 1968, 196th Light Infantry Brigade

been gone or how far they had moved was enough to set my nerves on edge. We didn't find any booby traps at the camps, and I didn't expect to. I'm sure the camps were used by different groups of NVA as they moved through the area.

We found a number of tunnel complexes and attempted to destroy them using hand grenades and C-4, but I'm not sure we were very successful. Sergeant Rouse normally handled the demolition work. At one tunnel I saw him wrap det cord around a bunch of claymores and then around a hand grenade that he planned to use as the detonator. The claymores with det cord attached were thrown back into the tunnel, and the grenade was positioned at the entrance. It didn't look safe to me, so I took cover. I looked up to see Sergeant Rouse running and then jumping for cover as he yelled, "Fire in the hole!" The claymores, det cord, and grenades exploded just as Sergeant Rouse jumped. He emerged covered with dirt. I guess the wide smile he had on his face meant that he was unharmed.

Although I think we were supposed to, we didn't make a habit of searching the tunnels. If somebody wanted to volunteer to go in, fine, but it wouldn't be ordered done. Most of the guys were simply just too big physically to fit into the narrow passageways of the tunnels, which left them free to say what they would do if only they were smaller. The tunnels were only searched if there happened to be a little guy who felt extra brave that day. I'm not sure why, but I volunteered to check out one of the tunnels we had discovered at an abandoned enemy camp. I was a seasoned veteran, had proven that I had what it took, and I was small. Watchdog was looking for somebody to do it, and I was the natural choice.

I laid my helmet on the ground beside the entrance, dropped my rucksack, removed my pistol belt and webbing, and after borrowing Watchdog's flashlight and .45 caliber pistol, I was ready to go. With no fear in my heart, except for maybe a small seed, I studied the entrance of the tunnel for signs of the enemy and listened intently for sounds that might give me a clue to what awaited me inside. As I prepared to enter the tunnel, I'm sure my confidence showed. Several of the greens stared in disbelief at what I was about to do. With the .45 ready, I crawled five or six feet back in to the tunnel to where it took a sharp turn to the left. Although I had volunteered and fully intended to check out the tunnel, I began to have second thoughts as that small seed of fear began to grow. With each movement, my fear grew stronger. Gruesome thoughts began to race through my mind as I shined the flashlight around the corner and peered into the next section of dark tunnel. I forced myself to move on. I crawled around the corner and moved forward with my flashlight providing the only light. The tunnel appeared to continue for another ten feet or so, and then it opened to a larger tunnel or a room or something, I couldn't be sure. As I contemplated my next move, my heart raced faster, and I could feel myself being overcome by the growing fear. Then my emotions exploded. I yelled, "THIS IS CRAZY!!!" Immediately I began crawling backwards out of the tunnel as fast as I could go. I crawled as if Ho Chi Minh himself was chasing me. I exited the tunnel like I had been shot out of a cannon. It had taken less than 15 feet of tunnel to transform me from a fearless soldier into a scared little boy.

After taking a few minutes to collect my composure, I told Watchdog that I wasn't going in any farther. He gave me an understanding smile, and then we threw several grenades into the tunnel and considered it "cleared."

Several days later I learned that Watchdog had volunteered to lead the brigade's Long Range Reconnaissance Team (LRRPs) and would soon be leaving the company, along with Sergeant Green, our platoon sergeant. I liked both of them and hated to see them go. I did get an opportunity to go with Watchdog on one last night patrol.

My Story, Vietnam 1968, 196th Light Infantry Brigade

The previous couple of weeks had been easy on us, and spirits were high. Our ten-man patrol left the company's night laager site on a moonlit night and worked its way off the high ground down to a trail that ran alongside several rice paddies that terraced up from the valley floor. I was walking point when I spotted what appeared to be a tunnel dug into the bank on the left-hand side of the trail. I stopped, stepped to the side of the trail, and motioned to the rest of the patrol to holdup. Watchdog worked his way up to me, and I pointed to the tunnel. The rest of the patrol held their position while Watchdog and I moved up the trail to check out the tunnel. I didn't really believe that anyone was in the tunnel or that it was a threat. We were just playing army, and that's how we did it. Things had been quiet, and we needed some excitement.

With our backs to the bank, Watchdog and I slowly worked our way up to the tunnel. I pulled the pin on a grenade, turned to Watchdog to make sure he was ready, and then slung the grenade hard into the tunnel. The problem was that the tunnel was only about six inches deep. The tunnel was nothing more than a shadow made by the moonlight. The grenade hit the bank and bounced back onto the trail. The darkness and our camouflage helped hide the stupid look on our faces as we took several quick steps up the trail and then dived for cover. "BOOM!" The grenade went off. The sound shattered the surrounding silence. We were extremely fortunate that neither of us were hurt. I sat up, looked at Watchdog, he looked at me, and then we both started a quiet laugh. My laughter turned into lasting giggles. I couldn't help it. Every time I looked at Watchdog I started giggling. We were actually having a good time. I was in the Central Highlands of South Vietnam on a squad size "killer" patrol, and I was having fun. Watchdog decided that it would be best if we called it short and headed back.

We had made so much noise that it wouldn't have been wise to go on.

I hated to see Watchdog leave; however, he was just one of a number of experienced men that had left the company after we had returned from the DMZ. Even the CO was now being followed around by Captain Bell, who would soon be taking command of Alpha Company.[23] To me, an experienced asshole was better than a nice guy who was "green." Although I hated the CO, he had experience, and I didn't want to see experience leave. I felt uneasy watching all of our experience go and not having anyone to look to for direction. The situation worsened when I realized that a lot of the guys were now looking to me to provide that direction. Without asking for it, I slowly began to take on more and more responsibility. I was introduced to Captain Bell as a NCO who could be counted on. On occasions I would be invited to the CP to provide input on terrain and the best routes. At times, my familiarity with our AO and ability to read a map even had the company FO (Forward Observer) checking with me to confirm our location prior to calling artillery.

As it turned out, a number of good soldiers in Alpha Company stepped up to the challenge and provided the needed leadership, and Captain Bell would prove to be an excellent company commander.

With confirmation that the NVA had moved out of our AO around LZ Center, Alpha Company began moving west, deeper into the Highlands. There was talk about a NVA stronghold located across the border in Laos, and we were moving west to counter the forces sent into South Vietnam.

---

[23] After the war I learned that Captain Oxford, Cherokee, had been relieved of command for the death of Larry McFaddin. Larry was the soldier who was sent back out of the perimeter to retrieve the starlight scope his LP had left behind when the VC advanced on their position.

My Story, Vietnam 1968, 196th Light Infantry Brigade

Each day brought more sightings and heavier contact. The Third Platoon lost a point-man, and several others were wounded when they walked into a well-placed ambush.

The deeper we moved into the mountains, the more nervous I became. The mountains were rugged and the jungle dense, leaving few places to set down a chopper. The terrain was beautiful, but strange and unfamiliar. As we worked our way through the lush jungle, a chilling thought stayed with me – "If I were the enemy, this is where I would want to be." We were a long ways from help, and I'm sure they knew it. I remember spending some of the most confusing days of my tour in these mountain jungles fighting an invisible enemy. I don't know if it was the first day, the seventh, or the third day, because they were all the same.

The day began with a point confrontation, followed by more incoming from several locations. The company wound up spread out all over the jungle, lying low, trying to figure out what the hell was happening and where the bullets were coming from. There was no logic to it. They wouldn't be on this side or on that side or located on the high ground or the low ground; they just seemed to be everywhere. Huey gunships helped us shoot up the jungle in search of the elusive enemy. Maybe the CO knew what was happening, but we grunts didn't have a clue. Each time there was a lull in the fighting and I began to relax, my nerves would be shattered by the snapping sound of an incoming bullet up ahead or maybe behind me. The Second Platoon made a sweep to the south of our position in an attempt to flush out the enemy, but only found more of the same and wound up getting a man seriously wounded.

Our efforts turned toward attempting to clear a place for a medevac chopper to sit down and securing the immediate area around the LZ. I was always amazed at the courage of the chopper pilots who would fly into a hot area, like the one we were in, to evacuate the wounded. I could hear the Huey coming and knew it was close, but I didn't see the Huey until it suddenly appeared over the trees and swooped down toward the yellow smoke that marked our LZ. The chopper was only on the ground a few seconds, just long enough to get the wounded soldier aboard, but I'm sure it felt like an eternity to the chopper crew. The chopper lifted up, and at tree-top level, darted off toward safety and help for our wounded buddy.

Eventually the incoming stopped, and we regrouped. That day, Alpha Company made very little progress toward achieving its objective, wherever or whatever it was.

After several hard days of fighting and never seeing an enemy soldier and making zero progress toward any objective, I came to the conclusion that once the NVA moved men and supplies into the rugged mountains of the Central Highlands, there was no way in hell that any army in the world could get them out. It didn't take a "General" to figure out what the problem was. The only way to stop them was to stop the flow of supplies before it got to the mountains. It would have been a simple matter to bomb the stuff in North Vietnam as it sat on the dock in Haiphong Harbor. For political reasons, our leaders elected to wait until the supplies had been spread out along thousands of miles of jungle trails before attempting to find and destroy it. Most of the stuff made it to where it was going, and we grunts suffered the consequences.

Watchdog's replacement arrived on one of the supply choppers. I don't remember his name because, like Watchdog, our new platoon leader was always called by his call sign, Stumpy. The name kind of fit his physique – short and stocky. My first impressions of him were good, however, like most of the officers, the few months they spend in the field would either make or break their career, so they had a tendency to be a little too aggressive.

My Story, Vietnam 1968, 196th Light Infantry Brigade

Stumpy did bring some good news with him. My R&R to Malaysia had been approved, and I was to leave on the next resupply chopper. I was ready. I needed some rest and relaxation. I had only been in-country for seven months, but it felt like I had been at war my entire life. Outfits that worked out of a base camp could relax when they returned from a patrol, but we stayed in the field continuously. LZ Center was as close as we got to the rear, and it was in the Central Highlands in the middle of a main NVA infiltration route and defended only by a rifle company. I was at war twenty-four hours a day, every day, and never got a break. At times I wasn't sure if there really was a United States and a place called home. I wondered if my mom and dad were real or if they were just a thought I had captured to keep me sane. If it hadn't been for the mail, I believe I would have lost it. The only things that were real for me were Vietnam, the War, and my mail.

I figured that if I played my cards right, I could be out of the field for over a week. This was an opportune time to be leaving; Charlie was making my life extremely uncomfortable. I did dread boarding the Chopper because so many of them had recently taken hits, but I was willing to take the chance. I wanted out of the field in a big way.

Alpha Company moved into position on top a small hill to be resupplied. Everyone was waiting for food and ammo, and I was waiting to go on R&R. We were normally resupplied every four days, and it had been six. Most of us were out of C-rations and had added hunger to the long list of discomforts.

Radio contact was made with the supply chopper, and smoke popped to confirm our location. As the chopper made its approach, it came under heavy fire and was immediately forced to turn back.

"Crack! Crack! Crack!" An automatic weapon sprayed the hilltop. Instinctively, I hit the ground. "Boom! Boom!"

Several mortars exploded on the hill. The attack sent us scrambling to the cover of the jungle on the side of the hill.

Word spread fast that Captain Bell was expecting the NVA to launch a ground assault and gave us orders to dig in. We worked feverishly to get the holes dug because of the immediate need. I didn't feel good about the situation. We may have made that big mistake that the enemy always seemed to wait for. We had screwed around and had run short of food and ammo, and thus far, the NVA had been successful in preventing us from being resupplied. The terrain was too rugged to chopper in reinforcements, and it would take several days for help to reach us on foot.

Despite a heavy pounding delivered by the gunships, the NVA didn't let the first chopper in that day. A brave chopper crew did, however, tumble out several boxes of ammo as they passed overhead, braving a hail of bullets.

We received automatic fire several more times before the sun went down. I had quit worrying so much about R&R and began worrying more about where my next meal was coming from and what the enemy was going to do next. That night for supper I shared a tin of peanut butter that I had been saving with two of my buddies.

Our over-active imaginations made for a long, sleepless night. Grenades were thrown several times at sounds in the night, and the PRC-25 crackled all night long as nervous LPs reported possible enemy movement.

The morning calm held, and we eventually realized that the NVA had apparently moved out during the night. Later that day Alpha Company was resupplied without any interference, and I boarded one of the departing choppers headed for the rear. Two days later I was enjoying all the comforts a fancy Hotel in downtown Kuala Lumpur, Malaysia could provide.

After returning to Vietnam, I spent the night on the floor in the terminal of the Da Nang Airport. I found an

My Story, Vietnam 1968, 196th Light Infantry Brigade

out-of-the-way spot on the floor and made myself comfortable, which was easy to do since most places I had bed down in the field were a lot less inviting than the corner I had found. After a good night's sleep, I hopped on a plane to Chu Lai, and shortly afterwards, reported to the company's rear headquarters. I was promptly put in charge of a work detail and given the job of securing one of the tents. I rounded up several guys in the area and went to work. It didn't take long to finish the job. I felt uncomfortable being put in charge of a group of men in the rear because I was younger than some of them, plus I didn't know anything about the Army except for the field. I made myself scarce the rest of the day to make sure I wouldn't be given another work detail.

 I ate supper in the company mess hall and then returned to the tent to settle down for the night. I walked back past a line of cots to where I had laid my gear. Although the tent was sized to hold maybe forty or fifty men, other than Mack, who was out of the field for some reason, and me, there were only five or six other guys in the tent. The group was gathered together in the far corner of the tent, and from the aroma in the air, I could tell that they were having themselves a good time.

 Mack left to go find a card game or something, and I lay back on my cot to relax. I ignored the muffled laughter coming from the corner until I heard a hell of a racket and turned to see a young soldier scrambling over several cots in attempt to get away from something. The soldier took refuge on the floor between two cots and then slowly raised his head and stared in the direction of another soldier slowly approaching him with a short-timers stick (short cane) in his hand. A dragon head carving on the end of the stick was being pointed in the direction of the soldier. The soldier had a terrified look on his face, and his eyes were glued on the dragon, watching its every move. The soldier was scared to death of the attacking monster, and it quickly became apparent that he was tripping on something other than marijuana. The dragon approached with a low growl coming from the soldier behind it, and the monster's intended victim stumbled over several more cots in an attempt to escape. I watched in amusement as the group tormented the young soldier with the wooden dragon head and may have chuckled several times as the frightened soldier frantically attempted to escape the dragon. The expression on the soldier's face was one of sheer terror. The dragon lunged at him again, and this time he made a mad dash for the door. The soldier's buddies tried to stop him before he got outside, but he violently slang one of the guys off as he made his way outside and up the side of the tent to the canvas top. The tent shook, and I could see the bulge in the canvas as the boy scrambled around attempting to escape. As they all raced outside to attempt to rescue their frightened buddy from the dragon, someone yelled, "He's going to break his god damn neck!" It only took them a few minutes to catch him. The dragon scared the soldier over to one side of the tent, and his buddies were able to catch and pull him off. I listened to the group giggling and laughing as they walked off, apparently to take their party elsewhere.

    Sometime that night Mack and I were awakened by the company clerk. He was all in a panic and was yelling for us to wake up. He had his steel pot on and was armed with his weapon and a flashlight. He informed us that an alert had been called. I got up and put my boots on and then walked outside to see what was going on. A group of soldiers had gathered in an area behind the battalion tents, so I strolled over to the group to see if I could find out what was happening. After learning that a VC soldier had apparently been spotted somewhere over by the airport, I walked back to the tent and went to bed. I couldn't believe that all the fuss was over an enemy soldier all the way over on the other side of the base. A few minutes later another soldier entered the tent and yelled, "Don't you guys understand, we are on alert! They have spotted some gooks!"

Mack rose up and yelled, "Hey mother, get the hell out of here!"

The soldier, apparently shocked at our uncaring attitude, slowly backed up and then turned and ran out the door to go play soldier. Mack and I went back to sleep and slept soundly the rest of the night.

Chapter Thirteen

Squad Patrols

When I rejoined the company after returning from Chu Lai, Alpha had moved back closer to LZ Center. We spent July and most of August conducting "search and destroy" operations. There was a lot of activity in our AO, and the VC were well armed. Most of the skirmishes were confined to the point. We either surprised them, and automatic fire was exchanged while they faded into the jungle, or they surprised us, and automatic fire was exchanged while they faded into the jungle. More often than not, at the end of the day, the CO had a body count to report. Alpha Company had a way of keeping the body count high. The company's "killer" patrols and ambushes proved to be effective against the Viet Cong. Considering the number of VC that were killed, our casualties were light. We did, however, pay a price, and it was usually the guys on point. It was a sobering moment when we waited for a medevac while a wounded buddy was on the ground fighting for his life. The confrontations were normally short, which meant that there was time to think while we waited for the chopper, time to be thankful that it was the "other guy," and time to realize that next time it might not be.

My Story, Vietnam 1968, 196th Light Infantry Brigade

The company made good use of squad-size patrols. They would enable the company to search more area, they could move faster and quieter, and could be sent in several directions at once to keep the VC off guard. I led more than my share of patrols because I could read a map better than most and had proven that I could direct artillery if needed. A squad-size patrol always brought with it the added danger of being an easy target should the VC decide to take the offense. I was always very cautious to avoid likely ambush locations. On many occasions, I detoured around a suspicious spot just because of a gut feeling.

Most of the patrols were routine, but others weren't. One mid-afternoon early in July, I was ordered to lead a squad-size patrol up a trail to check out some high ground for a potential night laager site. About a klick from the company, I rounded a bend in the trail and started up the side of a steep ridge when a burst of automatic fire cracked around us. I hit the ground and low-crawled to the cover of some heavy brush on the side of the trail, and my RTO followed. Phillips, who was behind the RTO, had just cleared the bend. He turned and ran back down the trail as fast as he could go. Not knowing exactly what was happening, the rest of the squad followed him. As I began to crawl through the brush toward the bend in the trail, my movement brought some probing bullets from the AK up on the ridge. I froze. Charlie had me and my RTO pinned down, and the rest of the squad had run. I was scared to move or even fire my weapon, fearing that it might give my position away.

Several more cracks filled the air as Charlie searched the jungle for us. The incoming was from one weapon, but that didn't mean that there was just one enemy soldier. A minute or so passed without any incoming. I wasn't sure if they had pulled out, or if they were just waiting for us to expose ourselves, or maybe they were trying to move in

Squad Patrols

closer. I needed to do something. Artillery wasn't an option. Although the fire seemed to be coming from a considerable distance up the ridge, the terrain was so steep that the actual horizontal distance between the enemy and us wasn't that far. I was located down range, so the slightest over shot would put the stuff right on top of me. I knew it was time to go. In a coordinated effort, we put our weapons on "A" for annihilate, opened up on the ridge, and made a run for it. Charlie didn't return our fire. He had apparently pulled out.

I met the rest of the squad down the trail a ways. They had regrouped, and all but Phillips and Baker were headed back up the trail to help me. Phillips and Baker didn't want to go back and face the enemy even if I did need help. They stayed down in the valley while the rest of the squad made their way back up the trail toward me.

My suspicions had been confirmed – neither Phillips nor Baker could be counted on. Although I was furious, I didn't let them see my anger. They were genuinely scared. The "SNAP" of an incoming bullet would petrify them. I could see it in their eyes, and I knew that there was nothing I could do to change it. Their experience outside the wire up north at Nhi Ha had destroyed them. They had only been in the field a couple weeks when it happened, and it was just a case of too much too soon, and neither one of them had been any good in the field since.

Upon returning to the company, I talked to Stumpy about the situation. Stumpy agreed to see what he could do, and we left it at that. I felt sorry for both Phillips and Baker.

Phillips and Baker were sent back to the rear within a couple days of that patrol. We parted friends. I was happy for them when they boarded a chopper headed for Chu Lai and jobs back in the rear.

On another patrol in July, Pineapple almost got to go home early. He had led a patrol down the north side of a hill into the jungle, and my squad was patrolling an area to the south. After completing my search, I was on point and was working my way through the jungle back up the side of the steep hill toward the perimeter. I paused when I heard some noise to my left. I was sure that I was the only patrol in the area, and my pulse quickened. I saw the bushes move and then saw a soldier and his oriental face. At the same time I pointed my weapon, flipped the safety off, and had already put pressure on the trigger when I realized it was Pineapple. I dropped the barrel of my weapon and felt faint. Pineapple looked up as if he expected to see me, smiled, and then took several quick steps up the trail to let me know that he wanted to race to the top. Pineapple won the race. My knees were too weak to make a race of it. I never told Pineapple how close he came. I get a sick feeling in the pit of my stomach every time I think about it.

    A couple of weeks later Alpha was working some small, rolling foothills at the base of the mountains. I was ordered to lead a patrol over several hills and then down to a trail, which joined the mountains to the flatland. The trail snaked its way around the base of LZ East as it made its way out of the mountains through the rolling hills to the flatland. In places the trail was concealed by heavy cover, and in other areas it was open. The patrol would take me an uncomfortable distance from the company.

    We made our way across the hills and then proceeded down the side of the last hill toward the trail located at the base. Midway down I stopped to assess the situation. Below and to the right of my position, I could see that the trail ran into a village that was mostly hidden by the trees. I stood in waist-high grass studying the hidden village below – a good 100 meters away. Just as I began to move on, I detected some flickering movement in the village through the openings in the overhanging trees. I immediately signaled for the squad to get down out of sight and be quiet. I parted the grass slowly – just enough to get a view of the village. I

Squad Patrols

had been concentrating on the village and had failed to see an armed VC soldier standing guard on the trail just outside the village. He was leaning against a tree and had a weapon at his side. I couldn't see much of the village, but I did detect a lot of movement. I knew the soldier had plenty of buddies. I was concerned about being spotted, so I didn't attempt to move any closer. I silently passed the word that VC were in the village and that I was to take the first shot.

I waited as the guys low-crawled through the grass to position themselves where they could get a view of the village. As I took aim, I noticed how small the sentry appeared, and as I squeezed the trigger and my weapon fired, a thought flashed through my mind – "What if he is just a kid?" He instantly fell straight down to the ground, and the rest of the squad opened up. A lone VC soldier ran out from the cover of the trees toward his fallen comrade in a hail storm of our bullets. About half way to his buddy, he had second thoughts and ran back to the cover of the trees. I don't know how in the hell we missed him, but we did. We sprayed the village down good with lead, and the VC didn't fire one round in return.

I immediately moved the guys down the hill to the trail. I stayed on the trail and spread the men out – half on one side of the trail and half on the other. We advanced our positions with no resistance. My gut feeling was that the enemy had run, but I wasn't sure. As I approached the downed VC soldier, my heart raced. I was relieved when I found a VC soldier, probably in his mid-twenties, lying on the ground. He had been shot in the chest and was unconscious, but still alive. An M-16 lay beside him.

We moved into the village, and I positioned guards to secure the area. We searched the hooches one by one and found nothing. From the looks of the village, it had long since been abandoned, and the VC that were passing through had disappeared into the jungle. Although I had led

My Story, Vietnam 1968, 196th Light Infantry Brigade

numerous patrols deep into the jungles and far from help, I was never able to shake the uncomfortable feelings that came with the responsibility. In the heat of battle, my preprogrammed response and training guided my actions, leaving little time for pondering the situation I was in, but when things settled down and thoughts were once again allowed to slowly move through my mind, that edgy, uncomfortable feeling would return. It had again settled in my gut, and I knew it would stay there until we got back.

I made radio contact with the CO and reported the contact. I was ordered to do what I could to keep the VC alive – the CO wanted a prisoner for interrogation. My heart was filled with seven long months of hatred, and there was no room for compassion, especially for a VC who was toting an M-16, which probably belonged to one of my dead buddies. I didn't want to help the wounded soldier and was ready to add the downed VC to our body count, but I had been ordered to help him, so I did – sort of. I told Mack, my RTO, to do what he could for him. Having no desire to help the wounded soldier, Mack whined, "Hell, I don't know what to do." I instructed him to apply some pressure to the wound to try and stop the bleeding and then patch him up.

As I proceeded to regroup the guys for the trip back, I turned to see Mack standing on the VC soldier's chest. He was applying pressure with his boot and the weight of his 6' 4" frame. Mack stood on the soldier's chest until the soldier died.

Grunts on both sides neither expected nor received any mercy. Mercy was reserved for the Air Force pilots and ranking officers.

Chapter Fourteen

Mines and Booby Traps

From time to time I would hear a firefight off in the distance echoing through the valley and knew that Bravo or Charlie Company had made contact. Sometimes we would get word about how they were doing. I remember hearing that six GIs from Bravo Company had been killed when a booby trap of some kind exploded at a night laager site. Occasionally we would hear the names of the casualties. Most of the time I didn't recognize the names, but sometimes I did. I heard that Watchdog had stepped on a mine and was severely wounded, and Sergeant Green had been killed.[24]

I'm not sure why, but VC booby traps and mines didn't really frighten me. Although I had seen a lot of old, uncovered punji pits with rotten bamboo spikes, I never did find or hear of anyone finding a fresh one. Booby traps and mines were never found on the main trails. The enemy used

---

[24] In 2003 I read a posting on the internet written by James Simpson (Watchdog) concerning the death of Sergeant Garry G. Green. Watchdog posted, "...When he was killed, he and I were standing together reading the map. It was not a booby trap, but an ambush by an NVA regiment at the top of the hill. I was shot in the head (still have the bullet in there), the side, and the stomach...."

the trails the same as we did. An NVA supply route ran through our AO and used many of the main trails. The Viet Cong couldn't place mines or booby traps on the trails without endangering their buddies from the north.

I did know that I had to be careful on secondary trails leading to the top of a hill or high ground where Americans might night laager. I especially knew to watch the existing laager sites. The VC knew that the Americans were basically lazy, and if they got an opportunity to use a site with existing foxholes, they would.

I spent considerable time on point and learned to locate trip wires. The booby traps that I found were not very creative. Most of them were simply a hand grenade tied to a tree or bush with a trip wire attached to the pin. The majority of the traps had been there so long that the wire had rusted, and the pin in the grenade corroded to the extent that it wouldn't come out even if you tripped over the wire and fell on your face. I did find several fresh traps, but they were where I expected to find them, and it was a simple matter to disarm them.

I know of at least one trap that I failed to detect. Late one afternoon in late July, I had been given orders to lead a patrol to the top of a nearby hill to check it out for a possible night laager location. I was walking point, and an easy-going, dependable fellow named Chapman followed me. Since I was on point, I let my RTO stay with Buckney, who was third in line. The rest of the patrol followed Alverson, the RTO. Scotty, our medic, had come along with us because we knew the hill had previously been used as a laager site, which significantly increased the danger. I made my way up a narrow trail that had heavy brush on both sides. As I neared the top of the hill, I could see that the thick vegetation along the trail opened up to a large clearing just up ahead on top of the hill. "BOOM!!" A tremendous explosion went off right behind me. My first thoughts were

Mines and Booby Traps

grenade and incoming. As I hit the ground, I opened up with my M-16 on full automatic, spraying the grass and bushes just a few feet in front of me. The rest of the patrol followed my lead and was throwing everything they had into the brush on both sides of the trail. It sounded like one hell of a firefight with the exception that there was no incoming. It took a few seconds for me to realize what had happened. I had walked over a mine, and Chapman had stepped on it. Chapman was lying on the ground surrounded by a thick cloud of yellow smoke and was screaming. The force of the explosion had caused the smoke grenade on his pistol belt to ignite. Scotty and Buckney immediately answered Chapman's screams. The sizzling hot smoke grenade was still on Chapman's pistol belt spewing smoke as it cooked what was left of his left leg. Scotty and Buckney slapped and pulled at the hot grenade with their bare hands trying to get it away from Chapman. They pulled the grenade lose, but not until they both had severely burnt their hands.

 I quickly positioned a couple of guys up the trail to secure our location while Alverson attempted to make contact with the CP. When he handed me the handset, the CO was on the horn. I had to force myself to stay calm as I informed Captain Bell that one of my men had stepped on a mine and was down, and that I needed a medevac as soon as possible. I pleaded, "Its real bad sir! I need that chopper right now!" I told him that the clearing on top of the hill was large enough for a LZ.

 Scotty's burns didn't slow him down. Both of Chapman's legs were still attached, but not by much. A large piece of his shoulder was gone, and bits of flesh torn from his legs had been trapped on the way up by his ammo pouches and webbing. Chapman was still conscious and was screaming as he thrashed around, attempting to move limbs that no longer responded. Buckney helped restrain Chapman as Scotty worked to save his life. Although I don't believe

Chapman could hear him, Scotty talked to him in a calm, reassuring voice as he squeezed needle topped tubes of morphine into his shredded limbs.

The PRC-25 cracked with the captain's voice. Captain Bell told me that a medevac chopper was on its way and that I was to move Chapman to the bottom of the hill and find a suitable LZ. The CO said the chopper pilot didn't want to set down on the top of the hill because of the possibility of additional mines. I turned to Scotty and asked if we could move Chapman. In a voice that left no doubt in my mind that what he said was fact, Scotty said, "He's losing a lot of blood and will die if we try to move him." On the horn, I told Captain Bell that we couldn't move Chapman and that I would check the top of the hill out for mines and secure the LZ. After conferring with the chopper pilot, the CO told me that the pilot agreed to land on top the hill if we cleared the area. I felt that if the Viet Cong had placed multiple mines on top of the hill, they wouldn't have placed one on the trail leading to the top, but I wasn't sure. I knew that the top of the hill was a potential mine field, and I had to check it out now. The chopper was on its way, and I didn't have much time. I couldn't ask anyone else to walk out into a mine field, so without hesitation, I moved up the trail toward the clearing at the top. Being brave or scared didn't have anything to do with it. It was just something that had to be done right then, and there was no time for considering the consequences.

I swiftly, but cautiously, followed the trail toward the top, and without having to ask, Kirk and several other guys followed me. We moved into the clearing, watching every step we made. I decided where we would bring the chopper down, and each of us took a section of the area to search. I studied the ground for signs showing that it had been disturbed but found nothing that would indicate a possible mine. It took just a few minutes for me to declare the area clear. I wasn't sure that it was, but it was as clear as it was going to get.

As the chopper approached, I popped smoke to identify our location and let the pilot know where he was to land. Chapman lost consciousness as Scotty and Buckney struggled to get him aboard the chopper. Chapman looked dead to me. His shredded fatigues had turned dark with blood, and the field dressings had already become saturated. I watched as the chopper lifted off, momentarily hovered while it turned to find the right direction, and then quickly flew off toward the rear and help for Chapman.

It had cost us a man to find out that the hill wasn't a suitable laager site. With our mission accomplished, we turned and headed back.

The massive flow of information my senses sent to my brain following the explosion burnt the experience deep into my memory. The war had made me a hardened soldier, and I hated the enemy. I knew the enemy would never show me any mercy, and I sure as hell would never show him any.

Chapter Fifteen

The Rigors of the Trail

The days of one-hundred-degree-plus heat continued into August. The rigors of the trail tested even the best of us. The seventy pounds of gear we carried, the scorching heat, the choking dust, and the constant danger made the long, hard marches more that some of us could take.

Alpha was on the move, and it was hot. We humped along a winding jungle trail that never seemed to end. Without warning, Jamison, who was just up ahead of me, collapsed. He fell to the trail, doubled over, grabbed his stomach, and began moaning painfully. Jamison was suffering from a severe case of heat exhaustion and cramps. I yelled for a medic. It only took a second for Scotty to reach Jamison. I helped Scotty remove Jamison's rucksack and webbing and open his fatigue top. Scotty went to work attempting to cool Jamison's body with cool water from our canteens. After his cramps had eased up a bit, Scotty dissolved some salt tablets in a canteen of water and had Jamison sip it slowly. Jamison's condition finally stabilized, and he began to recover. Others that day had to be medevac'd out of the field.

The Rigors of the Trail

You didn't get out of the field with Alpha Company unless it was serious, like your leg or arm being blown off. Heat exhaustion could be just as serious and would get you sent back as quickly as a bullet from an AK.

I became very much aware of the dangers that the extreme heat posed and decided that it was better to carry an extra canteen and suffer the pain of humping the added weight rather than risk the chance of becoming a victim of the heat. The small, gray pills I added to the water to keep from getting the shits worse than normal gave it a bad taste, but I drank it anyhow because I knew my body needed it. I normally carried four canteens, and on occasions would carry as many as five. Nothing would make me more furious than for someone to ask if they could borrow some water after a hard day of humping. My immediate reply was, "How many canteens do you hump?" When they said three, my response was, "Tough shit, I carry four!" A soldier who wanted to borrow water was either green and needed to learn a lesson, or he was lazy and wanted someone else to carry the extra weight.

A few days later, we were on another forced marched – an all-day hump. It was hot, and my rucksack felt like it weighed a ton. My fatigues were soaked with sweat, my legs ached, and my shoulders hurt like hell. We humped in single file down a trail that led across a small bridge spanning a narrow creek that ran four or five feet below. The shallow water was crystal clear and sparkled as it made its way over and around the rocks in the bottom. As I crossed the bridge, the running water mesmerized me. The heat was suffocating, my eyes burned with sweat, and the persistent pain caused by my rucksack straps was getting unbearable. I wanted desperately to stop, drop my rucksack, and refresh myself in the cool water below, but Alpha was on the move. The creek proved to be a little too inviting for one of the guys behind me. He didn't have enough strength to resist the

My Story, Vietnam 1968, 196th Light Infantry Brigade

pull of the water. He passed out and fell off the bridge face first into the four inch deep water and rocks. He was the first of six men to be medevac'd out of the field that day – casualties of the one-hundred-degree heat.

After a string of tough days, we were spread out on the trail trying to take advantage of what shade we could find while we waited for a supply chopper. The odor of my sweat-soaked helmet lying beside me filled the air. I continually wiped the sweat from my eyes. A few minutes later the chopper was on the ground, and several men, staying low to avoid the whirling blades, scurried around unloading supplies and ammo. "POP." An M-16 sounded. I made an instinctive move toward my weapon and then stopped. Something was wrong – only one shot. What happened? Word spread up and down the trail like wild fire. One of the boys in the Third Platoon couldn't take it anymore. A chopper was sitting there on the ground ready to take him home, and all he had to do was shoot himself in the foot, and he did. Apparently another soldier thought it was a good idea because there was another single "POP" and another passenger for the chopper. That day two GIs in Alpha Company had shot themselves in the foot to get out of the field.

The words "saddle up" always hurt. I wondered why they called us light infantry every time I felt the straps of my rucksack press into my sore shoulders. Even though I only carried what I felt was absolutely necessary, my pack was heavy. Like everyone else, when we were on the move, I didn't carry the heavy cans that came with the C-ration meals. The fruit was good, but the syrup was too heavy. I would eat what I could at the resupply site and then throw the rest away. Canned fruit and beanie weenies were just too heavy to hump. I always carried all the ammo I was supposed to because I knew from experience that I could need every round. Some guys were only concerned about

The Rigors of the Trail

their immediate need – relief from the torturous load they carried. On one occasion Stumpy caught our M-60 machine gunner throwing away six or seven rounds of ammunition. Come to find out, he and his ammo bearer had thrown away over half of their ammo. Other guys would crack open their claymore mines and remove the heavy explosive clay to lighten their load. An empty claymore is much easier to hump, and besides that, the C-4 burns hot and does a good job of heating C-rations. Occasionally, a green would hop off the chopper to join the company with an M-14 in hand, and it was obvious to everyone that he had a lesson to learn. If a new man insisted on being issued an M-14 rather than an M-16, he met no resistance. I heard stories about parents getting involved through their congressman to ensure their son wasn't issued the unreliable M-16. As long as the soldier carried at least twenty-five magazines of ammo like everyone else, he was welcome to the M-14. On the trail, added weight meant added pain. A few ounces could mean the difference between reaching the top of a mountain or passing out on the way up. It meant the difference between pain that was almost unbearable and pain that was. Carrying an M-14 instead of an M-16 added not ounces, but pounds, to a soldier's load. The M-16 weighs less than six pounds, and the .223 caliber ammo was less than half the weight of the M-14's 7.62 mm round. It never took long for the green to realize that he had made one hell of a mistake; nevertheless, he had to suffer the pain and wait for the next resupply ship before he could get rid of the chunk of iron he was humping.

The RTOs had a hell of a load to carry. They had to hump a rucksack, weapon, and ammo just like everyone else, plus they carried the radio. The PRC-25 radio was heavy and cumbersome, and the weight of the spare battery made it worse. Those who had to carry it called it the "prick"-25. The only good thing about humping the prick-25 was that you got the plastic bag that the spare battery came in. During the monsoon season, the plastic bags were worth their weight in gold. Most of the time the battery bag had to be used to cover the radio handset to keep it dry, but if the bag on the handset was still in good shape, the extra bag became a valuable commodity for the RTO. I always tried to be extra nice to the CP RTOs hoping they would pass an empty battery bag my way.

The night skies did provide some relief from the heat and gave us a chance to rest our weary shoulders, but the darkness also provided an environment that the Viet Cong preferred. Nighttime meant LPs, ambushes, and killer patrols. The night air was always filled with tension. Sometimes it was the harassing tactics of the Viet Cong, and other times it was our imaginations running wild. Only a true grunt knows what it is like to spend the night outside the perimeter watching for the enemy. A rustling in the brush or the sound of a cracking twig would activate the uncontrollable imagination of a nineteen-year-old GI manning a listening post. Many times a response from the LP would be triggered by nothing more than an active imagination. The quick, deep sound of an exploding grenade or the powerful sound of a claymore would break the silence of the night. The explosion would be followed by sounds of the GIs hauling ass through the bush toward the perimeter and safety.

Sometimes it wasn't our imagination. Alert LPs added several VC to the company's body count, and on many occasions blood trails and blood-covered bushes proved that it wasn't always our imagination. I led my share of the LPs and more than my share of night patrols and ambushes. By the time August had rolled around, my idea about duty and following orders had changed. My number one responsibility was to make sure that I and the guys who went out with me came back alive the next morning. My strategy was no longer to find and defeat the enemy; it was simply, "DO

The Rigors of the Trail

WHATEVER I HAD TO DO TO STAY ALIVE." If our commander-in-chief had wanted us to defeat the enemy, he would have let us take the war to North Vietnam where we could crush the NVA and Jane Fonda once and for all. Since the officers and senior NCOs in the company didn't go out on LPs or ambushes, I figured that I had the right to decide just how critical it was to the company's security for me to go to where I was ordered to go. If I thought the ambush location that had been selected was too dangerous and the purpose was just to increase the company's body count, I simply found a safer place to go – like a few meters out in front of one of the perimeter positions. I always made sure the guys in the perimeter foxholes knew that I would be out in front of them. They didn't mind the added security and surely wouldn't rat on me because the next time they had a tough ambush, they might want to do the same. I would lead the guys far enough away from the perimeter to be out of sight, which, if the cover was heavy, wouldn't be far. Before I would make my commo check, I waited about as long as it would have taken me to get to where I was supposed to go. I answered the hourly sit reps (situation reports) as if we were at the ambush site. I'm sure some of the officers knew what was happening, but they didn't say anything because they knew that they would do the same thing if our roles were reversed.

Even playing it safe was dangerous. It was another one of those warm evenings when I learned that I was to lead an ambush patrol that night. There had been a lot of light contact that day, and I didn't feel good about leaving the perimeter. When Stumpy pointed to the location on the map, I knew instantly that I wasn't going there. I figured the Command on Center had selected the site because Captain Bell had a little more concern for us that to send us so far, especially on a night like that night. The patrol was to take me down the jungle-covered hill to the main trail at the base, and then west on the trail for almost a klick to the ambush site at a junction of a secondary trail. I'm sure all the contact that day had the Command on Center excited about the prospects of increasing the battalion's body count, and the trail junction looked like a good place to do just that.

When I showed Buckney where we had been ordered to go, he responded with a simple, "Bull shit!" He knew me well enough to know that I would never risk the guys' lives to take them there. The "bull shit" was meant for the asshole on Center who pushed the pin in the map and said that's where he wanted us to setup. It was easy matter for him. He didn't have to walk the dark jungle and the dangerous trail to get to the place, and he didn't have to be concerned about the consequences if something went wrong once we got there.

I had it figured a bit different. The Viet Cong had learned that Americans get careless when they smell blood, and we had made contact several times that day. They knew that we would probably set up an ambush, and if we did, we would probably set it on the main trail and probably at the intersection of the dotted lines. I knew there was a good chance that the Viet Cong would never let us make it to the ambush site. I had no choice but to leave the hill down the side headed for the main trail since the CO may have suspected something if I had left headed out in the opposite direction. That sector of the perimeter belonged to the Third Platoon, and if I was going to stay just outside the perimeter in front of them, I would have had to let the guys at three, and maybe four, positions know. I didn't know them well enough to take the chance, plus several new men were among them and I didn't like the idea of spending the night within grenade-chunking distance of a bunch of greens.

At dusk I walked off the hill into the jungle knowing what I was not going to do, but still unsure about exactly what I was going to do. We pushed silently along a narrow

The Rigors of the Trail

foot path that guided us toward the bottom of the hill. Buckney, who was on point, stopped before he broke out into the open at the main trail. I quietly moved up and joined him. I motioned Buckney to hold his position and then slowly moved up until I could see up and down the main trail. I looked and listened for five minutes or better and then motioned for the guys to follow me. I moved straight across the trail and up the side of a jungle-covered hill. We worked into some heavy brush and made ourselves comfortable as we prepared to spend the night. I had thought about going up the trail a bit, but after seeing how open it was, I decided against it. I waited and then reported that we had reached the ambush site.

From our hiding place on the hill, I could see the main trail below through the openings in leafs, branches, and vines that concealed our presence. I made sure that everyone knew that if the enemy came down the trail, we would just let him pass unless we were detected, and we all knew that if that happened, we would be in serious trouble. We had no cover except for the vegetation we were hiding in, and it wouldn't stop a shower of AK bullets.

Sometime after midnight, things started to happen. I monitored the radio as one of the LPs reported some movement. "Boom!" I heard a grenade explode up on the hill. I learned from the CP RTO that the grenade was tossed from one of the perimeter foxholes toward some sounds in the jungle. I waited and listened. "What next?" And then my mind began processing some bad thoughts. "What if they attack and the CO calls for artillery support? If I were the FO, the first place I would hit would be at the bottom of the hill at the main trail right where we were setup!" I knew I had screwed up.

"Boom!" A claymore exploded up on the hill. "Oh shit!" I thought. I knew that the CO would order probing mortar and artillery fire if there was much more action. The tension slowly built in my body, and sweat poured from my face as I realized the predicament I had gotten us in. My hands began trembling, and I felt nauseated as I tried to decide whether or not I should report our actual location to the CO. If mortar and artillery shells began to fall, we would be in serious danger. I looked around at the guys hid away in the dense jungle, and they looked snug as bugs in a rug and apparently hadn't realized the predicament I had gotten them in, except for Buckney. I could tell he knew we were in trouble. My stomach was queasy, and I began to get sick with worry. I prayed. I asked him to help us make it through the night, and in those prayers, I made some promises to him that I never really ever kept. The words were so sincere that even today my conscience occasionally reminds me of the unkept promise I made so many years ago.

Things finally quieted down, but I didn't stop worrying. I actually got sick to my stomach. Fear and worry gripped my stomach and forced me to heave, and I felt the vomit enter my mouth. I held it. I couldn't spit for fear of making too much noise, so I put my face to the ground, opened my mouth, and let it silently flow out on to the jungle floor.

As the sun rose the next morning, the tension began to ease, and an unbelievable feeling of relief revived me. I said a sincere thank you, ended my night-long prayer, and then began preparing for the trip back up the hill to the company.

A week later on a warm, mid-August night, I was instructed to set up an ambush on a main trail a good half klick or so from the company. I positioned the men just off a main trail up on a ten-foot-high bank that dropped vertically down to the edge of the trail. The top of the bank was covered with tall grass and bushes. I had selected the position more as a hiding place than a place to spring an ambush. I placed a claymore on the edge of the bank facing down on the trail and moved back from the edge. From my

The Rigors of the Trail

vantage point, I could only see a small section of the trail, but I figured it was enough.

Sometime after midnight I was handed the PRC-25 handset. I listened to a conversation between the CP and a second ambush team that had been placed on a secondary trail. They reported hearing a lot of movement. The sounds were not coming from their trail, but sounded as if they were coming from the main trail and were headed toward my ambush site. I silently passed the word to the guys to prepare for some action, and then reported to the CP that I was ready. I picked up the claymore detonator, looked at the claymore, and then realized just how damn close I was to the mine. It was too late to change anything now. My heart raced and the sweat began to pour as I waited for the enemy in dead silence.

The silence soon gave way to a commotion coming down the trail. From the sound of the footsteps and clattering gear, I could tell that there was a bunch of them, and they were moving fast toward us. I pressed myself to the ground to shield my body from the coming blast. In the prone position, I could no longer see the trail – I didn't have to; I could hear what I needed to know. Prior to leaving the perimeter, I made sure the guys knew what our plan of action was. I would spring the trap with the claymore, and if it turned into a fight, we would throw our hand grenades. I stressed, "No M-16s, not unless things get real bad, and if that happens, it is every man for himself to get back to the perimeter." I couldn't begin to express in words the feelings that I had at that moment.

The enemy was moving toward my ambush site, and our claymore was setting too close to our position. Claymores were so routinely set out that sometimes they were not given a second thought – my mistake. A claymore is nothing but a rectangular-shaped piece of C-4 explosive enclosed in a plastic case. The mine is detonated by an

My Story, Vietnam 1968, 196th Light Infantry Brigade

electrical blasting cap which receives a charge from a hand-held "clicker" by way of the connecting wire. Glue holds a layer of steel balls on the inside surface of the mine face. When it explodes, steel balls are blasted toward the enemy, and the back half of the plastic case is blown backwards.

Even though the claymore was set too close to our position, there was no doubt in my mind about what I was going to do. I was going to detonate the mine and suffer the consequences. The rest of the guys were located somewhat behind me, and grass and bushes would provide them some protection. I waited for the enemy with the claymore detonator in one hand and a hand grenade in the other. I listened as the enemy approached and knew it was time. I could hear them passing on the trail below. I buried my face into the ground with the top of my helmet facing the claymore and squeezed the detonator – "BOOM!" A powerful explosion sounded. The back blast from the claymore hurt and covered me with dirt and dust, but I didn't move a muscle – none of us did.

There was a lot of commotion on the trail. From the sounds, I estimated that there was at least a platoon of them and knew better than to throw my grenade and turn it into a fight. We remained motionless. It was strange. Sounds were heard for another five minutes or so, but we never did hear any voices. I wasn't sure if they had moved on, or if they were searching for us, or what. It was a hell of a long night. Every sound was studied, and at times, I was sure Charlie was trying to slip up on us. Every accidental sound we made was amplified by the surrounding silence. I relied on my prayers to help me make it through the night.

As the darkness began to disappear, I felt that my prayers had been answered. The threat we faced diminished as visibility improved. I now dared to move enough to check my body for wounds caused by the back blast of the claymore. I apparently escaped unharmed, except for the shock my ear drums had received.

Daybreak meant that it was time to search our ambush site. I was concerned about checking out the trail because I had an uneasy feeling that the enemy might want to return the favor and set up something for us. I relayed my concerns to the CO. I was told to hold my position until Stumpy and the rest of the platoon arrived to assist me.

When the platoon arrived, we searched the trail and the surrounding area and found nothing – no bodies, no blood, no gear, nothing. The only thing I could figure was that I sprang the trap too late or too early, but I didn't really care. It was morning, and we had survived another one. One thing was for sure, it had been a long, hairy night.

It was now humping time again. The warm air that dried the mist that surrounded us told me we faced another one-hundred-degree day, but we could take it – we were grunts.

Chapter Sixteen

LZ West

Our search for the enemy took us across the Chang River southwest of LZ Center. A two day sweep along the river produced nothing. I didn't feel comfortable being so far from Center and was glad when we started looking for a place to go back across. We were soon waiting for the Third Platoon to cross the Chang and secure the far bank. As we waited, Miller, a black boy who had just joined the company, approached me and, with a concerned look on his face, told me that he couldn't swim. He was panic stricken at the thought of crossing the river. I tried to reassure him, explaining that there was nothing to worry about, and that if he needed help, I would be right behind him.

We moved along in single file getting closer to the river. As we approached the Chang and waited for our turn to cross, what little confidence I had given Miller was erased by the sound of the rapids and the sight of the swift current. As the Third Platoon worked their way across, I could see that the water was about waist deep, and from the cautious movement of the soldiers, it was apparent that the footing on the rocky bottom was treacherous. When the guys in the squad saw the fear on Miller's face, it was like sharks smelling blood. They began teasing him unmercifully. They had Miller convinced that he was going to drown. I felt sorry for him, but it was also sort of funny. He couldn't see past his own fears to recognize that they were just joking around.

Most of the Third Platoon had crossed when a "green" lost his footing and quickly disappeared as he was carried downstream. Lieutenant Maher, platoon leader of the Third Platoon, went after him. The new man managed to shed his rucksack and surfaced downstream. He worked his way over to the bank where a couple of guys helped him out of the water. It took him a few minutes to cough and spit out the Chang. Lieutenant Maher went down and never came up. His body was later recovered downstream. Lieutenant Maher had drowned attempting to save one of his men.

The joking stopped. I'm sure at that moment Kirk, who had instigated most of the ribbing, wished that he could take it all back. Attempting to reverse the damage, Kirk tried providing some words of encouragement to Miller, but it was too late. Miller was scared stiff when it was our turn to cross.

We took our time, making sure of our footing on the rocky bottom, and we all crossed safely. Miller had a wide grin on his face as he stepped out of the water and was helped up the slick bank by the two guys assigned to the task. As far as Miller was concerned, he had been given a new lease on life.

Most of our crossings had been at locations where the river was much wider and shallower, which made crossing relatively easy. Some of the guys questioned why the CO picked such a tough place to cross. I didn't. I figured the CO may have had reason to expect an enemy ambush, and he knew that Charlie wouldn't expect us to pick such a difficult place to ford the river.

That evening as we sat around the foxholes, Stumpy made his rounds telling us the good news. The First Platoon had been selected to man an abandoned fire support base called LZ West. There were three fire support bases in the AO: LZ East, LZ West, and LZ Center. When the 196th assumed responsibility for the AO, 2/1 took LZ East, 4/31 took LZ West, and we, 3/21, took LZ Center. The 4/31 had temporarily moved off LZ West, and during their absence, the 3/21 was to maintain a presence on the base. LZ West was located in the middle of the Hiep Duc Valley about seven or eight klicks west of LZ Center. Enemy activity in the valley could easily be monitored from the vantage point provided by the base. We were essentially going to be a platoon-size Observation Post (OP) for the next week or so. The guys viewed the situation as a chance to take a much needed break, a chance for the rot on our feet to heal, and a chance to let our sore backs and shoulders rest.

Stumpy told us that LZ West had not been hit for a long time and that the enemy knew better than to try because they would have to contend with the big guns on Center. I wasn't sure I liked the idea. I still remembered the hurtin' Charlie put on us other times the First Platoon had laagered alone. I was concerned, but on the other hand, the VC seemed to leave our four-man OPs alone because of the threat our artillery posed. The more I thought about it, the better I liked it. I needed some rest. We all did.

The First Platoon was air-lifted to the top of LZ West the next morning. Before long the chopping sound of the last Huey faded and allowed the jubilant sounds of a bunch of young men to be heard. We were acting like a bunch of school boys being let out of class for recess. We established a perimeter on the southeast end of the mountain using the existing bunkers. Stumpy assigned me two bunkers on the northeast side. The other squads manned one bunker on the southeast end, two on the south side, and what was left of a gun emplacement on the northwest side. Our northwest position was inside the old perimeter and used the chopper pad as a field-of-fire. All the bunkers and the abandoned command center on the north end of the mountain were left for Charlie. Stumpy established his CP in a gun emplacement located in the center of our perimeter. I didn't feel good about our perimeter. My two bunkers were located down the slope a good distance, and the curve of the mountain put the position on the right out of view. The guys positioned in the gun emplacement were located more to the rear of us than on our left and were also out of view. I felt that we were just too spread-out and would have been more concerned if we had been facing a real threat.

    We worked hard the rest of the day cleaning our bunkers and preparing secondary fighting positions that formed a much tighter perimeter around the CP. This was the first time that we had prepared secondary positions. The tighter perimeter of the secondary positions helped relieve some of my concerns. Miller and I worked on a large, two-man foxhole that had to be supplemented with sandbags in the front due to the slope it was located on. A partial wall of sandbags partitioned the hole into two fighting positions. If needed, Miller and I would share the hole.

    I was concerned about the potential for booby traps and had cautioned the guys, but as work on our perimeter continued, my fears slowly diminished. Nobody really minded the hard work because we knew that we could be lazy the rest of our stay on West once our positions had been prepared.

    Later that afternoon, a Huey flew in supplies, ammo, and a backlog of mail and packages. I eagerly waited to see if there was something in the bag for me. I hit the jackpot. The biggest package in the bag was mine. Mama had sent me a box full of canned fruit, candy, and a bunch of other good stuff. I stored my treasures nice and neatly on a shelf I built in the bunker. I was looking forward to the stay.

As the sun began to slowly disappear below a mountain ridge, we sat around our bunkers shooting the bull and enjoying our break from the war. We had worked hard that day and deserved a rest. I knew times were good when they started jammin' at Sergeant Rouse's bunker. I walked over to the bunker and found a comfortable sandbag to sit on. Several of the black guys had silky smooth voices and could put the Temptations to shame when they sang "My Girl," I wanted to join in, but I knew I would embarrass myself if I tried, so I just listened, enjoyed the moment, and dreamed of home. Eventually some of the white guys joined in and screwed it all up, but we still had a good time. I think maybe Alpha Company was somewhat different when it came to race relations because we spent so much time in the field. There was very little, if any, racial tension. Somehow or another we had all gotten into the shittin' mess together, and regardless of the color of our skin, we had to rely on one another to get ourselves out.

It was getting late, so I called the squad together to setup the normal guard schedule. The guys were tired and just plain worn out, and in a weak moment, I decided to give them a break. I asked if anyone had a problem with posting just one guard between our two bunkers rather than a guard for each bunker. It meant more sleep because of the shorter guard shifts, and we all needed it. Nobody had a problem with getting a little extra sleep. I had second thoughts about it. I knew I had just let my guard down, but at the moment, it seemed too late to do anything about it. Besides, I was looking forward to a good night's sleep with a roof over my head.

We drew straws for first shift, and Kirk won. He positioned himself between the bunkers while the rest of the squad prepared to sack-out. I was ready. I had made a bed in the bunker from ammo boxes and softened it with empty sandbags. It looked so inviting that I thought I would make it even better by taking off my boots. I had never before slept in the field with my boots off, but the bed looked so damn good that I couldn't help it – I unlaced them and pulled them off. I laid my head on a pillow I had fashioned from sandbags and covered up with my poncho liner. The cool, silky liner felt soothing to my tired, bare feet. I had selfishly taken the last guard shift so I could sleep all night (RHIP). My bed was comfortable and felt so good that I hated to fall asleep. I said my prayers and soon fell sound asleep.

"BOOM!!" I was shocked awake by a tremendous explosion. I was stunned. The bunker air was full of dust and dirt. "BOOM!!" Another explosion sounded. The bunker shook, and my eyes and mouth filled with dirt. My bunker had just taken two direct hits from RPGs (Chinese-Communist anti-tank weapon). I knew we were in trouble, and I screamed at the guys to get out as I jumped from my bunk and stumbled to the front of the bunker to find the claymore detonators. "Boom! Boom! Boom!" An explosion went off on top of the bunker and several more beside it. We were being bombarded with hand grenades, and I knew it was just a matter of time before one found its way inside. I squeezed two of the claymore detonators, and then the third, but nothing happened. The wires leading down the front of the bunker to the mines had been blown apart. I turned and grabbed my weapon and pistol belt, and without hesitation, ran out the back of the bunker with the guys scrambling up the hill ahead of me. Grenades, mortars, and satchel charges were exploding everywhere as we ran up the slope toward our secondary fighting positions. I jumped down into my position and turned to face the enemy. The other three guys kept running. They passed the secondary positions and went on up the hill. I saw one of the guys at the entrance of my second bunker start to run, but he had second thoughts and pulled back inside. I knew they had to get out before it was too late. I screamed at the top of my lungs, "Get out! Get out! Get back here!" The guys came running, but not one of them had a weapon, pistol belt, or anything. They had been jolted awake, were terrified, and just ran.

I had my pistol belt, three hand grenades, one bandoleer, and my weapon, and no one else in the squad had a weapon except for Miller. I knew he had carried his M-79 out of the bunker, but he had run on up and over the hill. I had one M-16 and three hand grenades to defend our side of the perimeter, and we were under a full scale ground attack. I threw all three of my hand grenades, one after another, and then pointed my weapon toward the enemy. The last thing I wanted to do was to use my M-16. I knew it could be fatal. The muzzle flash would give my position away, and I knew the enemy would try and eliminate it.

The flash of light from the bunker door meant that a grenade had found its way inside. The enemy had taken our bunker and had begun their advance. They moved up past the bunker and began throwing grenades into the perimeter. I knew I didn't have a choice; I opened up with my M-16. I emptied the first magazine into the tall grass around the bunker and then immediately dropped below the rim of the foxhole. I slapped in another magazine, hit the bolt release, and then stuck my weapon and right index finger up over the rim of the foxhole and blindly fired in the direction of the attacking enemy. I turned to see Miller jumping into the foxhole with me. He was yelling hysterically; "Sergeant Lyles, I've been hit! I'm bleeding! I'm bleeding! I'm bleeding!"

Even in the limited light provided by the moon, I could see that his left arm was dripping wet with blood, and I could also see that he still had his grenade launcher with him. I seldom used profanity, but there are times that no other words will do. I shouted, "Shut the fuck up and use that weapon soldier!" I don't know if it was the tone of my voice or the terrified look on my face that snapped Miller out of it. He immediately hushed, aimed his weapon, and started firing. I continued to empty one magazine after another. The gas tube atop the barrel of my M-16 was glowing red hot and looked as if it were about to melt. I continued firing my weapon on full automatic and feeding it all it would take. "Boom!" A grenade exploded beside our position. "Boom!" Another one exploded just to the front. I felt the shock of the explosions. The Viet Cong were zeroing in on us. I could hear the damn things hit, bounce, roll, and then explode. I knew that I needed to somehow get out of that hole, but I knew that I had waited too late. I had just pulled my weapon down again to reload when I heard a grenade hit the back wall of our position and fall to the bottom. I'm not sure if I totally cleared the hole or what, but I saw a flash of light and felt the slap of the grenade and was still in one piece. As I slid back into the smoke-filled hole, I thought that I might be dying. The smoke was so thick I could taste it. I could taste it and the dirt that filled the air. The grit had penetrated my mouth, eyes, and nose. Relying on instinct, I shoved another magazine in my weapon, raised it up over the rim of the hole, and started firing again.

Miller was lying in the bottom of the foxhole screaming. He was still alive but appeared to be in several pieces on the floor of our position. One of his legs had been nearly blown off. Miller was dying and needed help, but I didn't have time. I kept my M-16 hot and waited for the next grenade to find the hole.

Explosions were going off everywhere, and I was fighting for my life. Then, as suddenly as the attack had started, it stopped! They began to retreat. They had us beat, and with a little more effort, could have overrun us. Miller's M-79 had been silenced, and I was almost out of ammo and

My Story, Vietnam 1968, 196th Light Infantry Brigade

waiting for a chance to run. There was nothing else to stop them. I believe their plans were to sneak up on the bunkers, hit us hard, and then run before we had a chance to call artillery. They were probably surprised at how easy it was to take the bunkers and had not made plans for overrunning us, so they retreated as planned.

Scotty slid off into my foxhole to answer Miller's cries, and Jones followed to help him. Scotty worked under the red lens of a flashlight to save Miller's life. He squeezed needle topped tubes of morphine into what was left of Miller's legs and then kind of scooped up the muscle and flesh and packed it around the leg bone. Scotty wrapped several bandages around the mess to hold it all together. Several more guys ran down to help lift Miller out of the hole and take him to the chopper pad.

As Miller was being carried up the hill, the thought struck me, "Where in the hell is our artillery!" We were sitting next door to a fire support base and weren't getting any support. The Viet Cong were running down the side of the mountain, and we were just letting them go. A soldier from the CP crawled up to my position and said, "Stumpy wants your map and compass." Our platoon leader had lost his map and compass in all the confusion. The guys on LZ Center could see and hear the attack, but needed an azimuth before they could provide help, and Stumpy couldn't give it to them because he didn't have a fuckin' compass. I couldn't believe it. An officer responsible for a platoon of men couldn't find his map or compass. I told the soldier that my stuff was still in the bunker. Jones, who had stayed in the hole with me, immediately moved out toward the bunker to secure the map and compass. He didn't even have a weapon with him. We weren't sure if the enemy had totally pulled back or not, but that didn't stop him.

Jones came back with a couple of weapons, ammo, and the map and compass. I sent the map and compass to

Stumpy. He called in several barrages of HE, but it was well after the fact – the enemy had escaped.

Somehow in all the confusion and darkness, we were able to get Miller medevac'd out. I felt bad about yelling at him after he had come to me looking for help, but I didn't have a choice. I have always wanted to apologize to him, but I'm not sure that he even lived. In all the chaos that night, Miller, being green, probably didn't know what was going on. He was a terrified nineteen-year-old kid who didn't have any idea where all the hell was coming from. He only knew that he was hurt and needed help, so he came to me. I was experienced and knew that a grenade would be coming into our hole, and he was too green to know. The Vietnam War had lasted less than a week for Miller.

Needless to say, we stayed more alert the remainder of the night. Several grenades were thrown towards sounds in the night, and Stumpy called in another fire mission on some lights down in the valley. Our imaginations played hell with us until the sun began to rise the next morning.

I slowly began to realize that I hadn't escaped unharmed. I was covered with blood. Some of it was Miller's, and some it was mine. My left hand was swollen. A piece of frag had entered my ring finger between the knuckle and the first joint and had come to rest under the knuckle. I had cuts, scratches, and scrapes everywhere, and my feet were a bloody mess. I had run barefooted across several rolls of concertina wire we had pulled in front of our secondary positions. There was so much adrenaline in my body that I didn't even realize that I was barefoot until well after the battle was over.

Miller and I had been the only two hit; however, some of the other guys had bruises and scratches. Scotty made his rounds taking care of our wounds. After examining my hand and feeling the piece of metal still lodged in it, Scotty told me that he was going to send me to Center and let them look at it. There was a possibility that they would have to send me to the rear to have it cut out. I was hoping he would say that. The guys started congratulating me. It was sort of like winning the lottery, except, I was going to have to wait until after a visit to the medical bunker on Center to find out whether or not I won. Scotty cleaned and doctored my cuts and scrapes. The pain that had been absent all night had begun to return. I was sore and stiff, and it hurt to move, but I didn't complain. It felt great just to be alive.

    I had let my guard down. I had promised myself that I never would, but I did, and we paid for it. I began asking questions trying to figure out what in the hell had happened. I started by trying to find out who was on guard duty at the time. Alverson told me that after he had finished his shift, he had awakened Talley for his turn. Talley was a tall, skinny boy from Chicago who had only been in-country a month or so and hadn't seen much action. Talley apparently got up for a few minutes and then decided he was too sleepy to pull guard, so he went back into the bunker and climbed into his bunk. Alverson remembered seeing Talley crawl into his bunk and thought that his shift was over awful quick but didn't think anything else about it, figuring that he had dosed off during Talley's shift. I checked and found out that Talley never woke up the next man.

    When I approached Talley, he admitted going back to sleep. I couldn't believe his attitude. He thought we were safe up on the mountain, and he was sleepy, so he went back to bed. As Talley spoke, the anger in me built so fast that I thought I was going to explode. I came within a hair of blowing his shit away right then. I hated him and wanted him dead. Even before this situation, I didn't like him. He was a tall, skinny, goofy-acting smart ass. I had words with him on his second or third day in the field about the depth of his foxhole. He dug the hole deeper, but he let me know that he thought it was a lot of work for nothing. I wanted to kill him, and it would have been an easy matter, but I sucked it up and took it to Stumpy.

When I started talking about a court martial, I could tell Stumpy was cold on the idea. He pointed out that Talley was green and had a lot to learn. It didn't take me long to figure out what was going on. The night had been a disaster, and Stumpy had been in charge. First of all, we didn't have anyone on guard duty on my side of the hill, and that was my fault as much as it was Talley's. Secondly, when Charlie hit us, my squad ran and left their weapons behind, and third, the platoon leader couldn't call for artillery support because he had lost his map and compass.

When I realized Stumpy wasn't going to push the issue, I told him that if he didn't get Talley out of my squad right then, that I was going to walk back down the hill and kill him dead. Stumpy knew I was serious. Talley was called to the CP, and Stumpy chewed on his ass for a while and then reassigned him to Sergeant Rouse's squad. I don't think any of it even fazed Talley. He later acted like nothing had ever happen, and on occasions, even tried to talk to me.

I'm sure the official version of the night's events was that our artillery helped stop the enemies advance. We were all heroes for repelling the attack. I received a Bronze Star for my actions; however, like everything else that happened that night, it was screwed up too – the citation wasn't written accurately. It said that I returned to the blown bunker to retrieve the map and compass, and I didn't; Jones did. It couldn't have read right because if it had, it would have had to say something about all the stupid mistakes that were made that night – mistakes that cost a young man his legs and could have easily cost all of us our lives.

Stumpy later let me read what he had submitted, and I pointed out the discrepancies, but he made light of it and said I deserved it. I had single-handedly stopped a ground assault by what was estimated to be a reinforced platoon of

My Story, Vietnam 1968, 196th Light Infantry Brigade

Viet Cong, but of course, the citation couldn't say that. Sometimes I was real impressed with how well Stumpy had it together, and at other times, like this, he was unbelievably careless for someone with so much responsibility. He was a good officer, and I never had any doubt that he would be right beside me if things got bad. I considered him a friend. He was just young, and sometimes, like all of us, he made stupid mistakes.

Early that morning, an officer from the rear arrived by chopper to assess the situation. He and Stumpy stood atop the mountain talking while they watched us search the area below. I searched my secondary fighting position, looking for clues to why I had been spared. I didn't believe that I had totally cleared the hole when the grenade exploded. I found a partial answer to my question lying in the bottom of the hole on my side. It was half of a Chi-Com (Chinese Communist) grenade casing still intact – it had not split into fragments. When it exploded, apparently one big chunk was sent my way rather than a bunch of small pieces. The thing hit more on Miller's side of the hole, so the sandbag partition in the hole probably stopped some of the stuff, and almost clearing the hole probably helped me avoid the rest; that is, except for the small piece that hit my hand, if that's when I got it.

Both of my bunkers had taken hits from RPGs. We were all extremely fortunate to be alive. The hits were all low on the front wall of the bunkers. The slope on which the bunkers were built was steep, and the floor of the bunker was above where the rockets had hit. It was apparent that several grenades had exploded inside my bunker. The first thing I noticed was syrup dripping from a can of my fruit. I inspected the rest of the stuff that mama had sent me and found that none of it had survived.

When I found my boots, I was glad I hadn't been inside of them. They had holes all through them. One big gash opened up the toe of the right boot. They were barely wearable. I retrieved a pair of socks from my rucksack that was leaning against the outside bunker wall and put my boots on. They felt good, and there was no doubt in my mind that they would never come off again at night.

We slowly searched the tall grass on the side of the mountain looking for fallen enemies, but didn't find any. We did, however, find blood everywhere. From the amount of blood and its locations, we figured that four or five of them had been seriously wounded or killed. We apparently had given the VC enough time to pull their wounded back down the mountain. We found two RPG launchers, several rockets, and four or five grass baskets full of concussion charges that had been left behind. Blood was on everything. There was so much blood on one of the RPG launchers that I was sure that one of my hand grenades had got him.

The blood trails all converged and turned into a river of blood that followed a trail down the side of the mountain toward the valley below. The officer overseeing our search was all excited about the blood and the prospects of a body count. There was supposed to be a village down in the valley at the base of West where the Viet Cong may have held up or left their wounded and dead behind. We were ordered down the mountain to check the village out.

The clean-shaven officer didn't go with us, of course. He may have been concerned about getting his spit shined boots muddy or his pressed uniform dirty. He climbed aboard his Huey and flew back to where ever all the rear echelon assholes stay, and we prepared to go into the valley to search for the enemy.

One squad was left behind, and the rest of us headed down the side of the mountain following the trail of blood. We followed the blood to the bottom and straight into a small village of three or four hooches inhabited by elderly peasants. Stumpy followed the blood trail into the village with a vengeance. I figured the VC passed on through the village and probably gave the peasants hell in doing so. I don't think Stumpy really thought they had assisted the Viet Cong or were hiding them; I believe he was just looking to get even with somebody, and he didn't care whom.

Stumpy began pushing an old man around. The papa-san knew the words, "No VC, no VC," but they didn't do him any good. For a minute, I thought Stumpy was going to blow him away. By that time we had everyone rounded up in the middle of the village. Some of them were sobbing or crying, and others had been hardened to the brutality of war and showed no emotion on their stone faces.

Stumpy turned his attention away from the old man and walked into a hooch where a bunker had been found. Without giving any warning, he took a grenade from his pistol belt, pulled the pin, and threw it into the bunker. A muffled explosion sounded, and a cloud of dust and smoke belched from the bunker entrance. A figure appeared at the entrance of the bunker. Stumpy reached in and savagely dragged a woman from the bunker, out of the hooch, and into the open. She was probably in her mid to late thirties. There must have been a grenade sump or something in the bunker because she was still alive. I didn't see any blood on her except for some coming from her nose. She appeared to be dazed and unsure of what was happening. She attempted to stand up with the help of the old man, but he couldn't hold her, and she rolled over and fell back to the ground and began to cry out in pain. I guess Stumpy figured we had evened the score because he rounded us up and we headed back up the mountain, leaving the woman lying on the ground moaning painfully.

Soon after we had reached the top, a chopper lifted off from Center and headed our way. I knew it was coming for me, and I was ready. Our good deed down in the valley had made me sick. I was tired of war, and I wanted out.

LZ West

BRONZE STAR

DEPARTMENT OF THE ARMY
HEADQUARTERS, AMERICAL DIVISION
APO San Francisco 96374

GENERAL ORDERS
NUMBER 9507

18 December 1968

AWARD OF THE BRONZE STAR MEDAL

1. TC 320. The following AWARD is announced.

LYLES, GARY L US53811994 (SSAN), SERGEANT,
Company A, 3d Battalion, 21st Infantry, 196th Infantry Brigade APO 96256
Awarded: Bronze Star Medal with "V" Device
Date Action: 22 August 1968
Theater: Republic of Vietnam
Reason: For heroism in connection with military operations against a hostile force in the Republic of Vietnam. Sergeant Lyles distinguished himself by exceptionally valorous actions on 22 August 1968 while serving as a squad leader with Company A, 3d Battalion, 21st Infantry, 196th Infantry Brigade. On that date, Sergeant Lyles' platoon was positioned in a night defensive perimeter on Hill 448 when it came under a heavy mortar and ground attack by an estimated reinforced platoon of Viet Cong. After his bunker took a direct hit from two enemy anti-tank rounds, Sergeant Lyles disregarded his painful injuries and moved his men back to secondary fighting positions. After he had positioned all his men, he moved back to the blown bunker in an attempt to fire his claymore mines at the advancing enemy. Completing this task, he secured a map and compass left in the bunker, denying the enemy the use of the equipment. His timely actions contributed greatly to the successful defense of the perimeter and subsequent defeat of the enemy. Sergeant Lyles' personal heroism, professional competence, and devotion to duty are in keeping with the highest traditions of the military service and reflect great credit upon himself, the Americal Division, and the United States Army.
Authority: By direction of the President under the provisions of Executive Order 11046, 24 August 1962.

FOR THE COMMANDER:

OFFICIAL:

for R. S. TEMPLE, JR.
1LT, AGC
Asst AG

JACK L. TREADWELL
Colonel, GS
Chief of Staff

Chapter Seventeen

LZ Baldy

The Huey set down on LZ Center just long enough for me to hop off. I went straight to the medical bunker which was located adjacent to the chopper pad. They apparently knew I was coming because the medic used my name when he directed me to a treatment table. Several of the guys in the bunker had evidently seen the attack on LZ West and wanted to hear some details. I made light of it and provided no particulars other than to say that Charlie had blown me out of my foxhole with a Chi-Com grenade.

While a medic was examining my hand, he said, "You know you've got quite a reputation for staying alive." His remark caught me by surprise. Until that moment, I didn't realize that the soldiers on Center and those in the rear even had a clue of what was going on in the boonies. I found out that stories of what had happened in the field would filter back to Center and then to the rear. Anyhow, by the time the stories had reached the rear, they were something less than accurate. I actually heard one of the stories myself. Standing in line to get a hot meal on Center, I overheard a conversation between two rear echelon visitors. It took me a second to realize that they were talking about me. The story had it

LZ Baldy

that I sprang an ambush on a VC company and then had to fight hand-to-hand until reinforcements arrived the next morning. In reality, I fired a claymore at some noise and then hid in the bushes scared to death until the next morning when help arrived.

I did get some good news – I won the lottery. I was told that they were going to send me to LZ Baldy, a base camp back close to highway one, where they had better medical facilities. I knew I would only be out of the field a day or two, but that was better than nothing.

I caught the next chopper out and had one hell of a ride to Baldy. I think the pilot had been on one too many combat missions. I was the only passenger and figured that he and his copilot were trying to impress me or maybe scare me, I don't know. But one thing I do know; they did both. LZ Center sits on top of a steep mountain ridge. When the Huey lifted off, the pilot slowly moved us over to the edge and then sort of let the chopper fall off the side of the mountain nose first, staying just above the trees. As we approached the valley floor below, the chopper was pulled out of its dive to maintain a tree top level flight. We stayed barely above the jungle on the way out of the mountains headed toward the flatland to the east. We cleared the mountains and continued our low altitude race across the flatlands. I was watching the trees whiz by just below and expecting any moment to be smacked by a branch, when all of a sudden, the chopper made a ninety degree bank to the right and rolled back as it dropped down between the narrow banks of a small river. We followed the river east flying just above the water and well below the tree tops on either side. The speed is what impressed me; I didn't realize a chopper could fly so damn fast. We finally sat down safely at LZ Baldy. Trying not to let it show that I just had the shit scared out of me, I told the pilot that I appreciated the ride.

My Story, Vietnam 1968, 196th Light Infantry Brigade

I didn't know where the aid station was located, and there wasn't anyone at the landing pad to ask, so I started walking. Down the road a bit a jeep pulled up beside me, and I thought for a second that I was going to get a ride. It was an officer. He asked what outfit I was with, and I told him. He then proceeded to give me a ration of shit about how I looked and that I was out of uniform. He had diarrhea of the mouth and went on about my jungle cap and my ragged boots. The Viet Cong had given me an early wakeup call that morning, and I was tired, I was in pain, and I had taken about as much crap off the rear echelon asshole as I could take, but I knew I couldn't afford to lose my temper. My M-16 seemed as if it automatically knew what to do when we were in trouble. Fortunately for the ASSHOLE, he put the jeep in gear and moved on.

The guys in the rear didn't have the foggiest idea of what war was all about. They thought action meant waking up in the morning and learning, over breakfast, that a sixty millimeter mortar had hit the airfield on the other side of the base sometime that night. I learned after several trips to the rear that the true soldiers, the grunts, were disliked by most of the guys in the rear areas. I'm sure it was mostly because of the uncivilized way in which most grunts carried on when they got to the rear. Although less than ten soldiers out of a hundred in Vietnam were true grunts, it was easy to pick us out of a crowd. We were dirtier, smellier, and skinnier than everybody else. They didn't like us, and we didn't like them. When I thought about it, I didn't really have a good reason for disliking them. It was just that they had it so easy, and we had it so tough. Grunts were dying in the field while they played volleyball on the beach. There was such a contrast between the life they lived in the rear and the hell we had to endure in field. They received the same monthly combat pay as a Marine grunt on the DMZ who faced human wave assaults sent from across the border. The rear echelon soldiers went home as "Vietnam vets" with the same rights and privileges as the grunts who fought the war.[25] The only difference was that their chances of going home were a hell of a lot better than ours. It just didn't seem fair.

I finally found the aid station, walked in, and told the nurse at the front desk that I had a piece of grenade frag in my hand. I was directed back past a line of occupied treatment tables, separated by curtain partitions, to an empty table where I was told to wait. There was a wounded South Vietnamese soldier on the table next to mine. As I passed his table, I saw that he had multiple wounds and was covered in blood. He was crying with pain as several doctors worked over him.

While I sat on the table waiting for my turn and listening to the awful sounds penetrating the partitions, I realized that there was another side of war that I hadn't given much thought. In the field when someone was wounded, it normally only took a few minutes before he was medevac'd out. When the chopper flew out of sight, the whole thing was over. I realized that for the guys who were wounded, it was just the beginning.

I accompanied a medic back to a room where my hand was X-rayed, and then I was instructed to return to my table. Everything seemed so impersonal, and there wasn't a friendly soul in the bunch. Other than the bitchy nurse up front, nobody had even asked me my name or how I was hurt or anything. They just didn't care, but I figured maybe

---

[25] Even today I still have a problem with rear echelon veterans who seem to have bunch of war stories. Generally it takes me all of about 15 seconds to figure out that the story is a bunch of bull. I'm in awe of the troops who fought in the Ia Drang valley, at Dak To, at Khe Sanh, in Hue, in the Que Son and Hiep Duc Valleys, and other bloody places in Vietnam. Nobody needs to confuse a REMF for a soldier who fought the war.

that's the way they had to be to survive in the field hospital environment.

A doctor finally showed up with the X-ray, pointed to a bright spot on the film, and with few words exchanged, proceeded to remove the small piece of metal from my hand. After the doctor finished, a medic medicated and bandaged my hand. As he completed the task and turned to walk away, I was told that I could return to my unit. I hopped off the table and wasted no time making my way toward the door and out of that morbid, sandbag-surrounded building and into the bright sunshine.

Being about lunch time or a little after, I was hungry and started looking for a mess hall. I could almost taste the "hot" food. I found the mess hall, and they were still serving, so I grabbed a tray and filled it full. I was sitting at a table stuffing my face when I heard someone behind me say, "What the heck are you doing here?" I turned to see Vaughn standing there. Vaughn had left Alpha Company after being wounded in April and now had a good job on LZ Baldy. Lieutenant Gibbs, Alpha's executive officer, had pulled some strings and got Vaughn a job maintaining LZ Baldy's diesel engines. Lieutenant Gibbs went to bat for the guys who lived through the hell of April 13 when the First Platoon of Alpha was overrun. He figured that they had done their share and more, and didn't want to see them have to go back to the field, so he worked to find them jobs in the rear.

After greeting Vaughn, I explained that I had just came back to get patched up and that after lunch I was going to try to catch a chopper back to Center. We both agreed that I was getting gypped – only one day out of the field. Baldy wasn't the greatest place, but it was better than the alternative. Most of those stationed at LZ Baldy called Baldy "the field," and Chu Lai was the rear, but Vaughn and I both knew where the field was.

Vaughn's new job was to keep the camp's diesel generators running. Vaughn and a buddy took turns babysitting several diesel engines. One of them had to be there to watch the diesels at all times. Vaughn said as long as the lights stayed on, no one bothered them.

After chow Vaughn invited me down to his quarters for a beer. It sounded good to me since I wasn't exactly thrilled with the idea of going back to the field. We shot the bull as we slowly walked down the road toward his place. We walked up to a small building just big enough to accommodate two men. It was surrounded about waist high with sandbags and had the sandbag-surrounded diesel generators sitting beside it. Vaughn pointed to it with pride and said, "That's home." Vaughn gave me a tour of the generators and explained his job to me while his buddy fueled one of the engines. I asked how he put up with the constant noise, and he quickly informed me that the sound was the best part of it. Vaughn said once you get used to the hum of the diesels, you can't sleep without it. The inside of the shack was a hell of a lot nicer than a foxhole. It was stocked with a good supply of hot beer and soda, and the walls were plastered with plenty of girly pictures. It looked like a good place to spend the war to me.

Vaughn had it made. I knew several other guys like Vaughn who managed to find a way out of the field. Most of the good fortune was due to malaria, but several others found more creative ways to escape the danger of the jungle. I had a friend who was given a job in the rear after threatening to write his congressman to inform him that the Purple Heart he had been awarded was due to friendly fire and not due to enemy fire like the citation read. From time to time on LZ Center, everyone manning the perimeter would open up and empty several magazines of ammo in a display of power, and it was also a way of getting rid of old ammunition. During one of these displays, a drunken cook attempted to throw a grenade from his bunker in the middle of the perimeter to the jungle on the side of the mountain. The grenade fell short, and my buddy caught a piece of frag in the wrist. He used the incident to his advantage.

    I sucked the bottom out of the first can of beer, and it tasted good. I had developed a taste for hot beer. Each time we were resupplied in the field, each of us was given two beers and a can of soda. I always traded my soda for a third can of beer, and not wanting to hump the extra weight, I would down all three of them right there. The beer was hot and always good. After I had downed the first couple of beers, I began removing the entire top off the beer can with a P-38 (small C-ration can opener) so it wouldn't take so long for the beer to pour out. I had learned how to pour it down my throat without so much as a gulp. After a few more beers and some good rib-busting laughs, Vaughn told me that if I wanted to stay out of the field for a few weeks or longer, I was welcome to stay with him. The company didn't know when I would be back, and I was sure it would be a while before any medical reports reached the company, if they did at all. After another couple of beers, I agreed. As far as I was concerned that night, I was going to spend the rest of the war in Vaughn's shack. I was tired of fighting, and I didn't want to go back to the field. We told war stories and discussed the finer points of the wallpaper until I finally passed out. I slept all night to the hum of the diesels, and I didn't get awakened the first time to pull guard duty.

    The next morning I awoke with my head a little clearer and knew I had to go. After chow I said my good-byes to Vaughn and headed back to the chopper pad. There was a bunch of soldiers waiting at the pad for a lift to one place or another. After four or five Hueys packed with guys headed for Chu Lai departed, the LZ Center chopper set down. I waited as several boxes of medical supplies were loaded and then climbed aboard. I was the only passenger going to war.

Chapter Eighteen

Another Long Range Observation Post

When I returned from LZ Baldy, the First Platoon was still manning defensive positions on LZ West. We spent another four or five days on West before joining the rest of the company on LZ Center. Alpha Company had been selected to provide security for the fire support base for the next week or so and had arrived on the base earlier that day.

We worked hard that first day on Center. My squad had been assigned several tasks, including burning shit. Large, empty, artillery ammo cans were used to catch the stuff below the seat-holes in the outhouses. Small doors were available on the back side of the outhouses to access the cans. Somebody had to pull the cans out, douse their contents with kerosene, and then start the fires. Standing guard over the burning shit could prove challenging if the direction of the breeze was unpredictable. Getting caught in the rolling, black smoke could definitely ruin your day. I pulled rank when it came to burning shit, and nobody blamed me except for the guy who got the short straw.

The other jobs didn't require as much talent, just a strong back. We didn't mind the hard work, especially if we were working together where we could shoot the bull and joke around while we worked. Kirk would always keep us in stitches. He was a real character and enjoyed having fun. Kirk had made the mistake of staying out of school one semester at West Virginia and wound up in Vietnam. He proudly wore a gray "Hokie" t-shirt while in the field, and Stumpy soon learned that it was useless to try and get him in proper uniform. It was always "Yes Sir! Right away Sir!" But thirty minutes later, Kirk would become a Hokie again.

    I had been ordered to move a load of fence posts from the side of the mountain up to the top where they were to be used. After several trips toting posts with the hot sun beating down on our bare backs, Kirk said, "Hell, there has got to be a better way! I've got to hurry!" He dropped his load and took off running down to the bunker. He promptly returned with his helmet, his Hokie t-shirt, and an ink pen. He put on his t-shirt and tucked it in, and then proceeded to ink in a pair of Captain bars on the front of his helmet. When he put the helmet on, a serious "Company Commander" expression developed on his face. We all saluted him, and he took off running toward the chopper pad. We watched as Kirk talked to the pilot, who was increasing the RPM of the turbine engine just prior to lift-off. The next thing I knew, the chopper was hovering over our fence posts as "Captain" Kirk directed us to tie the stack of posts together and rig the load to the hovering chopper. Our job was completed in short order, and "Captain" Kirk gave us the rest of the day off.

    Even though some of the bunkers were spread too far apart, Center sat high on a mountain and was surrounded by an extensive mine field, so everyone felt relatively safe. Center meant hot meals and a chance to relax. Some guys relaxed more than others, especially after a visit to some of their artillery buddies. I knew marijuana was available and suspected other stuff was too. That night on Center, I was checking on my bunkers when I noticed that no one was on

Another Long Range Observation Post

guard at any of Sergeant Rouse's bunkers. It wasn't late enough to have started the normal guard schedule, but somebody should have been outside. As I walked up to Sergeant Rouse's bunker, I heard some laughter and giggling coming from the bunker. I pulled back the entrance flap and poked my head inside to see what was going on. The pot smoke was thick. The entire Second Squad, including Sergeant Rouse, was blown out of their minds. The Second Squad was packed into that one bunker, and they were having a ball. There was a pile of hand grenades lying in the middle of the bunker floor, and the detonators had been removed. My entrance didn't interrupt the party. I was immediately offered a hit, but I politely refused. I didn't have to see much to know that I didn't want any part of it. The guys were taking turns unscrewing the handle mechanism from a grenade and then bravely disarming the blasting cap by letting the handle spring up just enough to allow them to reach in and prevent the spring-loaded hammer from striking the cap. There was a round of laughter and hollering with each disarmed grenade. As I turned to walk out, Sergeant Rouse said, "Hey Lyles, we're just fixin' to break this up." I nodded my head in agreement and left.

Sergeant Rouse was a good squad leader and a friend, but seemed to have a problem with knowing when, and when not, to have a good time. He had been washed out of OCS (Officer Candidate School) in the final week for getting caught partying when he shouldn't have been. He probably would have made a good officer.

Sergeant Rouse's party ended a few minutes later with a bang. One of the guys let the hammer slip. I was told the next morning that they all just sat there looking at the dumb look on each other's face for five seconds, and then the blasting cap exploded. No one was seriously hurt – just a lot of small cuts. The next morning when I saw Sergeant Rouse and the orange mercurochrome blotches all over his face, I

My Story, Vietnam 1968, 196th Light Infantry Brigade

laughed. I laughed so hard my stomach ached. About the time I thought I was finished laughing, I would look at Sergeant Rouse's face again and then laugh some more. Sergeant Rouse didn't think it was nearly as funny as I did. For a while, I thought he was going to get into some kind of trouble – but he never did.

Early the next morning, I was called to Captain Bell's bunker. I was ordered to establish an OP (Observation Post) on a mountain ridge across the valley and southwest of Center. Me and four men I was to select would be choppered to the ridge where we would spend a week watching the surrounding valleys for enemy movement. Earlier in my tour, I had pulled a long-range OP and felt that I had done my share, but apparently not. The Viet Cong had been reluctant to hit our OP positions because of our artillery threat, until recently. They had hit us on LZ West, and a couple days later, attacked the OP on the ridge. The Viet Cong hit the OP hard, and it turned into an every-man-for-himself affair. All five of the guys were found the next day hiding down in the valley at the base of Center. Two of them had been seriously wounded in the attack. The CO wanted an experienced squad leader to lead the next OP to the ridge and had selected me.

The thought of five men spending a week on a ridge so far from Center was frightening. The CO said he was confident that I could handle the job, but that didn't make me feel any better. I asked the Second Platoon to supply a man and the Third to furnish two more. I put some pressure on Jamison, who was in my squad, and he reluctantly agreed to go. I directed the so-called volunteers to start getting the supplies together while I received instructions from the CO. He provided me with the radio frequency I was to use and the latest grid location codes that I would need for directing artillery.

Another Long Range Observation Post

Being tagged with OP duty was a lot like being given a death sentence. I could sense that others felt bad for me, but at the same time, they were glad it was me and not them. I felt a lump in my throat as the Huey lifted off LZ Center and headed toward the ridge on the other side of the valley several klicks away. The chopper set us down on a grass-covered mountain top that made up a section of the ridge. We worked swiftly to unload the ten cases of C-rations, extra radio batteries, trip flares, claymores, ammo, and plenty of hand grenades. With his mission accomplished, the pilot wasted no time getting the Huey airborne and headed on a course back toward Center and the safety we left behind.

As the sound of the chopper faded, an unexplainable feeling came over me, the ultimate feeling of isolation. Prior to the chopper lifting off, my mind was occupied with all the noise and motion that surrounded me. The whine of the turbine engine filled the air, and the down draft from the chopper blades caused the tall grass to swirl around us as we scrambled to unload our supplies. All the noise and commotion faded as the Huey moved off into the distance, and we were soon left with nothing but dead silence. There was an unbelievable contrast between the sounds when the chopper was on the ground and the dead silence that was left when it was gone.

We were alone. Five nineteen and twenty-year-old American boys sitting on a mountain in the middle of the jungle surrounded by experienced, hard-core enemy soldiers that knew we were there and wanted us dead. The thought of how much responsibility had been placed on my shoulders was overwhelming. It took me a minute or so to collect my composure. I had a job to do. The guys were looking to me to get them back safe, and that's what I was going to do.

I was convinced that we were going to be hit and knew I had better have my act together. The guys searched the top

My Story, Vietnam 1968, 196th Light Infantry Brigade

of the mountain to make sure we were alone while I established radio contact. I carefully surveyed the area to identify the locations where I wanted artillery rounds to be falling should we have a need for the support. I determined the coordinates for each "DECON" location and ordered a round of smoke from the guns on Center. I adjusted the smoke to pinpoint the predetermined strike and assigned a code to the location. With all the DECONs called in, I memorized the locations and codes so I wouldn't need anything but the radio handset to direct the artillery. If I wanted artillery falling in the ravine on the south side of the ridge, I ordered DECONs three and four. If we needed artillery support directly on top of the mountain in front of our position, I would order, "DECON-10, HE, fire for effect," and then get my head down. If things got real bad, I would order all the DECONs and then haul ass. Artillery would be falling everywhere except for our planned path of retreat. I decided to establish two positions – one for day and another for night. During the day we would have a good view of the valley to the southwest of the ridge, and at night we would move to a position that afforded more protection. I planned to spend the nights in an old bomb crater located down the side of the mountain a bit on the LZ Center side. We set out plenty of trip flares and claymores around the position. One claymore was aimed down a ravine that was to be our escape path.

After our night position had been prepared, we planned to stay away from it during the day. After dark, we would set up a GI dummy we had put together and position a couple ponchos as if they were covering sleeping GIs, and then quietly move off the top of the mountain down to the crater where we would hide for the night. I very carefully explained my plan to the guys. I was sure the Viet Cong would be watching us during the day and would know our location. Hopefully in the darkness of night they would hit

Another Long Range Observation Post

the wrong location. While they chucked grenades at the dummy, I would call in certain DECONs, and Charlie would run. If the artillery didn't force a retreat and the Viet Cong came on across the hill after us, we would fire the claymores and then start throwing our grenades. I stressed that nobody was to use their M-16. If things got worse, I would order all the DECONs and then fire the claymore in the ravine to clear our escape route. After that, it would be every man for himself. I told the guys that it would probably be best to hide in the valley until the next morning.

During the day, we took turns watching the valley below through binoculars. The first day was uneventful and the night long. About mid-day on the second day, we spotted a VC walking the dikes across an open paddy down in the valley. I made radio contact with Center, provided coordinates, and ordered a fire mission. The guns on Center rumbled, and we could hear the roaring whistle of the rounds as they passed overhead on their way to the rice paddy. The rounds hit in the rice paddy and sent a thundering echo though the valley. They missed their mark but sent the VC running. Anticipating his movement, I adjusted the coordinates and ordered, "HE, fire for effect!" The barrage of artillery left the VC lying in the paddy.

Over the next several days, we killed three more and sent others running. I was sure we were ticking Charlie off, and I was just as sure that he knew where we were. The more success we had during the day, the longer the nights were. The Viet Cong knew they would have to brave our artillery if they came after us. They also knew that if they shot us off the mountain, the Command on Center would just send five more to take our place. The VC had to decide just how bad they wanted us.

I was positive that we were going to be hit, and the only question in my mind was when. I waited for the attack, but it never did come. I knew my prayers had been answered when I saw the sun peeking over the horizon on the morning of the seventh day. The week had been ten years long for me. It was almost too good to be true when I saw the chopper heading toward us. We were packed and ready to go, but I knew we didn't need to let our guard down yet. I kept guards posted until the Huey was on the ground. I believe I held my breath until we were halfway back to Center.

As the Huey sat down on the LZ Center chopper pad, a crowd of spectators waited to greet us. My chest swelled with pride as soldiers from the mess tent, the CP, and from Artillery watched in awe as we grunts climbed out of the chopper. I'm sure some of them were wondering if they had the courage to do what we had just done. Captain Bell was there to meet us and congratulate us for a job well done.

Before walking back to his platoon, one of the guys told me that I had my "shit together," and if he ever had to go on another OP, he hoped that I would be the one leading it. His comments meant a lot to me.

I was glad it was all over and that I was back on LZ Center. I was glad to be back where most people in Vietnam would be afraid to go.

Chapter Nineteen

Helping Vietnamese Civilians

Alpha moved off LZ Center and, after a couple of days of hard humping, walked into the flatlands. We continued our march to the southeast for three or four days. Another section of flatland was being turned into a free-fire zone, and Alpha was to assist with the evacuation of Vietnamese civilians in the area. The Vietnamese were being moved to refugee camps to protect them from the Viet Cong and the war.

Alpha Company evacuated two small villages over the next couple of days. The civilians were moved out one chopper load at a time. They were mostly old men, women, and children. The Viet Cong were active in the area, so the young men and women were either Viet Cong, or they were dead. There was a lot of confusion, and it was obvious that some of them didn't want to leave their homes. Others wanted to take their livestock and other belongings, but soon learned that there wasn't room on the chopper. They were only allowed to take what they could carry in their arms, and nothing else. I remember one Huey attempting to get air-borne but couldn't because it was overloaded. The chopper lifted into the air a few feet and then settled back to the ground. Several Vietnamese were pulled off to lighten

My Story, Vietnam 1968, 196th Light Infantry Brigade

the load, and of course they didn't understand why. It added to all the confusion and brought cries from a woman still on aboard who apparently was being separated from her elderly husband. The young kids were frightened, and I'm sure they didn't understand what was going on. Vietnamese children are beautiful people, and it hurt me to see them so fearful. I tried to keep a smile on my face when I was dealing with the kids in an attempt to ease their fears.

As the Vietnamese were lifted into the air, they could see their homes burning and their livestock being killed. We were ordered to destroy anything the enemy could use. All the hooches were burned, and the water buffalo and chickens were killed. What rice supply wasn't bagged up and sent to the rear was destroyed. Kirk did all the hooch burning. He liked it for some reason. From time to time in the mountains, we would be ordered to burn the hooches in an area, and Kirk always volunteered for the job. The water buffalos were big, proud, fearless animals, but they were no match for the United States Army. It was amazing how much it took to kill one of them. Shooting a zigzagging chicken with an M-16 is a real challenge. It was sometimes comical to watch a cussing GI running around behind a zigzagging chicken, firing his M-16 without success. Eventually all the chickens fell just like everything else. We were told that we were helping these people, but I don't really think they appreciated it very much. I did know that if the area was being turned into a free-fire zone, they didn't have any choice but to leave. Once the free-fire zone was declared, anybody in the area was considered enemy and would be shot.

We moved back to the mountains and began conducting "search and destroy" operations. Most of the action was confined to the point, and since I spent a lot of time on point, I was treated to more than my share. The company commander decided which platoon would take lead, the

Helping Vietnamese Civilians

platoon leader would pick the squad, and it was up to the squad leader to decide which man would put his life on the line. I guess I walked point so much partly because I just didn't like asking someone else to do it, and partly because I was young and stupid.

Several days into the operation, I was ordered to lead a squad-size patrol to some high ground north of the company in search of the enemy. The patrol followed a trail that led alongside a series of rice paddies that terraced up from the valley floor and were nestled between two intersecting mountain ridges. The area made me somewhat nervous because of all the surrounding high ground and abundance of heavy cover. As I rounded a bend in the trail, I spotted a VC crossing the rice paddy. He quickly took cover behind a water buffalo, hoping that I hadn't seen him. When he saw me moving into position to get a shot at him, he made a run for it. The first burst from my M-16 missed him. I squeezed off several more rounds as he ran out of the paddy, up a small bank, and into a small village. I let go with another burst of automatic fire as he rounded the corner of one of the hooches. I wasn't sure if I had hit him or not. I cautiously moved the men across the paddy, and then we spread out to secure the village. Several men stood guard while the rest of us searched the four or five hooches.

The women and children looked on as we hunted for the VC. As I approached a hooch that had a bomb shelter located just outside the door underneath a grass awning, I spotted several drops of fresh blood leading to the entrance of the shelter. I immediately moved to the side of the shelter and yelled a warning to the guys as I pointed to the entrance. I expected the barrel of an AK-47 to be stuck out at any moment. Stooping down with my back up against the three-foot-high, dry mud wall of the shelter, I worked my way toward the entrance. I took a grenade from my pistol belt and started to pull the pin when a mama-san started screaming. She was apparently pleading with me not to throw the grenade, and at the same time, was moving toward the shelter entrance. She went down inside, and I didn't know what to expect next. A second later, she brought a small boy about nine or ten years old out of the bunker. He had been shot in the wrist. I had accidently shot the little boy when I sprayed the village attempting to hit the fleeing VC soldier. The mama-san apparently thought the boy was old enough to be considered a threat and decided it would be best to hide him. The wound looked nasty. One of the guys wrapped the boy's wrist with a bandage while I made contact with the CP. I explained the situation to the CO and requested a medevac. Because of the dangerous high ground, the CO decided it would be best if we brought the boy and the woman back to the company and medevac them out from there. I agreed and passed the word. I did my best to convince the mama-san that I wanted her and the boy to come with us. They were both scared. She didn't understand what I was saying, and I surely couldn't understand what she was trying to tell me. The mama-san finally decided that my smile meant that I wanted to help. She reluctantly joined us for our trip back. The mama-san and the boy walked with us as we made our way back down the ridge to the valley and then to a small, grass-covered hill where we joined the rest of the company. A few minutes later, the boy and the mama-san were put aboard a medevac chopper.

    Our daily operations were supplemented by early morning patrols that proved to be effective. Patrols sent out before daybreak to search hooches and small villages concealed in the mountain jungles were often successful. We had learned that the Viet Cong would use the cover if it was available. I volunteered on a number of occasions to slip up on a hooch alone. It wasn't that I was all that gung-ho, I just knew that if they saw or heard us coming before we saw them, it could mean big trouble, especially for the man on point. I felt that my chances were better if I went alone. Those confrontations were more personal than the rest of the war. It was a part of the war that even most grunts didn't get a chance to experience.

Early one foggy morning just before daybreak, I was walking point for a platoon-size patrol. Up ahead was our destination, a lone hooch partially hidden by the surrounding jungle. I stopped, kneeled down, and motioned for Stumpy. He quietly joined me. We decided it would be best if I snuck up on the hooch alone. Stumpy was to give me a fifteen minute head start, and then he and the rest of the platoon would follow.

I moved slowly up the trail toward the hooch, staying low and quiet and stopping from time to time to listen and watch for signs of the enemy. My life could depend on me seeing them first. I moved up to the edge of the clearing where the hooch sat and, after surveying the area, silently crossed a section of the open yard and took cover behind a well. An early morning mist hung over the hooch, making visibility even worse, which added to my uneasiness.

I heard voices coming from the inside. The well was located to one side of the hooch, so the entrance was out of view. I decided to stay right there behind the well and wait for Stumpy before attempting to take the hooch. Suddenly, a figure appeared from around the corner of the hooch and began walking toward the well. Through the mist I could see that he had something in his hand. A few more steps, and I could tell that it was a ladle, and he was apparently coming to the well for a drink of water. I knew I should have blown him away right then, but I didn't. I ducked back behind the three-foot-high well. When he got to within about ten feet, I stood up, pointed my weapon, and said, "Dung Lai!" (stop). I startled him. He stopped for a moment, and then began to back up slowly. I repeated my demand, "Dung lai! Dung lai!" and motioned for him to put his hands behind his head.

My Story, Vietnam 1968, 196th Light Infantry Brigade

He didn't stop. He kept moving slowly backwards. I realized I had made a mistake when I cleared the cover of the well. I knew that whoever was in the hooch had heard me, and I felt that the VC in front of me was stalling. I expected to see a blazing AK-47 come around the corner of the hooch at any moment.

    The tension grew as he continued to walk slowly backwards. He moved across the yard to the edge of the surrounding jungle. My repeated request for him to stop and put his hands behind his head went unheeded. He was 30 to 35 feet away from me when he attempted to run. I wasn't a very good shot, but at that distance he didn't have much of a chance. I knocked him down with several bursts of automatic fire. I immediately fell to the ground and turned toward the edge of the hooch. Another figure instantly appeared. I almost squeezed the trigger but stopped when I saw that it was an unarmed woman. I jumped to my feet and I shouted, "Dung lai! Dung lai!" But she paid no attention. She looked around, and not seeing her comrade in the grass, she walked right up to the barrel of my M-16, shouted something at me in Vietnamese, and then let out a laugh. My weapon was of no concern to her as she began taunting me. I didn't understand her words, but I knew their meaning.

    Stumpy and the rest of the platoon arrived at a run and quickly moved to secure the area. I pointed out the body to Stumpy. The VC had been hit multiple times spread from his chest to his upper thighs. When the woman saw the body, her laughter turned to screams. She thought he had escaped. The Vietnamese woman was taken prisoner, and the hooch and surrounding area was searched. Nothing of importance was found.

Chapter Twenty

Ambush in AK Valley

Alpha Company saw a lot of light action over the next couple of weeks. We worked the valleys, ridges, and mountains as we moved toward the western sector of our AO. I remember night laagering on a mountain called Nui Lon and leading patrols off it the next day. I had been in the area several times before and never liked it. The jungle on the sides of the mountain and the adjacent ridges was extremely thick and forced us to use the existing trails. At the base of the mountain, the thick, bushy growth gave way to a canopy-covered jungle. The sunshine penetrated the canopy only in spots, creating an eerie setting and an ideal place for an ambush. The enemy could move around in the dimly lit jungle under the canopy without fear of being detected from the air. If GIs were on Nui Lon, the enemy knew that they would have to come down one of the trails. The sparse vegetation under the jungle canopy gave Charlie a good field of fire. I led several squad-sized patrols off Nui Lon to search the surrounding area. I never did make contact and was surprised that the Viet Cong hadn't taken advantage of the terrain.[26]

Alpha Company eventually moved back east and began a sweep of a valley five or six klicks southeast of LZ Center. We had established a perimeter in the ruins of an abandoned village at the base of the mountain ridge and were enjoying a break. Several ranking officers from the rear had joined the CP early that morning. The CO seemed to be preoccupied with them and hadn't pushed us nearly as hard as usual. "Pop! Pop!" We received several rounds from a sniper someplace on the high ground on the far side of the valley. The incoming sent everybody scrambling for cover. After a few minutes and no more incoming, the danger seemed to have passed. No one had been hit, and I didn't really think it was anything to get concerned about, but the group of officers seemed to be awfully interested in something up on the mountain. They watched the mountain through binoculars, and there seemed to be some excitement about it as they passed the binoculars around. "Good," I thought. "The longer they play their game, the more rest we will get." The easy morning had already made me lazy, and I wasn't ready to hit the trail.

Sometime later the sound of an approaching aircraft interrupted my snooze. I sat up and listened, and then realized that it was headed our direction. The Phantom had our attention. Everyone started moving around trying to get into the best positions to watch the fighter. The group of officers and a bunch of RTOs stood together watching the

---

[26] After I had returned to the States, Alpha Company made the news when the guys jointly refused to move down Nui Lon after taking heavy causalities on several earlier attempts. The guys refused direct orders to move down the mountain until the battalion commander, who was choppered in from Center, convinced them that the enemy had moved out of the area. Alpha's company commander was relieved of command. No action was taken against the men.

Ambush in AK Valley

fighter approach. They pointed first in that direction, and then in the other direction. I got the impression that the CO was putting on a show for our guest. I watched the Phantom roll down into the valley and head toward the high ground. "Over kill," I thought. I expected the jet to use its cannons on the sniper, or whatever else it was that the officers were watching. I was surprised to see two bombs drop from beneath the jet and the high drag fins pop open as they sailed down toward the top of the mountain ridge. I had seen a number of air strikes and knew that we were too close for the pilot to be using bombs up on the high ground. I scrambled for the cover of a shallow tunnel dug into the side of the hill a few feet away. I was a little unsure if I would need the cover or not, but decided to play it safe. It was apparent that many of the guys felt the same way and had started moseying toward cover.

The rest of the company, including the officers, stood watching the show. None of the officers in the company had been with us during our battles with the NVA when we had to use air support. This was their first air strike, and I'm sure that was why it was called. The greens and the officers watched as the bombs hit and exploded, sending clouds of earth rolling into the sky. They watched as the stuff went up and over, and then almost one by one they realized that some of the stuff was going to fall on us. Several good-sized rocks hit the ground, and then came a shower of rocks. I hunkered down in my hole and was immediately joined by several more. As the last of the rocks hit the ground, I heard a "What the shit?" and several "Fucks!" Then I heard someone yell for a medic. A large rock had hit one of the guys on the shoulder and had broken his collar bone. There were several more injuries, but not as severe.

Several days later after our visitors had departed, we entered AK Valley to make a sweep. I dreaded it every time we patrolled the area. Alpha had not swept AK Valley one time without making contact, sometimes heavy contact. The First Platoon had been overrun close to the east end of the valley. We spent several days in the valley, and to my surprise didn't get shot at the first time. We spent the night of October 23 on a grass-covered hill at the east end of the valley, and the next morning stayed on the hill to be resupplied. Choppers brought in supplies, ammo, hot meals, beer and soda, and clean fatigues. It was an easy morning, and we didn't saddle up until about noon time. Stumpy called me over and told me that the CO wanted the First Platoon to leave some men behind to set up an ambush for Charlie. The company had recently sprung several successful ambushes at resupply sites. Viet Cong supply squads would frequently move into an area after the Americans had left to scarf up anything that had been thrown away. Most of the time these squads were unarmed and an easy target. The top of the hill was relatively open, so our movements could be easily monitored from several vantage points. I was concerned that if the Viet Cong expected an ambush, he may elect to surprise us rather than us surprising him.

After voicing my concerns to Stumpy, we decided against leaving anyone behind. Stumpy presented an alternate plan to Captain Bell, and he agreed with it. The plan was for us to leave the hill with the rest of the company, and then after twenty or thirty minutes, I was to lead my squad back to the hill and slip up on any Viet Cong that may be there. More choppers than usual had visited the hill, so we knew that the Viet Cong would show – we just didn't know when. Stumpy wanted to be part of the action, so he decided to go along with us.

The company left in a single file down the side of the grass-covered hill and into the jungle, with my squad bringing up the rear. A couple of hundred meters down the trail in the thick cover of the surrounding jungle, we stopped and let the rest of the company move on. We took cover in some heavy brush on the side of the trail and stayed motionless for twenty minutes or longer. I decided it was time and looked over at Stumpy. He gave me the nod.

I took point, and Mitchell, a black boy from Chicago, dropped in behind me. Buckney was behind Mitchell, and Stumpy and the rest of the squad followed him. We silently moved back up the trail toward the hill. We cleared the cover of the jungle and moved swiftly to some tall grass at the base of the hill. They were there! I couldn't see them, but I could hear them talking. Occasional laughter from the top of the hill reassured me that we hadn't been detected. My heart was pounding hard. We had hit the jack pot. I estimated that there were five or six of them searching the top of the hill for things we had left behind.

We dropped our rucksacks and started up the side of the hill on our hands and knees. About mid-way up, I knew we were making too much noise. The sound of breaking twigs and the rustle of the grass was too much. I signaled for Stumpy and the squad to stay put and then motioned for Mitchell and Buckney to come with me. Stumpy knew I was right and nodded in agreement. The three of us began low-crawling toward the enemy. I slowly parted the grass as I moved quietly up the side of the hill. Each move was slow and deliberate. We managed to reach the top but were still concealed by the tall grass. The only thing I could see from our position was the very top of some of their heads. I could hear voices, laughter, and see black hair moving about above the grass. I was unsure of what to do next. I knew we needed to get a little closer.

Up ahead, I heard a rustling in the grass, and then my heart stopped when I realized someone was coming through the grass in our direction. It was an old mama-san searching the grass for something the Americans may have thrown away. I pressed myself down into the grass, hoping to avoid detection. She moved closer, and I knew it was inevitable –

she was going to see us. She looked in our direction, hesitated momentarily in disbelief, and then let out a shrill scream. Without hesitation, I reached out and grabbed the woman's arm and slung her to the ground as I ran toward the clearing ahead. I broke into the clearing with my M-16 ready to knock down several of the unarmed VC supply squad. I was stunned at what I saw. Sitting in the clearing was a complete platoon of armed Viet Cong – "Boo Koo" VC. A group of twenty or more armed soldiers had accompanied an unarmed supply squad to the hill. Most of them were sitting around in the grass enjoying our discarded C-rations when I sprang out of the grass and surprised them. My first thoughts were to turn and run for my life, and I don't know why I didn't. Instead, I opened up on full automatic and downed one of them that was standing only a few feet in front of me. I sprayed the area, and they scattered. They scrambled toward the edge of the hill.

As Mitchell broke into the open, his first shots knocked down a VC to my left who had already raised his weapon toward me. We didn't slow down. We had totally surprised them, and they just scattered. I hit another one as he rose up out of the grass and started to run. As I jammed another magazine into my weapon, I ran down the side of the hill a short distance to get a better angle on the fleeing VC. I could see ten to fifteen of them spread out on the side of the hill and were running for their lives. I emptied a whole magazine at the fleeing soldiers and didn't hit a one. I jammed in another magazine. I took my time and picked out a VC that was carrying an M-16, aimed, and fired. My first burst was too high. He ran to the right following a trail down the side of the hill. I squeezed off another burst and hit him in the head. He collapsed straight down to the ground.

There was a trail at the base of the hill and then a ten foot or so high cliff on the other side of the trail. Some ran

Ambush in AK Valley

up the trail, and others jumped off the cliff. I took aim at another, and then suddenly, an uneasy feeling gripped me. VC were lying in the grass on top of the hill behind me. In my haste to kill VC soldiers, I had made a mistake. I had VC behind me and VC in front of me, and I was in the open. I was concerned that some of them might reach the bottom, regain their composure, and start shooting back. Thanks to Stumpy, I didn't have to pay for my mistake. He led the rest of the squad as they charged out into the opening. Just as they cleared the grass, a VC woman jumped up out of the grass on the edge of the hill and started to run. Somebody immediately knocked her down with a burst from their M-16. Some of the squad chewed up the jungle at the base of the hill with their M-16s while the rest searched the grass for enemy soldiers.

As our targets faded into the jungle, the shooting slowed, and then it stopped. We cautiously searched the grass on top of the hill. We found a Viet Cong soldier lying in the grass trying to play dead. Several hard jabs with the barrel of an M-16 quickly revived him. He had a terrified look on his face as he slowly rose to his knees. We were less than a klick from where the First Platoon had been overrun back in April, so I knew that these were the Viet Cong responsible for the slaughter. These were the VC that showed no mercy when they bayoneted Perez and killed all the others. It was all I could do to keep from blowing his head off.

A second VC was found in the grass, and he also surrendered. Stumpy had his hands full trying to keep us from killing the VC. Stumpy already had his body count and wanted to add to his success by bringing back some prisoners, but the rest of us wanted nothing but revenge. The prisoners were tied up, blindfolded, and placed under guard.

I walked down to the VC soldier I had killed on the side of the hill and picked up the M-16 he had been carrying. The only other thing I wanted from him was his NVA jungle cap. It was still partially on his head and was full of blood. I pulled it from underneath his head, poured the blood out, and then shook off as much blood as I could. I took my helmet off and put on my blood-soaked trophy.

The guys searched the dead and the backpacks that had been left behind and helped themselves to the enemy's belongings. As he held up a wad of Vietnamese money he had found on one of the soldiers, Kirk shouted, "Hey, more money!" We found a packet of papers in one of the backpacks that looked to be important, some medical supplies, and a little bit of everything else.

The girl that had been killed was young and attractive. It seemed such a waste, but I knew that if the tables had been turned, she would run a bayonet through me without even blinking.

I thanked Mitchell for his first shot. He grinned and said that he had seen worse on the streets in Chicago. One of the guys said something about starting a collection of ears like our Marine buddies on the DMZ. Stumpy convinced him that we were more civilized than the Marines, so he decided to let the dead keep their ears.

I should have killed more VC than I did, but I just couldn't hit what I was shooting at. I was always amazed at how bad a shot the enemy was, and I had learned that we weren't much better. It seemed to me that nobody could hit anything they were shooting at in the heat of battle.

The attack had been a total surprise. The Viet Cong were completely disorganized as we routed them from the area. They never fired the first shot in return. When we left the hill headed back toward the company with our prisoners, the old mama-san and our war souvenirs, we left six dead VC as partial payment for the boys who died back in April. The handiwork of several of the guys in the squad left the girl lying on the ground nude with her legs spread and a cigarette sticking in her vagina.

BRONZE STAR MEDAL
(With first Oak Leaf Cluster)

DEPARTMENT OF THE ARMY
HEADQUARTERS, AMERICAL DIVISION
APO San Francisco 96374

GENERAL ORDERS
NUMBER 601

23 January 1969

AWARD OF THE BRONZE STAR MEDAL

1. TC 320. The following AWARD is announced.

LYLES, GARY L US53811994 (SSAN ███████), SERGEANT,
Company A, 3d Battalion, 21st Infantry, 196th Infantry Brigade APO 96256
Awarded: Bronze Star Medal with "V" Device (1st Oak Leaf Cluster)
Date action: 24 October 1968
Theater: Republic of Vietnam
Reason: For heroism, not involving aerial flight, in connection with military operations against a hostile force in the Republic of Vietnam. Sergeant Lyles distinguished himself by exceptionally valorous actions on 24 October 1968 while serving with Company A, 3rd Battalion, 21st Infantry, 196th Infantry Brigade. On that date, the company was conducting a combat operation ten miles west of Tam Ky. While walking point, Sergeant Lyles spotted a platoon of Viet Cong, armed and carrying packs. Volunteering to engage the enemy, Sergeant Lyles and three comrades quickly closed with the insurgents. After crawling two hundred meters up a steep hill, they were detected by a Vietnamese woman, who warned the enemy of their approach. Disregarding the danger to his own safety, Sergeant Lyles grabbed the woman and pulled her out of the ambush site. Before the hostile force was able to react, he rallied his men and assaulted the insurgents. Firing his weapon on full automatic, he completely disorganized the hostile force and routed them from the area, killing six insurgents and capturing two weapons. In addition to this, he detained two enemy soldiers, the Vietnamese woman and captured a packet of documents which greatly aided subsequent operations in the area. Through his timely actions, he contributed greatly to the success of the operation and the subsequent defeat of the enemy. Sergeant Lyles' personal heroism, professional competence, and devotion to duty are in keeping with the highest traditions of the military service and reflect great credit upon himself, the Americal Division, and the United States Army.
Authority: By direction of the President under the provisions of Executive Order 11046, 24 August 1962.

Chapter Twenty-One

The Monsoon

The monsoon rains brought with it all the miseries I had remembered from my first few months in-country. I don't know which was worse, the heat and dust of the summer, or the mud and rain of the monsoon. I was a bit better prepared to deal with the hardships than I had been back in January. I had learned the little tricks that made life somewhat bearable, and most importantly, I learned to control my state of mind. Once I got it in my head that the misery caused by the rain was mostly mental and that I had a job to do whether I was wet or dry, the little things like water running down the crack of my butt and water-diluted C-rations no longer bothered me.

I used plenty of plastic bags to keep my writing paper, matches, and stuff dry. I learned that I could dry out my spare pair of socks by putting them in my fatigue top next to my body. I learned to fold the excess material of my pants legs over and use boot laces to tie the fatigues to the top of my boots and then wrap the laces up my leg to make the fatigues fit tight up to my knee. This would help keep the leeches out and provide less area for mud to stick. I had learned to build a variety of one-man sleeping shelters using

The Monsoon

my poncho and whatever else was available. My favorite shelter was built by tying sticks together to make two crosses, and then pressing the crosses in the ground just far enough apart to accept my poncho as a roof. I attached the poncho at the three ends of each cross to form a shelter with a roof, but no sides, and use the various lengths of string and twine I had collected to secure the shelter. How high I positioned the poncho above the ground depended on how hard it was raining. The design didn't obstruct my vision and allowed me to roll out on either side in the event that I had to get to the foxhole in a hurry. Some of the guys used two-man shelters formed by attaching two ponchos in the conventional pup tent style. Every once in a while, I would sleep in a two-man shelter, but never felt good about it. Although I stayed drier, I couldn't see anything except for the view out each end. Other guys simply wore their poncho and lay on the ground. It wasn't nearly as comfortable as a shelter, but at least they could wear their poncho while pulling guard duty.

Rainy nights during the monsoon season were cold. Many nights I sat in the mud on the edge of my foxhole on guard duty with my teeth chattering. The poncho liner was a necessity. It was a blanket made of nylon type material that seemed too light to keep you warm. It took discipline when you were cold and wet to wrap up in a soaking wet poncho liner that seemed to make things worse. The liner had a remarkable ability to hold in the heat. Before long, your body heat would warm the water trapped in the liner, and you soon realized that your teeth had stopped chattering and you were actually halfway comfortable.

It was just plain tough when you felt someone shaking you at 0230 in the morning to wake you up for your guard shift. You had to pull back that warm poncho liner and crawl out of your shelter into the cold rain, sit down in the mud at the foxhole, and watch the dark jungle through the falling rain drops.

The monsoon provided an environment that permitted the leeches to crawl out of the creeks and rivers into the grass that we walked through. Some areas had thousands of leeches clinging to the grass and reaching out, searching for a passerby to attach itself to. The leeches could be washed off with mosquito repellant, but not before they had made a small sore. The sores didn't heal fast in the moist environment. They normally grew into large, circular, running sores that never seemed to heal. My sores didn't seem to get too bad, but some of the other guys had sores which I'm sure left lasting scars. At one night laager site, the leeches were so bad that we had to watch one another's face for the bloodsuckers. Sometime that night a medevac chopper had to be called in to evacuate a boy because a leech had crawled up into his penis and he couldn't get it out. The chopper brought in a supply of prophylactics which Scotty passed out. He suggested we wear them that night to protect our private parts from the leeches.

I took extra good care of my feet. I switched socks often and did my best to keep my feet clean and free of jungle rot. The wool socks and boot inserts aided in pulling the moisture away from your feet, and with a little extra care, you could keep your feet healthy. There was no sympathy in the Army for anyone with bad feet. If you let jungle rot develop on your feet, it only meant that humping was going to be that much tougher. You had two choices – keep up or fall behind and join the Viet Cong.

I did feel that the rain gave me an advantage when I was on point. The sounds I made were masked by the rain beating the jungle, and even when it was not raining, the ground was soft and let me move silently along the trails.

My M-16 proved to be just as dependable in the mud and rain as it was in the dust and dirt. As long as I cleaned it

The Monsoon

once a day, greased the round kept in the chamber, and only put 18 rounds in the magazine, it was ready when I needed it. The only thing that would rust on the weapon was the little spring-loaded bolt cover door. The bluing never lasted long, and it soon became susceptible to rust. Almost everybody just let it rust, and that was probably best because it destroyed a shine that could easily get you killed. I couldn't stand to see the rust on my weapon, so I would scrub the door with a wire cleaning brush and grease to remove the rust. The clean metal forced me to put black tape over the door to cover the shine.

The only problem I ever had with the M-16 during the monsoon season, and it happened twice, was that the rear circular sight would retain a water droplet. On one occasion, I was working my way down a trail toward a small village when I saw two armed VC soldiers standing in the village talking to an old mama-san. I raised my M-16 to take aim and then hesitated a second when I realized I couldn't see through my rear sight. It had a water droplet in it. As I lowered my weapon to blow the water out of the sight, they saw me and ran. I only got off several single shots in their direction before they dodged behind one of the hooches. I remember Captain Bell being somewhat upset because I hadn't fired on automatic, but I didn't bother to explain.

The same damn thing happened again when I saw a squad or more of armed Viet Cong on the far side of a narrow rice paddy moving at a run as they made their way up a trail toward some high ground. There was only one clearing where I could get a good, clean shot. I took aim as a VC toting an M-16 entered a clearing, only to find a water droplet in my rear sight. This time I didn't even get a shot off before he had disappeared into the jungle. After that, we blindly fired into the jungle and lobbed in several M-79 rounds, but it all proved to be ineffective.

My Story, Vietnam 1968, 196th Light Infantry Brigade

The experiences taught me to check my rear sight from time to time when it was raining. I added the lesson to the list I passed on to the greens that joined the company. I had learned many things that weren't taught in Basic Training or AIT. Some of them had been passed on to me when I was green, such as grease the round kept in the chamber and only load 18 rounds in the 20-round magazines. Other lessons I added myself, like keep the water blown out of the rear sight, never run the claymore wires down the front of the bunker, and use caution when you throw a grenade into a black jungle because I had learned the hard way that they will bounce back if they hit a tree.

The company spent most of October in the mountains. All of Alpha's AO was in a free-fire zone, but there were still a lot of Vietnamese peasants living in the area. They were mostly the young and the old that did their best to stay out of the way of the war, but sometimes they didn't. I know of more than one instance where an old papa-san was shot when he was mistaken for the enemy. The old men were reported as dead VC just the same in interest of keeping the company body count high. The civilians generally had little to fear from a company-sized unit because the soldiers still felt bound by the laws of civilization that the company brought with it to the field. Smaller platoon and squad-sized units were another matter. The law was whatever the group of nineteen-year-old soldiers and their twenty-two-year-old leader wanted it to be. Put a nineteen-year-old American boy in an environment like the isolated jungles of Vietnam in the middle of a war and he can be just as nasty as any soldier in history. In a free-fire zone deep in the mountain jungles, small patrols often walked that hairy edge between acceptable behavior and the barbaric behavior they were capable of. Although the First Platoon only fell off that edge a few times, I'm sure others were much worse.

The Monsoon

We continued searching the mountain jungles for the enemy using a lot of platoon-sized patrols. The Second Squad was on point as First Platoon humped a trail through the heavy jungle. The column stopped moving, and we waited. Then the point man passed word back to send up Max, our machine gunner. I followed Max and his ammo bearer to the front of the column to see what was going on. Stumpy was with the point at the edge of a large, open rice paddy. The jungle had opened up to a large rice paddy, which lay in a valley and gave way to the flatland to the east. They were watching something on the far side of the paddy a good 250 to 300 meters away. Max immediately spread the bi-pod on the barrel and positioned the weapon at the edge of the paddy, and his ammo bearer took a prone position beside him. Stumpy said, "Do ya see the gook?"

After slowly scanning the rice paddy, Max responded, "I don't see him."

Stumpy said, "Behind that water buffalo," as he pointed in the direction of the animal off in the distance. Max still couldn't see the enemy. Stumpy smacked Max's helmet and said, "Right there behind the water buffalo... behind the water buffalo."

Then Max finally caught on, "Oh... behind the water buffalo!"

Max snuggled in behind his M-60, took aim, and squeezed the trigger. "Rat-tat-tat, rat-tat-tat." The first bust sent the animal running across the paddy. Max followed the animal, using short, controlled busts from the M-60, and the water buffalo fell to the paddy.

Stumpy had given our machine gunner an opportunity to fire his weapon. Humping an M-60 in the bush is pure punishment. Humping it without getting an opportunity to squeeze off a few rounds from time to time is worse. Stumpy had given Max a chance to fire his weapon at the expense of someone's water buffalo.

My Story, Vietnam 1968, 196th Light Infantry Brigade

At mid-day the First Platoon moved into a village that was nestled in the jungle on the side of a mountain. It was another one of those miserable days of continuous rain. We searched the village and found a young woman hiding in a bunker inside one of the hooches. When she was marched outside, no one in the village came to her aid or even acknowledged her presence.

Peasant women were normally old, and the results of a hard life showed on their faces. Their teeth were always stained reddish brown from the betel nuts they chewed, and their feet and hands calloused as a result of years of hard work. The girl obviously didn't belong in the village. She was a good looking woman, probably in her late teens or early twenties. Her teeth were white, and her hands and feet were smooth. Tran, the company's Vietnamese interpreter, had accompanied us on the patrol. It took just a few minutes for him to determine that she was Viet Cong. She was tied up and placed under guard.

With the day already a success, Stumpy decided to stay in the village rather than to continue up the mountain. He wanted to take advantage of the shelter that the village provided and get out of the rain for a while. I was instructed to take my squad and secure the hooches located farthest up the side of the mountain, and the Second and Third squads were to stay with the CP and secure the main part of the village. The Second Squad took charge of the prisoner and put her down into a bunker that was in one of the hooches. I posted guards at strategic locations around the hooches, and the rest of us took cover inside.

The rain never let up. We stayed in the village all afternoon taking turns standing guard in the rain. The two old mama-sans that were in the hooch I had chosen to occupy were nervous at first, but later became somewhat friendly when they saw that we were going to behave ourselves. I made a point of picking up some trash and several empty C-ration cans that had been thrown on the earth floor of the hooch, which I think went a long way toward easing the tension.

One of the guys took advantage of the fire and pot of water in the hooch. He boiled several eggs that the mama-sans seemed willing to give him. The first egg he cracked open had a chicken in it. With a scowl on his face, a long "SSSShhhh...it!" came out of his mouth as he drew back to throw the egg out the door. The mama-san yelled at him in a scolding manner and proceeded to take the egg from him. We all stared and several "YUCK!"s could be heard as she swallowed the beginnings of the chicken that was inside.

A soldier from the Second Squad stuck his head in the doorway of my hooch and said, "Stumpy wants to see you. He is having a squad leader meeting."

I grabbed my weapon and a bandoleer, made my way down to Stumpy's hooch, and walked inside. Something was wrong; I could see it on Stumpy's face. The other two squad leaders, along with two guys from the Second Squad, were in the hooch. "What's up?" I asked.

Stumpy responded, "We've got a problem." The guys from the Second Squad had gotten carried away guarding the prisoner and raped her. When Tran found out about it, he was furious. He ranted and raved and promised to report the incident to the company commander just as soon as we got back. Stumpy said that Tran was serious, and we were in for some big trouble. I didn't understand it. Tran had a real hatred for the Viet Cong. He was the last person in the world I would have expected to have cared. I once saw him get carried away interrogating a VC prisoner. He slammed a forty-five pistol up side the prisoner's head, knocking him to the ground, and then began firing wildly into the ground around him. Tran worked himself into frenzy and then shot the VC in the head. Tran was choppered to LZ Center so he could tell them he was sorry and it wouldn't happen again, and then he returned to the field that same day. There must have been more to the story than what Tran was telling us, or either he had a soft spot for a pretty woman, and she was pretty, especially to a bunch of grunts who had been in the boonies forever. Whatever the case, Tran was mad, and he was serious when he said he was going to report the rape. It had been two of the black boys in the Second Squad who had been given responsibility for watching the prisoner. They were good soldiers and could always be counted on. The only explanation they could offer was, "Hell, I don't know – it just happened."

The solution was simple; a sniper could get him on the way back. Whoever got a chance was to "Just do it!" We were instructed to go back to our squads and explain the predicament and make sure that nobody had a problem with what was proposed. We all needed to be in agreement.

I went back up the hill to the squad and talked to the guys, and then returned to the CP. Nobody in the platoon had a problem with killing Tran if that's what it took to shut him up. After all, war is awful damn dangerous. The decision had been made, and the problem was close to being solved when Tran walked into the hooch. He saw me and the other squad leaders, the guys from the Second Squad and Stumpy, sitting in a huddle, and I'm sure he saw the look on our faces. I think it took him all of about a second to figure it out. His attitude did a 180. He started laughing and said, "I make a joke." Tran said he hated VC, and he didn't care what happened to her. He continued to make light of it in a room filled with solemn silence. He made several remarks about how good our prisoner looked and that he may want some of it himself before we went back, but no one bought it.

Stumpy gave the order, "Saddle up." I walked past Tran on my way out of the hooch and never acknowledged his presence. As far as I was concerned, he was a dead man.

The Monsoon

With our blindfolded prisoner in tow, we headed back. On the trail Tran tried to stay close to Stumpy, while Stumpy kept trying to put some distance between them. The tension mounted as everyone waited for it to happen. I figured one of the guys from the Second Squad would pull the trigger. Every step of the way I expected someone to shoot Tran, but it never happened. When we walked into the company perimeter, everyone seemed relieved, and I'm sure Tran knew how close he had come. Stumpy turned our prisoner over to the CO, and, to my surprise, nothing else was ever said.

Several days later, our platoon approached a hooch situated at the base of a mountain and partially hidden by the surrounding jungle. As we moved along a foot path through the jungle toward the hooch, a small dog darted onto the trail up ahead, and with several sharp barks, warned of our approach. Kirk quickly moved up the trail into the opening, only to hear someone moving through the jungle up the mountain to the rear of the hooch. Apparently the VC who had been at the hooch had fled, leaving an old mama-san and a young woman behind. Knowing better that to give chase, Stumpy gave orders to secure the area.

It was getting close to time to start heading back, so Stumpy decided to stay at the hooch and take a break before hitting the trail. Stumpy escorted the two women into the hooch where he halfheartedly attempted to interrogate them. He learned nothing and only confirmed that they didn't know English and he didn't know Vietnamese. It was obvious that they were both scared as they nervously squatted together against the wall of the hooch. The old woman chewed her betel nuts as her eyes followed the GIs. Stumpy walked back outside to inspect the perimeter, while Kirk and Alverson continued to search the small hooch. Alverson took no care to avoid making a mess of the place and took delight in watching the range of expressions that appeared on the old woman's face as he decided what to break and what not to break. The sight of Kirk's cigarette liter and the closeness of the grass thatch of her home to its flame brought a verbal plea from the old women. I knew Kirk and Alverson were just joking around and meant no real harm, but our host didn't. Of course, if the hooch had burnt, it would have still been just a joke to the young soldiers.

I dropped my webbing in a comfortable corner of the hooch and sat down on the earthen floor to take a much needed rest. Kirk and Alverson kept pestering our host. "I think the mama-san likes me," Kirk said as he sat down beside the old mama-san and put his arm around her. Not wanting to anger the young soldier, she pleaded politely for him to leave her alone as she squirmed gently trying to free herself. Alverson walked over and sat down beside the younger woman and scooted up beside her. She made a low, crying sound and moved away, and Alverson and Kirk both chuckled.

Changing tactics, a scowl slowly formed on Kirk's face, and then he angrily pointed his finger at the old women. "You VC! You VC!" he yelled. Kirk accusingly then pointed his finger toward the young woman and shouted, "You VC! You VC!"

"No VC! No VC! No VC!" they pleaded.

Kirk began putting on a show. It was all several of the guys could do to keep from busting out laughing. It was a joke for the Americans and a life or death situation for the Vietnamese women. Kirk dragged the mama-san out of the hooch, and Alverson followed with the younger women. By that time several others joined in the fun. Alverson had help tying the women to a small tree in the yard. The young woman began to cry, and the mama-san sobbed and pleaded in Vietnamese. Kirk yelled, "Anyone got a safety pin?" He was promptly handed a large safety pin as he searched his

The Monsoon

pockets and pulled out a 196th insignia patch. He pinned the 196th patch to the crotch of her black pants. "There, that ought to really piss Charlie off," Kirk said.

Stumpy said, "Ok, that's enough; time to go; saddle up!" It was time to start heading back.

We got our stuff together and fell in line for the march back to the company. Alverson wasn't through. He ran over, picked up a ladder that was lying beside the hooch, and walked over and put it over the old mama-san's head, supporting the weight of the ladder on her neck. She cried out. One of the greens asked whether we ought to leave her like that, and Kirk said that the young bitches Viet Cong husbands would be back in the village within five minutes after we leave, and he could take it off. I knew Kirk was right. I just hoped that if I ever got captured, it wouldn't be by him, or by her for that matter.

Chapter Twenty-Two

The River

Alpha's maneuvers during October and on into November produced a lot of point action and a number of small skirmishes with the Viet Cong. Most of the skirmishes followed the same pattern. The company's strategy generally involved sweeping an area where the Viet Cong had been spotted, with two of the platoons forcing the enemy toward the third platoon. It never worked exactly as planned, but it normally forced a confrontation. One of the platoons would make contact, and a firefight would ensue. We normally killed several VC during the initial phase of the contact, but after that, it would end up with us just shooting up the jungle.

Even without enemy harassment, humping the mountains was never easy, but by now I had learned to take it in stride, as did most of the guys. Some never learned. They fought it every step of the way, making themselves miserable in the process. Mack, Stumpy's RTO, was one of them. He was a big boy, six feet four or so, and had a hell of a time moving through the thick jungle. His weapon or his radio or something was always getting caught up in the vines and undergrowth.

The River

    We were working our way through some thick jungle as we moved down the side of a mountain, and as usual, Mack was being detained every few steps by a pesky vine or branch. At first I could hear him mutter a cuss word or two under his breath as he worked himself free, but eventually he became quite vocal. A vine reached out and raked him across the face with its sharp prongs, and another grabbed his leg. Mack fought back with brute strength. Like the bull he was, he began forcing himself through the jungle, dragging vines and all. He growled loudly as he bulled his way through the heavy undergrowth. Eventually, the jungle got the best of him, and the vines attached to his radio, rucksack, and neck stopped him in his tracks. He gave up and flopped to the ground with the assistance of the spring-loaded vines. He landed on his butt. He just sat there and began to cry. His tears turned to anger, and then he began to cuss. He cussed loud enough for Ho Chi Minh to hear him in Hanoi, and he used a vast arsenal of four-letter words. He cussed the vines, the jungle, Vietnam, the war, and the United States Army. Out of breath and with tears on his face, he looked up to see Stumpy looking down at him. Stumpy had gotten tickled watching Mack's antics, and with a smile on his face, said, "Get off your ass Mack! We've got a war to fight." With much of his tension relieved, Mack got up, pulled the vines loose and continued down the mountain.

    After a hard day of humping, I looked forward to the best part of the day, especially if we had been given a break from the weather. The time after foxholes had been dug and before the start of guard duty was enjoyable, that was, of course, if it wasn't my turn to lead the LP. We got along well with one another and didn't mind poking each other with a well-placed joke or two. We sat around the foxholes cleaning our weapons and talking about home, girls, and that new '69 Camaro we were going to buy when we got back to the world.

My Story, Vietnam 1968, 196th Light Infantry Brigade

I welcomed the opportunity to get some sleep after a long, exhausting day. It had gotten easy for me to fall into a restful sleep because I knew from experience that I could rely on myself to carry out my preprogrammed response if I should be suddenly awakened during the night. I usually rested well, but occasionally would be bothered by a recurring nightmare that caused me some restless nights. I had dreams about being in battle and not being able to find my weapon because I had laid it down somewhere. I would wake up in a cold sweat and be unbelievably relieved to see my M-16 lying on the ground beside me. I would reach out and pull it over to me. The comforting feeling of the cold plastic and metal up against me would allow me to fall back to sleep. It was my best friend, and I had to take care of it.

During the first week in November, Alpha moved deeper into the mountains headed toward the Chang River. There were several point confrontations along the way that added to the company's body count. I remember waiting in line on a trail that weaved up the side of a mountain and listening to an exchange of fire between our point and the Viet Cong. After the contact, we continued up the trail. Our point had killed one of the VC soldiers and left him lying on the trail. It was a gruesome sight that attested to the power of the M-16. I didn't see where the bullet went in, but when it came out, it cleanly popped the entire top of his skull off, leaving what was left of his brain exposed.

I was on point when we reached the Chang River. I hated crossing the river. It was a perfect place for an ambush, and I expected one each time we crossed. There were only certain places where it could be crossed on foot, and I'm sure the enemy knew every one of them. The "FORD" locations were clearly marked on my map, so they weren't a secret. Crossing the river at someplace other than one of the designated locations had in the past proved to be costly. It taught us that you can't swim with several bandoleers of

The River

ammo hanging around your neck and a seventy pound rucksack on your back.

Each time Alpha crossed the river, four or five volunteers would cross first to secure the far bank before the remainder of the company made the crossing. I was on point, so it was sort of my place to volunteer. I had crossed first once before and hoped I would never have to do it again, but here I was, fixin' to risk my life again. It was just something I had to do.

The area we choose to cross was wide and a little over waist deep in the middle. Like before, about halfway across, I was overwhelmed by a feeling of helplessness. I moved slow, making sure of my footing as I studied every detail on the far bank of the river. I felt that if I could see them before they started shooting, I might have a slim chance of getting out alive. If I didn't, I knew my chances would be zero. The tension mounted with every step and reached a suffocating peak a few feet from the bank. At that point, it was simple – if they were there, I was dead. I was relieved and able to breathe again when I reached the far side, stepped out of the water, and climbed up the bank. The five of us secured the area, and the rest of the company crossed safely.

Alpha Company began a sweep of an area along the river. On the first day, the Second Platoon stayed with the CP to provide security, while the Third Platoon was sent on a patrol up the river, and we were sent down the river. Our Third Squad took point and was followed by the platoon CP, which consisted of Te, the company's Kit Carson scout, Stumpy, his RTO, and Scotty. My squad was in line behind the CP, and the Second Squad brought up the rear. We were following a trail that paralleled the river. We had moved a considerable distance downstream when the trail turned away from the river and headed up a small hill into some heavy woods. The Third Squad had already entered the woods when all hell broke loose. "Crack! Crack! Crack!

Crack!" The snapping sound of incoming filled the air. Te was hit immediately and collapsed to the trail in front of Stumpy. The Third Squad began returning fire while the rest of us scrambled into the woods for cover.

The slight slope of the hill provided us some protection from the lead that was coming from the thick jungle on the far side of the hill. We lay with our faces in the dirt as bullets from at least five or six automatic weapons cracked over our heads. The enemy incoming slowed, and then quit. The way it stopped worried me. If it had been the Viet Cong breaking the engagement and running, the incoming would have stopped suddenly. This didn't. The incoming from one or two weapons stopped, followed by a third, and then the rest. After a moment of silence, we received another burst or two of automatic fire. I got the impression that they had held their position.

We were no longer returning fire, but the situation was still very tense. I was sure we had run into the NVA and was waiting for their next move. Stumpy was on the horn calling a fire mission while I worked to get the guys spread out into a perimeter of sorts. I expected any second to hear the sound of incoming shells and the rumble of the guns on Center. After several uneasy minutes and no artillery, I knew something was wrong. Stumpy was still on the horn. I couldn't hear what he was saying, but I could tell by the expression on his face that something was wrong. It was bad wrong! We had wandered too far south and had run into Bravo Company, which had moved too far north. Somebody on Center had sense enough to recognize that two nervous first lieutenants were attempting to call artillery in on one another.

Scotty worked feverishly to save Te's life, but there was nothing he could do. A bullet from an American's M-16 had put a nasty hole in his chest. Te died there on the trail while we waited for a medevac chopper. A stupid mistake

The River

had cost him his life. I never did hear anything else about the incident.

Several days later, I was walking point for the company as we moved alongside the Chang River following the same trail. The narrow trail snaked along the river and was lined with heavy cover. The CO passed the word to "Take ten." I dropped my rucksack to the side of the trail, took a swig of water from my canteen, and then sat down and leaned back against my rucksack to take a much needed break.

I was shooting the bull with Kirk and Scotty behind me when I thought I heard something up ahead on the trail. I immediately put a finger to my mouth signaling to those behind me to be quiet. The signal was silently passed back from soldier to soldier. I could hear Vietnamese voices up ahead. They were on the trail walking toward us. My pulse quickened as I rolled over on my stomach and took cover behind my rucksack.

I cautiously tried to work myself as far to the side of the trail as I could for more cover and to give several of the guys behind me a line of fire. I was scared! The trail made a slight bend up ahead, and because of the heavy cover, the enemy would be within twenty feet of me before I could see him. I didn't know what to expect. It could be a couple of VC, or it could be a company of NVA, and I prayed that it wasn't the NVA.

The high-pitched voices grew closer, and it was obvious that they didn't know we were waiting. I wanted more cover, but I knew I couldn't move. I held my breath and stayed perfectly still with my weapon pointing toward the bend in the trail. I had made it clear that I was to take the first shot and intended to let the first two round the bend before I opened up, but the tension in my body peaked as the first VC walked into view. I opened up on full automatic. He fell to the ground as the one or two VC behind him turned and ran.

My Story, Vietnam 1968, 196th Light Infantry Brigade

In an attempt to throw some more lead at the fleeing VC, I jumped up and ran toward the bend with Kirk following. As I rounded the bend, the VC were already out of sight, but I let go with another burst from my M-16, and Kirk fired his M-79, hoping to lob the grenade on the trail up ahead. Instead, Kirk's round hit a tree branch up high and not too far ahead of me. "Boom!" A piece of the exploding grenade slapped me on the inside of my left knee. My pursuit of the enemy stopped as I fell to the ground holding my knee. I had a small hole in my fatigues and could see a little blood. I wasn't sure if I had a ticket to the rear or not because it wasn't very painful, but I hoped that Kirk had done me a favor.

Scotty arrived at a run and immediately cut my fatigues open to get to the wound. When Scotty wiped the blood away, the sight of a clean, round hole brought a grin to my face. I told Scotty that he could call that medevac now. Scotty continued working, and in one quick move, like squeezing a pimple, he forced a small piece of metal to the surface and out of my knee. "What in the hell did you do that for!" I yelled. "Put it back and call me a damn chopper!" I was half joking, but I was also half serious. I had just missed a golden opportunity to get out of the field. Scotty said he wished he could send me back, but they had been on him awful hard for sending guys out of the field with such minor wounds. He said they would just turn me around and send me back, and that he would be in more trouble than he already was. I quit fussing and let Scotty finish patching up my knee.

After searching the dead VC, Kirk and Alverson propped him up against a tree, folded his arms and crossed his legs, and then put a beard of shaving cream on his face and a cigarette in his mouth. Their intentions were to piss Charlie off, and I'm sure they did just that.

Chapter Twenty-Three

Ambush

I had been looking forward to mid-November. The 196th had a practice of pulling their men out of the field one month prior to their DEROS date. By rights, I should have left the field on November sixteenth, but on the eleventh of November, I was promoted to Staff Sergeant, E-6, and was told that due to the shortage of experienced NCOs, I would have to stay in the field.

Even with less than a month left in-country, I continued the ritual of throwing away my malaria pill. Once a week, Scotty would hand the pills out. When he handed me my pill, Scotty would make an about-face, and I would throw the pill over my shoulder. Early in my tour, I took the pill, but quickly learned the wisdom in discarding the medicine. A number of guys had lucked out during the year and came down with malaria. Malaria meant a mandatory thirty-day stay in a safe hospital with real beds and hot food. I planned to continue throwing away the pills until the last day. As far as I was concerned, having malaria was preferable to spending one day in the field.

November sixteenth came and went, and I was still in the field patrolling the flatlands. We were conducting "search and destroy" missions and using a lot of squad-size patrols to cover more area. I was ordered to take my squad and make a sweep of an area to the north of our position. The area was mostly rice paddies, hedge rows, and wooded areas that concealed a hooch or two. Most of the hooches had long since been abandoned, but others were still occupied by old papa-sans and mama-sans who apparently refused to let the war drive them away from their homes.

The terrain forced me stay out in the open more than I liked. To get to some of the wooded areas, we had no choice but to walk the rice paddy dikes spread out in single file. We were an easy target, and the enemy could, at a glance, determine that we were only squad strength. It was an uneasy feeling to be walking a dike in the middle of a rice paddy bordered by thick hedge rows and woods. It was just another one of those things you had to do.

After crossing several open rice paddies and searching the wooded areas along the way, I began to feel a little edgy about being so far from the company. We followed a trail out of a wood line and into the open. The trail was bordered on one side by a wide open rice paddy and an open flat on the other. I was concerned about being out in the open again, but we had to cross it to get to the last section of woods I was to search before heading back.

The trail was rather wide and looked to have served more than just foot traffic. About a third of the way across, the trail made its way up the gradual incline of a knoll. "CRACK! CRACK! CRACK!" Suddenly, cracks of incoming bullets were everywhere. I dived to the side of the trail and scrambled to the cover of a small ditch that ran alongside. It was nothing more than a rain-washed gully less than a foot deep in most places.

The guys rooted in to make the most of the available cover. The incoming was intense and appeared to be coming from the hedge row on the far side of the rice paddy. Bullets kicked up dirt in front of us, and others made intense, bullwhip-sounding cracks as they passed within inches over our bodies. It wasn't a quick hit and run. I was sure they had been watching us, knew our strength, and knew we were a long way from help. They had let us walk out into the open and then sprang the ambush, intending to kill every one of us, and if it hadn't been for that small gully, they would have. They probably intended to kill me and my RTO with the initial burst of fire to eliminate the artillery threat. It gave the guys a split second to dive for the ditch before the rest of the enemy weapons opened up.

We were pinned down. The guys slowly began to return fire while I maneuvered myself into position where I could reach the radio hand-set. They never let up. I had the feeling that they were attempting to hold us down while others were moved into position to get a better shot at us. I had to do something fast. I reached down and pulled my map and my bootlace tethered compass from my leg pocket. I had studied the map just before we walked out into the open, so I knew our location. I exposed myself just long enough to obtain a quick azimuth on the hedge row. With the map lying in the bottom of the ditch, I rotated it into proper alignment with the compass, and then using the azimuth, quickly determined the coordinates of the enemy's location. I screamed into the radio hand-set, "Stumpy-one to Apache!!! Stumpy-one to Apache!!! Fire mission, fire mission!!!"

My request for artillery support was relayed to the guns on Center by the company FO. The normal practice was to order a round of smoke, make adjustments, and then order the high explosive (HE), but I didn't have time for that. The grease penciled "Xs" marked on my map identified the coordinate codes. I continued shouting, "From Bravo-Alpha-Tango, west two-point one, north one-point-three… Hotel Echo, fire for effect!!" The FO didn't question my request for high explosive. I'm sure he could tell from the desperate tone of my voice that I was in deep trouble.

I put my face into the ground and waited for the artillery, hoping that I had done the right thing. Artillery didn't always hit exactly where you wanted it to. I was calling artillery in on a hedge row less than a hundred and fifty meters away. The slightest error on anybody's part could put the artillery right on top of us. "Fire for effect" meant for the guys on Center to throw everything they have.

I could hear the roaring whistle of the rounds as they passed overhead. The incoming fire stopped immediately as the enemy braced for what was coming. They probably figured out about that time that they hadn't killed me.

The artillery shells began falling – tremendous explosions right on target. The artillery was hitting perfectly right on the edge of the paddy and in the hedge row. I made an adjustment to move the fire power down the hedge row and ordered another round of HE. The artillery shredded the heavy growth that lined the rice paddy, sending smoke, dirt, and dust billowing into the air. Just as soon as the second artillery barrage let up, I yelled, "Move out! Move it!!" We made a run for the woods to our rear. We made a clean break without a shot being fired.

In the cover of the trees, I made radio contact with the CO and informed him that we had escaped the danger. I requested another fire mission. I wanted to give the enemy one more round of hell. I was so impressed with the accuracy of the artillery and so pumped up that I just wanted to do it again. The CO informed me that if I threw any more artillery at the enemy, battalion regulations would require us to search the area for a body count. I wasn't about to take the men across that rice paddy, so I canceled my request. We moved out, headed back toward the company without anybody receiving so much as a scratch. Sometimes it just amazed me how bad a shot the enemy could be. By rights, several of us ought to have been killed.

I knew I had done my job well, and I'm sure it showed on my face when we walked into the perimeter. Word of our ordeal spread fast, and I got a pat on the back for a job well done.

About sunset that same day, Stumpy and I were called to the CP. Captain Bell asked me if I thought I could lead a night patrol back to the area where I had been ambushed. The CO felt that the VC would take advantage of the hooches in the area, and he wanted to surprise them. I was surprised, almost shocked, when Captain Bell said he wanted to go with us. It would be a first for me – the company commander on a squad-size patrol? I told Captain Bell that I felt I could get us there and back if he could handle the Viet Cong in the village. He simply said, "Good."

It was a classic killer patrol. Of course, with the CO coming along, we did everything by the book. We painted one another's face with a camo stick and double checked to ensure our dog tags and sling swivels on our weapons were taped up. Pistol belts were stripped, and our helmets were replaced with a variety of jungle caps. By the time we were ready to go, we were almost invisible. In the cover of the woods, we could only be seen if we smiled, and we weren't smiling.

I took point and lead the patrol out of the perimeter in single file through the woods and down the trail to the edge of the first rice paddy. I stopped before I broke the cover of the woods and kneeled down on one knee to survey the area. I probably spent more time making sure it was safe to cross than I normally would because the CO was with us, and I wanted to keep him happy.

We walked the dikes across the paddy and continued on. Although I had traveled the route once before and had memorized that section of the map and felt certain about our direction, I got an uneasy feeling when we passed through several areas I didn't remember. I kept the thoughts to myself and continued moving silently, hopefully toward our objective. It took us well over an hour to reach our destination. I had never before traveled that far from the company at night on a squad-size patrol. I was relieved to see the hooches up ahead that I had been looking for.

I stopped, kneeled down, and signaled for the CO to join me. I pointed to the hooches. The CO had told me that he wanted to be the first to enter the village, and that sure didn't break my heart. Without speaking a word, the captain laid out the plan. He pointed to himself and several squad members, and then to the second hooch. Stumpy and the rest of us were to take the nearest one.

I let Captain Bell have point, and I fell in behind Stumpy. We moved down the trail toward the hooches and then broke into a run. Before I had entered the village, the silence was broken by the automatic fire from an M-16. Three VC had run from the second hooch, and the CO and several of the guys gave chase. Stumpy and I took the first hooch, only to find that we had startled an old papa-san and mama-san. Stumpy was worked up as bad as I had ever seen him. He began kicking things around as he angrily searched the dimly lit hooch. He turned his attention toward the old man and gave him a sharp kick, "Where VC, where VC, where VC?" He raised his rifle butt. "Where VC?" Stumpy was crazy with anger, and I believe if the CO had not been with us, he would have knocked the old man's head off.

Finding nothing in the hooch, we moved out to go help the CO. The three VC had crawled into a tunnel in the side of a dirt bank at the edge of the village. Stumpy and I arrived just as a man and a woman emerged from the tunnel with their hands held behind their head. The third was dragged from the entrance of the tunnel. He had been hit several times as he tried to make his way into the tunnel and had been killed. The CO threw a grenade back into the tunnel, and the explosion belched dust and dirt from the tunnel entrance. After the dust cleared, the CO shined his flashlight back into the hole. It didn't appear to be too deep. One of the guys took the flashlight and went into the tunnel. Two weapons were brought out, an AK-47 and an old French rifle.

The prisoners were tied up and blindfolded. With all our trophies in-hand, I cautiously led the patrol back through the woods and across the rice paddies to the laager site. Captain Bell was thrilled with our success, and I could tell it was hard for him to maintain that "Company Commander" composure. He actually smiled a couple of times. The captain asked me to mark his map with a grease pencil showing the route we took and the location of the hooches. It surprised me that he didn't know, and I realized that he had totally relied on me to get us out there and back.

The actions of that day should have boosted my confidence to an all-time high, but they didn't. They did just the opposite. That day was a turning point in the war for me. I was a short-timer with only three weeks left in-country, and I had almost been killed. And for what, I didn't know. Until that day, I had never once thought that I might not make it. Even when a grenade dropped to the bottom of my foxhole, I knew I was going to make it; even in the face of a NVA human-wave attack, I knew I was going to make it. But now, I was unsure whether or not I would survive the next three weeks. I couldn't shake the feeling. I had seen others, like Green who was killed on the DMZ, lose their confidence and knew it could prove fatal. In an emergency, my actions had always reflected my confidence. I acted as if I was going to live, and I did. Those who didn't have that confidence expected to be killed, and they were. I had developed a case of the short-timer jitters. I was sick both mentally and physically. My stomach was queasy, and I felt like I was going to BARF!

Chapter Twenty-Four

Short-Timer

At the end of November, Stumpy left the field for an assignment in the rear and was replaced with a green first lieutenant. Within a day or so, our new platoon leader was joined by an E-7 platoon sergeant. The new in-country platoon sergeant supposedly had some Korean combat experience. They were both a little too gung-ho for me, but then again, all new officers and NCOs seem to start out that way.

I pulled my last ambush in Vietnam with about two weeks left before my DEROS date. The weather was terrible. It was raining hard and was supposed to get much worse. A severe storm was predicted to come inland that night. The CO believed that the enemy might attempt to move men and supplies through the area while the Americans were covered up braced for the storm.

I led my men out at dusk and positioned them on a sloping bank that overlooked a main trail. I had chosen the location very carefully because I was certain that Captain Bell was right. From our vantage point, I would be able to see the enemy walk out into the open about thirty meters to the left-front of me and then follow the trail as it passed to

Short-Timer

within ten meters of our position. I knew that the short-timer jitters wouldn't let me sleep, so I planned on staying awake all night.

Sometime after midnight, the storm hit. The wind violently thrashed the jungle around us, and we were pelted by blown debris. Sheets of rain soaked us, and we stayed as close to the ground as possible to escape the fury of the wind. The guys covered up with their ponchos and pressed their faces to the ground to protect themselves from the violent weather. I didn't. I kept my eyes on the trail. The rain beat my face while I watched for the enemy. I was sure that they would take advantage of the weather. The wind and rain played tricks on my mind. At times during the night, I was sure I saw the Viet Cong coming down the trail, but after some tense moments, decided that it was nothing more than the jungle dancing in the wind and rain.

The storm finally broke, and the light of morning arrived. It had been a long night, and I had a lot of time to think. I had made a decision. As far as I was concerned, the war was over. I had done my share and more, and I wasn't going to do anything else. I didn't care about the Army, duty, Communism, or the war. All I wanted was to go home alive. I wanted to go home to my mama. I didn't belong in Vietnam; my home was thirteen thousand miles away on the other side of the earth.

That morning after I had returned from the ambush, I had a long talk with our new platoon sergeant. I told him that I wasn't going on another ambush or LP and that it would be a lot easier for both of us if he didn't ask me to go. I told him that I was a short-timer and wanted to go home in one piece. He got madder than hell, but I didn't care. I was tired of war.

I was never asked to go out at night again. The new platoon leader and platoon sergeant knew that I had a good reputation, and I guess they decided to leave it alone. Besides, I was in good with their boss, Captain Bell.

A couple of days later, while conducting "search and destroy" operations in the flatlands, our platoon received sniper fire from the ruins of an old French plantation house. My squad was ordered to take the house. I moved the men up to the house and sent half of the guys around one way and the rest around the other side. I stayed back and directed the operation from a distance. I wasn't taking any chances. Somehow the VC slipped away, and I didn't care. The platoon sergeant didn't like the way I handled the situation, and he let me know it. He didn't like the way I was doing my job, and he didn't like me, but I couldn't have cared less. I knew that eleven months from then, if he was still alive, he would understand.

I didn't know very many short-timers during the year; 1968 had been tough on Alpha Company. I now understood what it meant to be a short-timer and dismissed all the negative thoughts I had about the short-timers I had known. I now understood the mental pain that Sergeant Huff was experiencing when I was so unsympathetic.

On December 7, 1968, in an open field of tall grass, I boarded a chopper for the last time. The Huey was headed to the rear. As the Chopper lifted off the ground, I was in shock. I couldn't believe I was really going home and that my ordeal in the jungles of Vietnam had come to an end. I felt as if I had been at war my entire life, and now it was actually over. I tried to keep my emotions from flowing as I waived to the guys standing below in the tall grass that swirled around them. I felt guilty leaving them.

Short-Timer

LETTER OF APPRECIATION

DEPARTMENT OF THE ARMY
Company A, 3d Battalion, 21st Infantry
196th Infantry Brigade, Americal Division
APO San Francisco 96256

AVBFBBACO 5 December 68

SUBJECT: Letter of Appreciation

TO: SSG Gary L Lyles, US53811994
705th Infantry Battalion, Division Maintenance
Fort Carson, Colorado

On this occasion of your departure from Company A 3d Battalion, 21st Infantry, 196th Infantry Brigade, Americal Division, APO San Francisco 96256, I wish to take this opportunity to commend you for the outstanding meritorial service performed during your tenure with this unit.

The duties of an Infantry Squad Leader is one of challenge and responsibility. You performed these duties with diligence, and professionalism, your tireless energy and interest have been of inestimable value. Your enthusiasm and your willing cooperation coupled with your ambition have contributed immeasurably to the high morale and prestige of your squad.

Your ability to read a map better than any man in the company (officers included), and experience as a fully qualified adjuster of indirect fire has increased the effectiveness of the company numerous times. The small unit patrolling activities such as "Killer Patrols" which are sent out to destroy the enemy infrastructure, and night patrols, which take advantage of the enemy's false confidence in his superiority at night has been one of your many successful accomplishments. Your professionalism and competence have strongly influenced the actions of other squad leaders in the company.

In your future endeavors should you be assigned as an instructor of map reading, weapons, patrolling or leadership, you will have direct bearing in the development of newly trained soldiers, which will mold the structure of our Army for tomorrow. I know that your attributes will be a great asset to your new commander, and I wish you continued success.

HAROLD I. BELL
CPT, Infantry
Commanding

My Story, Vietnam 1968, 196th Light Infantry Brigade

The chopper sat me down in Chu Lai. I walked from the chopper pad to our base headquarters in full combat gear. As I walked into the company area, I was warmly greeted by a couple of my buddies. They accompanied me to the company's supply room – the same place I had visited one long year ago. My duffle bag was pulled out of the back where it had been stored for the last year. I had a lot of help transferring my personal stuff from my rucksack to my duffle bag. I stripped my pistol belt and webbing and laid the gear on the counter with my empty rucksack. I pulled the liner out of my helmet and removed the cloth helmet cover. I started to throw the cover into the trash can but had second thoughts when the ink pen scratching on the cover brought back a rush of memories. The buck sergeant stripes, which had been so proudly inked in, hadn't been updated with the rocker that didn't seem to mean as much. A short-timers calendar, which I had become so proud of, was displayed on the left side. There was a mark for each day I had spent in Vietnam, and the words "SHORT-DEROS DEC. 16, 1968" had been added beside the calendar. The letters "TENN." on the right side let everyone know where I was from, and the initials "F.T.A." let everyone know what I thought about the Army. A list of the places, which detailed my travels, had been written in on the right side in the available space – "LZ Center, LZ Colt, LZ Baldy, LZ West, LZ East, Nui Loc Son, LZ Ross, Tam Ky, Camp Evans, Quang Tri, Hill 35, Dong Ha, Chu Lai, Hill 29, Vung Tau, Nhi Ha, Da Nang, and Cam Rahn Bay." I folded the helmet cover and placed it in the duffle bag with the rest of my personal belongings.

   A green buck sergeant stood in the supply room watching the spectacle as he waited to start the long, tough year that lay ahead of him. He asked me if he could have my M-16. Until that moment I hadn't thought about having to give up my weapon. It was the friend I had slept with and cared for during the longest year of my life. It had never

Short-Timer

once failed me and always knew what to do when we were in trouble. I felt like I was betraying my best friend when I handed it to the sergeant. I felt naked. I had taken care of it, and it had taken care of me through some tough times, and now I was just giving it away. The anguish I felt overwhelmed me as I watched him pull the bolt back to inspect the barrel. Being embarrassed at the emotions I was showing over an assemblage of plastic and steel, I forced a smile onto my face and asked the "green" to take care of my weapon. I eased my mind by promising myself that I would try somehow to buy me another one when I got back to the States.

I took a long shower and tried to wash the painful memories of the war down the drain along with the layers of dirt and mud I had brought out of the jungle. After I showered and shaved and put on a clean uniform, I looked as good as any rear echelon soldier.

I spent the remainder of that day processing out of Chu Lai. At one of the in/out processing buildings, I was mistaken by a couple of rear echelon soldiers as a new man just arriving in-country. They handed me a picture of a dead VC soldier and said, "This is what war is really like." The picture was rather gross and was an attempt to scare me and provide them with a good laugh. The horrified expression that they expected to see never developed. I didn't say a word. I just turned and walked away. I kept the picture for almost twenty years and then decided to burn it to make sure that my two sons would never have to see anything like it. The two soldiers were just a couple of rear echelon assholes who didn't know "shit!" I almost hated them.

The next day I hopped a ride on a plane to the out-of-country processing center in Cam Ranh Bay. Prior to busing a group of us to the airport the following day, our duffle bags were emptied and the contents searched. I assumed they were looking for weapons and explosives, but found

My Story, Vietnam 1968, 196th Light Infantry Brigade

out that they wanted more when they relieved me of a NVA gas mask and several other souvenirs I had collected from NVA soldiers up north on the DMZ. After gathering my trophies in May, I had humped the extra weight up and down the mountains of Vietnam until I was able to store them in the rear when I went on R&R. I had paid heavily for the stuff, but because of some Army regulation, they simply took them from me. I'm sure that today some ex-rear echelon officer periodically shows off the war trophies he had collected during the war.

On December 9, 1968, I boarded a brightly-colored Braniff airliner for the trip home. We were welcomed aboard by beautiful stewardesses with the longest legs I had ever seen. They were wearing mini-skirts, which had come into style while I was in the jungle. I had heard about them but didn't believe it until then. As I sat down and buckled up, I knew my long ordeal had come to an end. I was excited. The jet engines roared as the airliner raced down the runway. When the landing gear broke contact with the Republic of Vietnam and the plane lifted into the air, everyone aboard shouted with joy. I couldn't help from yelling. I had no control over the sounds of utter joy that flowed from my mouth. I was going home!

I remember the airliner sitting on the ground in Washington State and feeling the cold December air rush into the airplane as the door was opened. The cold air felt great, and I knew I was home!

My first priority was to find a phone and call home, and I did. I called my mama and told her that she didn't have to worry anymore.

The next evening I sat with Mann and a group of other Vietnam vets at a table in the lounge of the Seattle-Tacoma airport waiting for my flight to Memphis. When I ordered a beer, I was asked for my ID. Upon producing an ID that showed that I wouldn't turn twenty-one years old until midnight that night, I was refused service. Mann, who had survived the slaughter of the First Platoon in April and the battles at Nhi Ha the following month, the miserable monsoon, the scorching heat, and a bout with malaria, went wild, and I thought for a time he was going to get us all thrown into jail. He finally calmed down, and I drank my Coke.

Four days after I had been pulled out of the jungle in Vietnam, I was home sitting at the dining room table talking to my mama and dad as if I had never left. The next day on December the twelfth, I bought that new 1969 Camaro I had so often talked about while sitting around the foxhole with the guys. I felt very fortunate; 58,286 young men never got an opportunity to buy the car they had talked about.

A month and a half later, I was hospitalized suffering with malaria at Fort Carson, Colorado.

THE END

Glossary

AIT – Advanced Infantry Training

AO – Area of Operation

APC – Armored Personnel Carrier

C-4 – Plastic explosive

Charlie – Viet Cong – VC – Victor Charlie or just Charlie for short

Chicom – Chinese Communist

CO – Commanding Officer

Concertina – Military Barbed Wire

CP – Command Post

DEFCONs – Coordinates for an anticipated artillery strike

DMZ – Demilitarized Zone

Dung Lai – Vietnamese for Stop

EM – Enlisted Men

Glossary

FO – Forward Observer

HE – High Explosive artillery

KIA – Killed In Action

Klick – 1000 meters (.62 miles)

LAW – Light Anti-tank Weapon

LP – Listening Post sent out to provide early warning

LRRP – Long Range Reconnaissance Patrol

LZ – Landing Zone

MOS 11B10 – Military Occupation Specialty, Infantry

NVA – North Vietnamese Army

OCS – Officer Candidate School

OP – Observation Post

P-38 – C-ration can opener

RHIP – Rank Has Its Privilege

RPG – Rocket Propelled Grenade

RTO – Radio Telephone Operator

SITREP – Situation Report

WIA – Wounded In Action